Managing RISK in
Communication Encounters

Vince Waldron dedicates this work to Kathleen—a courageous risk taker and the wellspring of safety for our family. The adventure continues. . . . Thanks to Jeff Kassing, my longtime colleague, coauthor, and friend, for his insight, amazing work ethic, organization, and, most important for a project like this, great sense of humor. Looking forward to our next project.

Jeffrey W. Kassing would like to dedicate this work to "my girls," Lindsey and Quinn, for giving me a warm and comfortable place to land after a tough day at the office; to my parents, Amy and Don, for unending support and bolstering along the way and for a lifetime of examples of how to be good and humane to others; to my brothers, Dono and Brum, for teaching and showing me how to be a good teammate, a respectable colleague, and an accommodating peer; and to my coauthor and friend Vince, the single best mentor a colleague could seek. Thank you for including me on this project.

Managing RISK in Communication Encounters

Strategies for the Workplace

Vincent R. Waldron • Jeffrey W. Kassing

Arizona State University

Los Angeles | London | New Delhi
Singapore | Washington DC

For information:

SAGE Publications, Inc.
2455 Teller Road
Thousand Oaks,
   California 91320
E-mail: order@sagepub.com

SAGE Publications India Pvt. Ltd.
B 1/I 1 Mohan Cooperative
   Industrial Area
Mathura Road, New Delhi 110 044
India

SAGE Publications Ltd.
1 Oliver's Yard
55 City Road
London EC1Y 1SP
United Kingdom

SAGE Publications
   Asia-Pacific Pte. Ltd.
33 Pekin Street #02-01
Far East Square
Singapore 048763

Printed in the United States of America

Library of Congress Cataloging-in-Publication Data

Waldron, Vincent R.
Managing risk in communication encounters: strategies for the workplace/ Vincent R. Waldron, Jeffrey W. Kassing.
     p. cm.
Includes bibliographical references and index.
ISBN 978-1-4129-6667-2 (pbk.)
   1. Communication in organizations. 2. Interpersonal communication. 3. Business communication. 4. Risk—Sociological aspects. 5. Conflict management. I. Kassing, Jeffrey W. II. Title.

HD30.3.W345 2011
650.1′3—dc22   2009035794

This book is printed on acid-free paper.

10   11   12   13   14   10   9   8   7   6   5   4   3   2   1

Acquisitions Editor:	Todd R. Armstrong
Editorial Assistant:	Nathan Davidson
Production Editor:	Astrid Virding
Copy Editor:	Gillian Dickens
Typesetter:	C&M Digitals (P) Ltd.
Proofreader:	Ellen Brink
Indexer:	Molly Hall
Cover Designer:	Arup Giri
Marketing Manager:	Helen Salmon

Contents

Preface

The contemporary workplace is fraught with risk.

This book helps students understand the crucial role that communication plays in managing, even optimizing, the risky situations that nearly all of us encounter at work. These are the situations where communication really *matters* because something important—identity, career, relationships, organizational productivity—is endangered if we fail to communicate well. Some of these encounters have highly significant personal implications: How do I manage a workplace romance? Deal with a difficult team member? Express my most intense emotions? Others have organization-wide consequences. How can I promote innovation in a change-resistant organizational culture? How should employees respond to management's unethical conduct? What communication behaviors facilitate cohesion and productivity in a culturally diverse workplace?

Our focus on the negotiation of risk could not be more timely. In the time it took to write this book, about a year, the American economy has been in freefall. American companies shed workers at an alarming rate, corporate profits plummeted, the housing market crashed, and some of our most respected financial institutions failed. Although the causes of this debacle are many, we argue that the most fundamental of these involves a failure by individuals and organizations to respond prudently and responsibly to risk. Consider: In recent years, uncounted home buyers put themselves at risk by purchasing unrealistically large mortgages with unpredictable interest rates. They were lured by lenders who put aside traditional safeguards in order to maximize short-term profits. The risk associated with these bad loans was disguised by financial traders who packaged them into inscrutable "derivatives" that could be passed along to naive purchasers. Had any one of these parties—home buyers, lenders, traders—engaged in more responsible communication, the real estate meltdown might have been averted.

This book starts with the idea that the management of risk is, among other things, a *communicative* phenomenon. It is through communication that risk is detected, assessed, transformed, and maintained at desirable levels. After all, if home buyers had asked more penetrating questions, lenders explained risks more clearly, and brokers communicated more transparently about derivatives, many of the economic losses could have been avoided.

Indeed, risky situations are managed by communication: the language we choose, the cues we attend to, the tactics we use, the communication rules we follow, the interactions we participate in, the processes our organizations create.

Managing Risk in Communication Encounters: Strategies for the Workplace begins by introducing the reader to the concept of risk. In Chapter 1, we explore individual, relational, organizational, and communal risk. We argue for a link between perceptions of risk and organizational ethics—the perception of risk is sometimes an early warning that organizational practices are unethical or potentially harmful. Indeed, we argue that risk is a *good* thing because of this "signal" function. Our Risk Negotiation Framework (RNF), which is applied throughout the text, is introduced in this first chapter. It conceptualizes risk management as a communicative process with four phases: attending, sensemaking, transforming, and maintaining. We emphasize the historical and contextual influences that make a given situation more or less risky. The RNF suggests that the communicative practices of employees (and organizations) lead to three potential outcomes: increased risk, relative safety, and optimization. Regarding this last possibility, we suggest that, when handled skillfully, risky situations have *transformative potential*—they can make organizations more productive and employees more satisfied.

The body of the text presents nine chapters, each detailing a kind of risky encounter likely to be faced by students. We organize the chapters around the levels of analysis: individual, relational, and organizational. Encounters that primarily involve risk to *individual* employees involve the delivery of negative feedback (Chapter 2), managing emotion (Chapter 3), and resisting bullying and harassment (Chapter 4). The second section examines risks that are more *relational* in nature. It includes chapters on optimizing relationships with peers and supervisors (Chapter 5), monitoring romantic relationships (Chapter 6), and dealing with difference (Chapter 7). The third set of chapters focuses on situations with consequences for the productivity and cohesion of larger units of the *organization*. We explore the challenges of expressing dissent (Chapter 8), proposing innovation (Chapter 9), and responding to difficult team members (Chapter 10).

Chapter 11 closes the book with a discussion of emerging risks. We examine such topics as the virtual workplace, the increasingly transparent boundary between private and work life, intergenerational communication, and the growing popularity of temporary work arrangements. We close with a cautionary tale, drawing lessons from the financial crisis that has recently rocked the United States and encouraging the reader to apply them to the risks they might encounter in their own career.

Managing Risk in Communication Encounters: Strategies for the Workplace is an engaging, research-based text designed for students who will soon be entering the workforce. It argues for the importance of individual and relational communication behavior, even as it prepares students to be responsible organizational citizens in a world of sweeping cultural and organizational change. It brings new meaning to the old adage: nothing risked, nothing gained.

The authors thank Corrine Ricks, who carefully copyedited a substantial part of the text. We acknowledge our colleagues in Communication Studies at ASU for their collegiality and support. Few employees enjoy such a low-risk work environment. We are grateful to the many students who helped us collect workplace narratives and sometimes shared their own work experiences. In reporting these stories, we changed names, combined narrative elements, and altered details so as to preserve the anonymity of our sources. At Sage, Todd Armstrong provided valuable editorial guidance, and Aja Baker helped with logistics. We are grateful to them both.

We wish to thank the following reviewers for their helpful comments throughout the writing and development of this book: Mary Helen Brown (Auburn University); Debbie S. Dougherty (University of Missouri); Kathy Krone (University of Nebraska-Lincoln); Vernon Miller (Michigan State University); Michael E. Roloff (Northwestern University); Patricia M. Sias (Washington State University); and JC Bruno Teboul (DePaul University).

1

Introduction

*A Theoretical Model for Managing
Workplace Risk*

*A new coworker was overwhelmed by his job and actually for-
got to attend one of our weekend events. He was confused
about the schedule. My boss was livid, because we were short-
handed. On Monday, she reamed him, yelling and threatening
to fire him. I heard it all and thought it was unfair. I wasn't sure
what to do, but I was upset about the poor treatment. I decided
to let her calm down and then talked to her privately. I told her
I understood her anger, but the new guy wasn't really at fault. He
didn't know he was "just expected" to be at every event. She
seemed calmer and eventually apologized to him. The situation
blew over. We have all been working together ever since, with no
big problems. I think my boss knows she overreacted and I did
the right thing.*

Elena, age 26

❖ THE ANATOMY OF WORKPLACE RISK

As Elena's account reveals, the workplace can be a complicated and some-times risky place. What do we mean by risky? We mean that employees sometimes face circumstances that threaten their identities, work rela-tionships, and the health of their organization. These are the situations that even veteran employees describe as "dicey," "difficult," and "challeng-ing." Elena found herself in such a situation—one in which relationships with her boss were put on the line. We all face these kinds of communica-tion challenges. These are the situations where your communication behavior really *matters*. Something you care about—your identity, ethical principles, a valued relationship, the organization's success, even your career—may change for the worse if you fail to respond appropriately. Something important has been made vulnerable. It is placed at risk.

This first chapter introduces various forms of workplace risk, and we explain how, for us, the management of risk is a *communicative* process. Through our Risk Negotiation Framework (RNF), we identify factors that make work more or less risky. Particular attention is paid to what we call the risk negotiation cycle, a series of four communicative phases that apply to nearly any risky situation. This section is particu-larly important because the risk negotiation cycle is applied in each of the next nine chapters. Each one examines in detail a risky situation that you are likely to face at some point in your career. Some of them you may already face on a regular basis. Throughout this book, we argue that the communicative practices used by you and your cowork-ers function to make you safer or more vulnerable.

Before moving ahead, we should note that at work, risk can be a very good thing. If you pay attention, your sense that a work situation is risky can be a valuable signal—a warning that you are in danger of damaging a valued relationship, engaging in unethical conduct, or endangering an important organizational goal. We revisit this vital "sig-nal function" of risk in the concluding chapter of the book (Chapter 11). Risky situations also offer what we call transformative potential. They are opportunities for you to change things for the better; they can be positive turning points in your work relationships and your career. Elena, who works in the community education department of a large hospital, made the most of such an opportunity. She certainly took a risk by questioning her boss's outburst. Uncertain about how to pro-ceed, Elena might have worried that the supervisor's anger would be directed at her. Did she have a right to question a leader's judgment? As it turned out, Elena's communication transformed the situation in positive ways. Much to his relief, the new employee's job was pre-served. The relational tension in this small office was alleviated.

Elena's boss seemed to appreciate her constructive approach. Also important, Elena acted in accordance with an ethical principle that she highly valued—a commitment to relational fairness.

Elena's success can be attributed in part to her communication practices. For example, by letting the supervisor "calm down," this relatively young employee exhibited expertise in emotion management (Chapter 3). In choosing to express her concerns in private, she helped the boss save face (Chapter 2). As we learned, Elena conscientiously maintains an open relationship with her supervisor through regular, open, and constructive communication (Chapter 5). This communicative history allows employee and supervisor to feel comfortable on the occasions when Elena feels compelled to speak her mind (Chapter 8). Certainly Elena's defense of her new colleague will be a positive turning point in their coworker relationship.

Of course, risk management involves more than relationships. At Benson's Family Restaurant (see Textbox 1.1), reluctance to adapt to changing circumstances put the whole business at risk. But one employee's efforts to propose a credible alternative averted the threat. Although work circumstances differ dramatically, your communication practices are likely to be essential tools in negotiating the risks faced by your own organization.

Textbox 1.1	**Transforming Risk: Advocating for Change at Benson's Family Restaurant**

For several generations, the Benson family made a good living from its downtown restaurant. Local business people loved its down-home "country-style" food and the personalized (if leisurely) service they received from the always chatty servers. But sales plummeted when several new restaurants opened nearby. Even regular customers limited their visits to once or twice a week. Helen, the family matriarch, was reluctant to change the family's business model. She dropped hints about closing the restaurant and settling into an overdue retirement. Helen Benson's word had been law for 20 years, and her decisions were rarely questioned. But Jake Benson, Helen's grandson and current manager of the restaurant, decided to give it a try. He quickly convened focus groups of the family's former customers, offering a free meal in exchange for their honest feedback. It became obvious that these former regulars had abandoned Benson's Family Restaurant for two reasons. In contrast to Benson's lineup of country-style (read "fried") lunch choices, the competition provided heart-healthy meals. Also important to time-starved businesspeople, the new establishments promised to deliver meals in "10 minutes or less." Bolstered by the focus group evidence, Jake prepared a proposal for his change-resistant grandmother. He proposed a complete remodel of the menu, "call-ahead" ordering, and streamlined service. To his surprise, she agreed to the changes. For at least another generation, Benson's Family Restaurant will remain a vibrant component of the downtown restaurant scene.

❖ FORMS OF RISK

In work contexts, risk is best understood as a phenomenon that affects multiple levels of social organization. It affects individual employees, work relationships, whole organizations, and even larger communities. As suggested by Figure 1.1, each level is "nested" within the levels above. For example, sexually harassing communication puts the individual victim at risk of losing the sense of respect and safety that all persons desire. But harassment is also a relational phenomenon—a misuse of power that disadvantages the victim. At the macro level, organizational norms amplify the risk experienced by the victim, particularly if they fail to provide a safe means of reporting and resisting harassment. And of course, community norms (and laws) ultimately determine how sexually harassing behavior is defined and punished in our workplaces.

Individual Risk

At the individual level, risk takes multiple forms. We explore some of these in the paragraphs below.

Career Risk. Many employees face the threat of job loss or the interruption of a career. The risk may be due to poor performance, but often the risk stems from changing economic conditions. For example, large numbers of auto-making jobs have shifted from the United States to other countries. Technology can make some job skills obsolete. The modern economy requires flexibility as organizations and their workers adjust to rapid change. Employees can no longer count on an implied social contract in which employers offer job security in exchange for loyalty and hard work. All of these trends create the potential for careers to be more temporary, varied, and unpredictable.

Identity Risk. The values, attitudes, behaviors, and expectations we associate with our "self" form our identity. Identity is neither concrete nor unitary. Different aspects of identity are expressed in our interactions with other people, including romantic partners, family, friends, and coworkers. Identity is linked to the expectations that others have of us. The expected and acceptable behaviors available to us in a given situation comprise a role. Roles are particularly important at work, where they are enforced by explicit reward systems, regulated by procedures, and monitored by supervisors and peers. The ethical standards we ascribe to are important parts of identity.

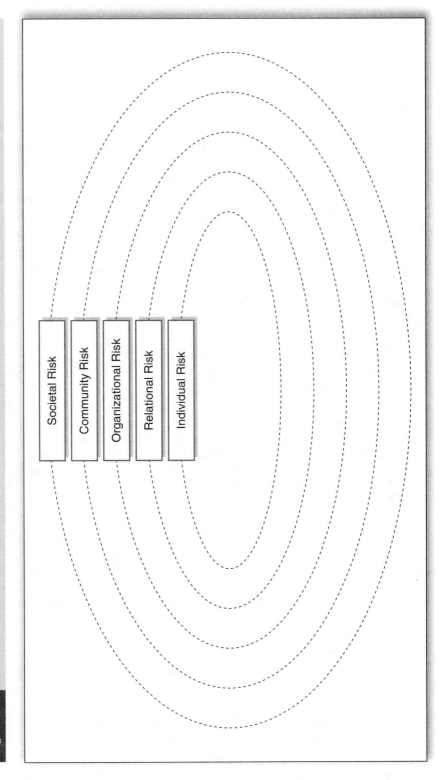

Figure 1.1 Levels of Risk

Societal Risk

Community Risk

Organizational Risk

Relational Risk

Individual Risk

Our identities are put at risk in several ways, some of which involve our work role. Behavior that is inconsistent with your role at work may put you at risk. Your organization may take action to encourage role conformity. Another threat is role loss, when we are removed from a role, asked to share it, or the role itself is eliminated. But identity risk extends beyond the work role. Workers sometimes experience a deeper loss of self—a sense that their work is crowding out or suppressing valuable aspects of their personal identity. As an example, consider that service workers (including restaurant servers) are required to suppress "negative" emotions, like the indignity that arises when customers are rude. For some, these continuous attempts to suppress "real" emotion take a personal toll (see Chapter 3). As suggested in Textbox 1.2, some types of work can dull our emotional responses. Minh wonders if work-induced alterations to our emotional makeup extend to our personal relationships.

Textbox 1.2   Emotional Numbing in the ER

In recounting his emotionally exhausting training as a medical intern in the busy emergency room of a county hospital, Minh was disturbed by the emotional numbness he experienced, even when his patients were suffering. Toward the end of a demanding 24-hour-long shift, he found himself ministering to a woman in the deep throes of labor. As she screamed in pain, he stood by nearly asleep on his feet, completely detached from the scene unfolding around him. "Let's get it over with," he urged her, not bothering to offer comfort or assurance. Later he regretted the lack of emotional empathy he experienced that day. Minh wondered if his emotional responsiveness had been permanently altered by the medical training. What would he feel when his wife was in the throes of labor?

Health Risk. Some careers, such as those in law enforcement, put employees in physical danger. So too does dysfunctional communication between coworkers when the stakes are high (e.g., communication between airline co-pilots). But the more pervasive risks may be those that stem from job-related stress. The communicative and psychological demands of certain kinds of jobs (e.g., nursing or teaching) are associated with high rates of "emotional burnout." Dysfunctional work environments, including those characterized by harassment or bullying, also put employee health at risk (see Chapter 4). The National Institute of Occupational Safety and Health (2009) provides credible information on the physical risks of job stress (see Textbox 1.3).

> ### Textbox 1.3 — What the Research Says: Risking Your Health on the Job?
>
> **Cardiovascular Disease**
>
> Studies indicate that psychologically demanding jobs that allow employees little control over the work process increase the risk of cardiovascular disease.
>
> **Musculoskeletal Disorders**
>
> Job stress may increase the risk for development of back and upper-extremity musculoskeletal disorders.
>
> **Psychological Disorders**
>
> Several studies suggest that differences in rates of mental health problems (such as depression and burnout) for various occupations are due partly to differences in job stress levels.
>
> **Workplace Injury**
>
> Stressful working conditions may interfere with safe work practices and set the stage for injuries.
>
> **Suicide, Cancer, Ulcers, and Impaired Immune Function**
>
> Some studies suggest a relationship between stressful working conditions and these health problems. However, more research is needed before firm conclusions can be drawn.

Relational Risk

As important as individual qualities are, they are often muted or magnified by the nature of work relationships. It is at the relational level that factors such as trust, liking, openness, and power disparities make communication more or less risky. At work, we manage numerous relationships, including those with supervisors, team members, support staff, technical experts, suppliers, and customers. All of these can be put at risk by poor communication. Of course, our relationships extend beyond the workplace. Some coworkers are also friends. These blended relationships are both rewarding and sometimes complicated (see Chapter 5).

Romantic relationships at work can be particularly complicated (Chapter 6) because power disparities can place one of the parties at risk. Ethics codes discourage some forms of romantic behavior, and even those at the highest levels of an organization can experience unintended negative consequences. That was the case for Harry Stonecipher, the powerful president and CEO of Boeing, the American aircraft manufacturer (see Textbox 1.4). After discovering that the married Stonecipher sent sexually explicit e-mails to a female executive, Boeing's board of directors requested his resignation. Finally, and perhaps most important, our work has implications for our personal relationships. Sometimes work becomes so consuming that it displaces or distorts relationships with partners, family, and friends.

Textbox 1.4   Power, Romance, and Ethics: A Cautionary Tale

Harry Stonecipher, a hard-charging 68-year-old former executive, was called out of retirement to lead Boeing back from a series of high-profile ethics scandals. By all accounts, his brief encore was successful. In announcing his resignation, a company press release (Boeing, 2005) noted that "Boeing is in excellent shape with significant momentum due in large part to Harry's forceful leadership." However, as reported by *BusinessWeek* (Holmes, 2005), Stonecipher was tripped up when he flaunted the company's ethics policy. An anonymous employee apparently discovered explicit e-mails exchanged by the married Stonecipher and a female Boeing executive. The board found that the female executive was not harmed by her relationship with the powerful CEO. Nonetheless, it concluded that "the facts reflected poorly on Harry's judgment and would impair his ability to lead the company."

Organizational Risk

Organizational-level processes subsume individuals and their relationships. The operating procedures, tasks, reward systems, cultural norms, and organizing structures of a given organization determine what counts as "risky" behavior at the individual and relational levels. For example, some companies reward employees for "blowing the whistle" on unethical behavior. In others, employees must suppress their ethical concerns unless they are willing to put their jobs at risk (see Chapter 8). When we speak of organizational risk, we mean that the core functions and values of the organization are threatened. The failure of employees to complete tasks productively and efficiently is one such risk. Lapses in quality fit here as well. So do losses in sales and the failure to serve customers well. We also find that some organizations are put at risk because of ethics violations. Companies lose public respect, and sometimes a great deal of money, when they flout their own ethical standards or those of the industry. Some are at risk of violating the law.

Communal Risk

The larger social context must be considered in any discussion of organizational risk. After all, organizations don't exist in a vacuum. Instead, they are shaped by cultural, political, and economic forces, and they often try to influence those forces. At the community level, a given organization shares its resources with those who live in close proximity. The organization's actions may put the community at risk (see Textbox 1.5). This is most obvious when an organizational mistake leads to a health crisis. Imagine a restaurant chain that serves tainted food or a petroleum company that fouls the local water supply. Of course risk works both ways. The actions of a local government or citizen's group may restrict the organization's business practices or cause it to forfeit profits.

Textbox 1.5 **What Happens When a Town Implodes?**

The tiny faming community town of Postville, Iowa, has seen hard times before (Rubiner, 2009). Falling prices for its agricultural products, foreign competition, and bad weather have all taken a toll. But nothing compares to the current disaster, which has been attributed to the risky actions of a single businessperson. During an immigration raid, 389 workers were arrested at Agriprocessors, a meatpacking company and the town's major employer. Eight months later, Postville is still grappling with what its leaders describe as a "humanitarian and economic disaster." Many of the workers were deported, and those who remain must rely on the community for food, legal services, and help in paying their rent. Immigrants, from countries such as Guatemala, barely survived the cold Iowa winter as unemployed workers. Government coffers are empty. Businesses and landlords are suffering, and Agriprocessors has filed for bankruptcy. The problems apparently stem from the risky actions of CEO Sholom Rubashkin, who now faces federal charges for helping illegal immigrants obtain false papers. Rubashkin has denied guilt.

Societal Risk

At the societal level, risk stems from cultural and economic forces. These sometimes take the form of sweeping change—the kind that affects industries or even national economies. In the United States, one such trend is to outsource organizational functions such as human resources or customer relations. These moves save the organization money but put large numbers of employees at risk for unemployment. Outsourcing can make the organization more vulnerable as well because contractors may not be under its control. For example, some U.S. companies have outsourced their customer service function to companies operating in foreign countries where labor is relatively cheap. However, language differences have complicated communication and frustrated customers, leaving some companies in a difficult position.

Some social influences are more subtle, even invisible. But they are reflected in the taken-for-granted assumptions that help us decide what is "normal" at work. For example, in the United States, our culture teaches us that success in business requires long hours of work. In the popular press, profiles of successful leaders offer admiring descriptions of their Herculean work schedules and highly constrained personal lives. Of course, these executives, and those who internalize their values, may put themselves at risk. Their health may suffer. The time available for parenting and other family duties may be woefully inadequate, resulting in frayed social bonds. Because societal assumptions about work are rarely questioned, we often don't realize how they put us at risk. Uncovering risky societal assumptions is an important task of this book.

❖ A COMMUNICATIVE APPROACH TO RISK

Risk is often considered a psychological concept. But as communication scholars, we focus on the behaviors and processes that give risky situations their meaning. The key elements of our approach are presented in an upcoming section of this chapter. Before considering them in detail, though, we discuss five different ways that the concepts of risk and communication are connected (see Figure 1.2).

Figure 1.2   Connections Between Communication and Risk

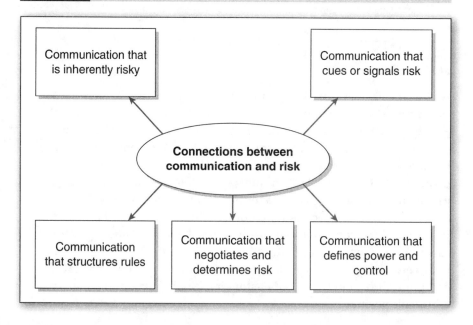

First, certain communication behaviors are inherently risky because they are used to harm or hurt. Insults, sarcastic comments, and threats are examples. Second, communicative behaviors cue us to the possibility of risk. Verbal warnings are common, as when a coworker lets you know that another employee is having a bad day. But nonverbal cues are important too. Both verbal and nonverbal communication helped Jenna, a 26-year-old paralegal, recognize that "things weren't right":

> I walked into the coffee room and conversation just stopped. It was an uncomfortable feeling, like I was barging in on their party. I asked my coworkers about what was going on, but they just said, "nothing much." They didn't look me in the eyes or smile, like they usually would. All of them left the room, but not the one I was closest to. "Haven't you heard yet?" she said. "Jay [my boss] wants to talk to you. And he isn't happy about something."

Risk is communicative in a third way. Organizational life is structured by communication rules, many of which are unspoken. Our opening narrative illustrated one such rule: "All employees are expected to attend weekend events." Rules are often enforced formally. You might receive a poor performance evaluation if you skip the required events. Informal enforcement comes from peers, who might give you the "cold shoulder" if you fail to help out on weekends. Breaking the rules is sometimes necessary, but doing so puts you at risk, even when you do it unintentionally.

Fourth, a communicative approach focuses our attention on risk as a negotiated or managed process. Our perceptions of risk unfold over time, so we can't assume that psychological perceptions of risk will remain static. Rather, work situations become more or less risky as the participants initiate discussion, experience emotional reactions, ask questions, make sense of the answers, and collectively revise the meaning of the situation. As an example, imagine that a salesperson detects a quality problem in the company's much anticipated new product line. Would it be risky to share this observation with management? Communicating "bad news" can seem risky, particularly if the recipient will take the news poorly and possibly "blame the messenger" (see Chapter 2). Then again, the supervisor may interpret the news as valuable feedback—a useful early indication that adjustments must be made to meet customer expectations. So the risk originally perceived by the salesperson may be diminished as the parties explore this different way of thinking about the feedback.

A fifth and final connection between communication and risk involves the "enactment" of organizational power structures. By defining roles, maintaining reward systems, and regulating interactions, organizations define which behaviors are safe and which are risky. However, it is through our own routine behavior that we signal (often subconsciously) acceptance of organizational mandates (Giddens, 1979). For example, by agreeing not to discuss "forbidden" topics, such as our level of compensation, we signal acceptance of this restriction. By standing by silently or by censoring the speech of coworkers, we help management impose a system of controls. In this way, our communication helps define the parameters of risky behavior.

❖ A RISK NEGOTIATION FRAMEWORK

Figure 1.3 presents the elements of our Risk Negotiation Framework. The elements of the framework are addressed here only briefly. In subsequent chapters, we use them to analyze nine different risky situations that you are likely to face at work.

Historical Factors

The organizational present is inevitably shaped by the past. For example, the act of providing constructive feedback to a team member feels riskier if he or she "blew up" during a previous feedback session. So *relationship history* is a major influence on current encounters.

At the relational level, patterns of maintenance communication may be the most important historical variable (see Chapter 5). Relationship maintenance involves routine communication—the kinds of daily interaction that define and sustain our relationships with coworkers and supervisors (Waldron, 2003). *Organizational incidents* will also influence the climate of risk. Having observed a safety violation at your workplace, you will feel more comfortable reporting it if past reports have resulted in praise or even a safety award. Relationship history and organizational incidents combine over time in our *work experience*, which in turn serves to inform our sensibilities about what's risky in our respective workplaces.

Context

Context is the constellation of expectations, resources, and social relations that define our workplace. As Figure 1.3 illustrates, risky episodes

Figure 1.3 Risk Negotiation Framework

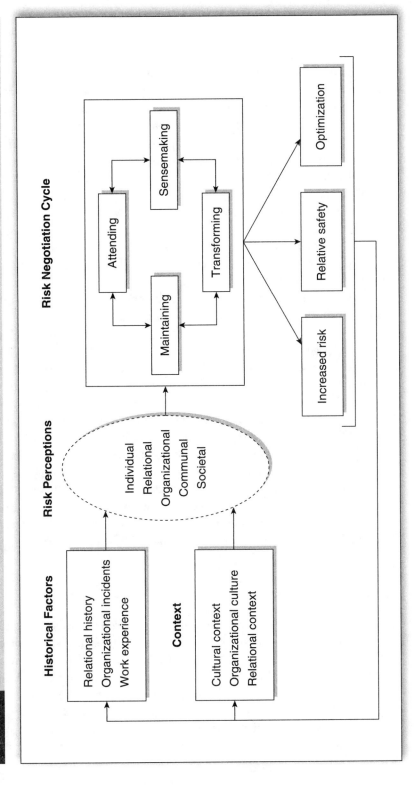

Risk Negotiation Cycle

Sensemaking

Attending

Transforming

Maintaining

Optimization

Relative safety

Increased risk

Risk Perceptions

Individual
Relational
Organizational
Communal
Societal

Historical Factors

Relational history
Organizational incidents
Work experience

Context

Cultural context
Organizational culture
Relational context

occur within a larger *cultural context*. For example, gender norms dictate which kinds of behaviors (e.g., assertiveness, use of sexual humor) are interpersonally safe and which are risky when performed by men or women. Cultural differences can make business negotiations with international partners appear riskier than those with domestic partners. Of course, each organization is defined by its own *organizational culture*, as indicated by dress codes, jargon, business values, and other symbolic behaviors.

These cultural factors are profoundly important in understanding work life, but in our approach, the *relational context* gets considerable attention. It is through our interactions with others that risk is negotiated. As we mentioned above, relational context is determined in part by the partners' history of interaction. It is further defined by relational qualities such as trust, power, liking, respect, openness, and inclusion in decision making. As a case in point, members are less likely to offer suggestions for improving their workplace when their leaders are disliked, distrusted, and unlikely to include employees in decision-making processes (Waldron, 2003).

The relational context is also defined by formal and informal communication rules. These regulate the frequency, direction, and quality of communication in a given relationship. Rule violations may put employees at risk. For example, the employee who secretly "goes around the boss" in reporting an ethics violation may be violating the rule that says something like, "Go to your direct supervisor with all problems first." This rule violation puts the employee at some degree of identity risk. Will she or he be labeled a traitor or "tattletale"? The goal of preserving a supportive supervisory relationship is sacrificed in such situations (see Kassing, 2007), and the employees' effectiveness in the work unit will be undermined if the supervisor attempts retribution.

Risk Perceptions

As we see it, employees' perceptions of risk drive their communicative behaviors. These perceptions are formed in part from historical influences and our understanding of the cultural and organizational context in which we find ourselves. Risk perceptions are fluid, changing as we engage in communication with the other parties participating in a given episode. The salient dimensions of risk can be any of those we discussed earlier: individual, relational, organizational, communal, and societal. So, our perceptions of risk may track along any one or perhaps several of these trajectories at once. Although just simply listed in Figure 1.3, keep in mind that these levels of risk are nested, as illustrated in Figure 1.1; they spill over from one to another much like the rings formed when a rock is dropped into still water.

Raul, a middle manager at a large bank, was criticized publicly and (he felt) unfairly by his boss. The situation occurred in a business meeting, in front of senior managers and Raul's own staff. He reacted this way:

> I felt angry—humiliated and betrayed. [I] felt like I had been stabbed in the back, with no way to defend myself or explain my position. Because of the audience, I probably would not have confronted the senior management person in this meeting, even if time permitted. . . . He forever damaged my credibility. (Waldron, 2000, p. 67)

Raul feels that his identity was attacked (individual risk), but his narrative also suggests that his relationship with his boss was put at risk. Raul was so demoralized by this situation that he interviewed for a management job at one of the bank's competitors. His boss's public criticism put the organization at risk of losing one of its few Spanish-speaking managers.

Perceiving the potential for unethical behavior is an important part of the RNF. Workers put themselves and others at risk when they ignore or suppress ethical warning signs. In an infamous example, executives at Enron, a major player in the energy industry, deceived investors and their own employees about the company's business activities and its financial health. As a result of their behavior, they risked their own careers, destroyed the company, and put the savings of investors and Enron retirees in peril.

❖ THE RISK NEGOTIATION CYCLE

In our framework, employees negotiate perceptions of risk through a cycle of communication involving four interlinked phases (attending, sensemaking, transforming, and maintaining). The two-way arrows in Figure 1.3 indicate that the process may proceed forward, from one phase to the other. However, it is possible for the cycle to stop and return to an earlier point. As we see it, the cycle can continue indefinitely, shaping the risk perceptions of the participants. The cycle may wind down, though, as risk perceptions stabilize or the risk is diminished through the communication practices of the participants.

Each of the four phases is enacted through some combination of four communication tools: strategies, tactics, language use, and non-verbal cues. Communication strategies are general approaches that communicators use in seeking their goals. For example, you might use the strategy of "feigning ignorance" as you enter a situation that appears risky. The general idea is to appear ignorant, so people will fill you in. At the tactical level, one way to implement the strategy is to use an innocent question ("So, is something unusual going on here?"). Language use refers to how we employ words, including labels and metaphors. Your innocent question would have a different meaning if you asked, "Is something *illegal* going on here?" Finally, nonverbal cues, such as facial expressions or tone of voice, are important in risk negotiation. If you asked the question above in a loud or menacing voice, the situation would feel riskier to the other employees, who might feel they are being accused.

Attending

The risk negotiation cycle is initiated with the task of detecting and attending to the nature and magnitude of a potential risk. At this point in the process, the cues are often nonverbal, as when a worker detects that the boss is in a bad mood by recognizing certain facial expressions. A manager notices that something is amiss in an employee's demeanor. Coworkers suspect that a peer is lying due to her odd behavior. Certain verbal messages signal that caution is warranted. A supervisor reveals too much personal information—a sign that a more intimate relationship is desired. During the attending phase, employees form their initial perceptions by observing closely, noticing warning signs, and comparing the current situation to past encounters.

Sensemaking

During the sensemaking phase, the employee's communicative task is to more fully explore the meaning and magnitude of risk. It may start with a review of the relevant cultural, organizational, and relational rules. Having developed amorous feelings for a coworker, an employee asks, "Is it OK for me to date someone at work?" But ultimately, sensemaking is a collective process, whereby employees offer speculations about motives and goals, explore hypothetical explanations, and negotiate over the magnitude, clarity, and seriousness of the situation. For example, having observed a pattern of tardiness in a peer, employees may gather in the break room to discuss the significance of the offense. What are the office norms? How late is *late?* Does the tardiness suggest that something is wrong at home? What are the effects on our work? Is it right to let this behavior go unreported? Emotional reactions may be communicated and even socially constructed during this phase. Through discussion, coworkers spread feelings of fear, fan the flames of indignation, or collectively build the courage to confront risky situations.

Transforming

Through individual initiative or collective action, employees can change risky situations—for better or for worse. Transformative communication practices address the individual, relational, and organizational threats we identified earlier. Although approaches vary across situations, transformative behaviors are those that protect identities, preserve or strengthen relationships, and alter organizational practices that are unsafe, unethical, and ineffective. Reconsider the case of the tardy office worker. By approaching the situation tactfully ("Some of us are worried that you have been running late. Is there anything we can do to help you out?"), a coworker could preserve a supportive relationship with the truant peer even as the rule-violating behavior is questioned. This kind of risk negotiation episode may clarify why the employee is late (car problems) and even yield a transformational solution (offering to carpool).

Maintaining

Once employees perceive that risk levels have changed, they may engage in practices that stabilize risk at current levels. To revisit the case of the tardy coworker once more, employees could monitor arrival times until they are convinced that their coworker has established a habit of punctuality. They may look for evidence of backsliding and, once it is observed, quickly address the issue in team meetings. Or these concerned peers could engage in collaborative recall, telling and retelling the story of how the once-tardy worker "saw the light." Humorous teasing could be integral to this maintenance process, as coworkers embellish this story of redemption and solidify their identity as a highly cohesive team. All of these activities ensure that the risk of recurrent tardiness remains acceptably low.

In contrast, another form of interaction intentionally confirms that risk is, and will remain, high. We see this when coworkers repeatedly warn each other about the consequences of unsafe work practices.

In doing so, they may issue gentle reminders, recount stories of past accidents, or fantasize about the rewards they will receive if they meet annual safety goals. These kinds of interactions stabilize heightened perceptions of risk and demonstrate the constructive role that risk can play in the workplace.

❖ OUTCOMES OF MANAGING RISK

The Risk Negotiation Framework encourages us to think of risk as an episodic process. While it is certainly the case that some episodes sustain a certain level of risk indefinitely (as with the safety-minded workers), most build to some kind of resolution or outcome. We envision three types of outcomes: increased risk, relative safety, and optimization. The first of these, *increased risk*, is an indication that the risk episode exacerbated vulnerability or increased the potential that something valued by the participants will be lost. This increased vulnerability is often attributable to ineffective communication by the participants, who may have enacted behaviors that threatened identities, harmed relationships, impeded task performance, or created an ethical lapse. As shown by the feedback loop at the bottom of Figure 1.3, this episode becomes part of the history and context shared by the participants. Its memory will affect the tenor of future encounters.

More successful risk negotiation cycles increase perceptions of safety. Through their interactions, the parties may discover that risk was fueled by misperceptions or misunderstandings. Having communicated about the risk, they feel less vulnerable. In the case of the truant team member, peers protected the coworker by handling the problem themselves. Had they complained to a supervisor, the team might have increased the risk of negative sanction and disrupted cohesion (see Chapter 10). Actions of this kind increase *relative safety* in the sense that the participants perceive less risk after the episode than they did when it began.

Optimization transcends concerns about safety and risk. Having negotiated a risky situation, the participants realize some kind of gain. For example, the episode may result in strengthened relationships among the parties. Or, previously untapped communication competencies are sometimes uncovered. Successfully negotiating a risky situation may instill confidence in a previously hesitant employee. Another instance of optimization might be a positive change in the relational rules or organizational procedures that make work unnecessarily risky. It is not uncommon for risky situations to yield creative solutions.

In fact, successful entrepreneurs often deliberatively expose themselves to risk and sometimes find themselves at odds with more conservative coworkers and managers (see Chapter 9). When risky situations lead to optimization, this too is recorded in the memories of the participants. Possibly, these employees become more open to the transformative potential of risky situations and more empowered when facing them.

❖ CONCLUSION

Whether they do so intuitively or through deliberate analysis, employees can learn to assess and manage risk. Doing so requires an appreciation for the tensions that inevitably arise from the melding of individual goals, relational dynamics, and organizational mandates. It also requires an understanding of how community and societal values shape our work experiences. Each chapter of this book presents a risky work situation that people are likely to experience early in their careers. Chapters 2 through 10 conform to a standard organizational structure. Each chapter begins by introducing a risky communication situation and explains why it is important. We then review several key research studies. The studies help us provide an evidenced-based analysis of the concepts that help employees manage risk when encountering situations like this. We are particularly concerned with communicative strategies, tactics, and behaviors. Therefore, each chapter includes a summary table titled Communication Options. The chapters continue with an application of the risk negotiation cycle and its four phases: attending, sensemaking, transforming, and maintaining. Throughout each chapter, we explore the communicative practices that are likely to lead to increased risk, relative safety, and, sometimes, optimization. Ultimately, we want to illustrate that risk negotiation episodes can bring opportunities for positive and powerful change. If nothing else, they challenge us to hone our communication competencies. In embracing the positive potential of risk, we are not above resorting to a well-worn cliché—nothing risked, nothing gained.

❖ REFERENCES

Boeing. (2005, March 7). *Boeing CEO Harry Stonecipher resigns* [Press release]. Retrieved from www.boeing.com/news/releases/2005/q1/nr_050307a.html

Giddens, A. (1979). *Central problems in social theory.* Berkeley: University of California Press.

Holmes, S. (2005, March 8). What Boeing needs to fly right. *BusinessWeek.* Retrieved June 6, 2009, from http://www.businessweek.com/bwdaily/dnflash/mar2005/nf2005038_1218_db042.htm

Kassing, J. W. (2007). Going around the boss: Exploring the consequences of circumvention. *Management Communication Quarterly, 21,* 55–74.

National Institute for Occupational Safety and Health. (2009). *Stress . . . at work* (Pub. 99–101). Retrieved June 8, 2009, from http://www.cdc.gov/niosh/docs/99–101/

Rubiner, R. (2009, January 28). *Iowa: What happens when a town implodes?* Retrieved June 19, 2009, from http://www.time.com/time/nation/article/0,8599,1874205,00.html

Waldron, V. (2000). Relational experiences and emotion at work. In S. Fineman (Ed.), *Emotion in organizations* (2nd ed., pp. 64–82). London: Sage.

Waldron, V. (2003). Relationship maintenance in organizational settings. In D. J. Canary & M. Dainton (Eds.), *Maintaining relationships through communication: Relational, contextual, and cultural variations* (pp. 163–184). Mahwah, NJ: Lawrence Erlbaum.

2

Delivering and Seeking Feedback

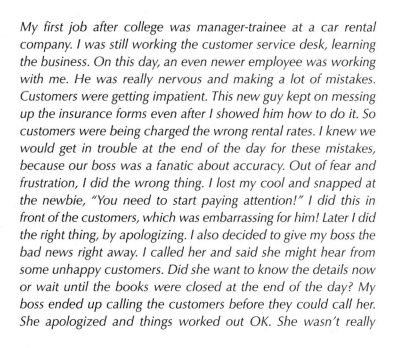

My first job after college was manager-trainee at a car rental company. I was still working the customer service desk, learning the business. On this day, an even newer employee was working with me. He was really nervous and making a lot of mistakes. Customers were getting impatient. This new guy kept on messing up the insurance forms even after I showed him how to do it. So customers were being charged the wrong rental rates. I knew we would get in trouble at the end of the day for these mistakes, because our boss was a fanatic about accuracy. Out of fear and frustration, I did the wrong thing. I lost my cool and snapped at the newbie, "You need to start paying attention!" I did this in front of the customers, which was embarrassing for him! Later I did the right thing, by apologizing. I also decided to give my boss the bad news right away. I called her and said she might hear from some unhappy customers. Did she want to know the details now or wait until the books were closed at the end of the day? My boss ended up calling the customers before they could call her. She apologized and things worked out OK. She wasn't really *angry. She even thanked me for telling the truth and avoiding a negative surprise.*

Vickie, age 26

Vickie's story has much to tell us about the communication of feedback, particularly negative feedback. In this situation, Vickie's impatient reaction damaged both her relationship with her coworker and the customer's experience with the car rental company. Reprimanding her coworker with a general directive embarrassed her colleague in public. There is no doubt the nervous newcomer was already "paying attention." A better response from Vickie would have been to provide reassurance and specific directions (e.g., "Go ahead and check this box if they want to decline the liability insurance."). Specific directions delivered in a quiet, assuring voice would have helped her coworker through a challenging situation, and impatient customers would have seen their business was being handled in a calm, professional manner.

Fortunately, Vickie redeemed herself by communicating the bad news to her supervisor. Most employees suppress negative performance information out of fear of retaliation, especially when communicating up the chain of command. They often fear the "kill the messenger" mentality that prevails in some organizations. But Vickie's approach was skillful. Why? Because she reported the bad news quickly before things got worse, a strategy called preemptive feedback. Vickie made it possible for her supervisor to head off a customer service problem with a few conciliatory phone calls. Had Vickie waited, her boss would have been waylaid by a negative surprise. Instead, Vickie got credit for being honest and concerned for the good of her company.

This chapter addresses the sometimes difficult process of communicating negative feedback. We discuss performance feedback because nearly every employee receives it, formally or informally, from a supervisor. A deeper understanding of why employees and supervisors struggle with this communication task may help you be more adaptable and less defensive when your performance is critiqued. After all, constructive feedback is essential if we are to correct our inevitable mistakes and help coworkers improve performance. In fact, it is sometimes beneficial to seek feedback rather than waiting for it to be delivered. Delivering constructive criticism is an essential part of any manager's job, and seeking feedback is important for all employees.

This chapter also considers the related challenge of communicating bad news. Inevitably, things will go wrong at your workplace. Performance will falter. Requests will be denied. Ethical violations will occur. Customers will be unhappy. At some point, bad news must be delivered to coworkers or management. How should it be communicated? To deal with these kinds of situations, members of organizations must develop competence in delivering undesirable messages. To put it another way, communicating bad news in a manner that preserves work relationships and employee morale is an important skill.

The term *feedback* may have first appeared in a 1948 volume penned by cybernetic theorist Norbert Weiner, although the concept had been applied much earlier (see Waldron, 2008). For Weiner and similar-thinking engineers, feedback was the signal that indicated a discrepancy between the goal of a system and its current level of performance. Feedback loops allow machines to adjust performance continuously, as when a thermostat signals a cooling system to turn on or off depending on current and desired temperatures. Negative feedback is corrective, while positive feedback indicates that no change in performance is needed.

The feedback concept was so useful in the world of machines that researchers studied its application in human organizations, believing that effectively communicated feedback should improve the performance of individual employees and workgroups. Indeed, feedback is a crucial kind of workplace communication. Of course, relationships complicate the feedback process, particularly those that involve differences in power. A series of important early studies (Rosen & Tesser, 1970; Tesser & Rosen, 1972) established that most people would rather say nothing than deliver negative feedback, a tendency labeled the "mum effect." Later, organizational researchers confirmed that the communication of negative feedback to employees can be a troubling and difficult task for leaders (Larson, 1989). And for members, upward communication of negative information is even more problematic because of the power differences involved. Criticizing your boss can be a risky undertaking.

Choosing an appropriate medium for delivering feedback is another consideration (Timmerman & Harrison, 2005). It may be tempting to avoid face-to-face communication when delivering negative performance information or alerting workers to bad news. Written messages or e-mails distance the sender from potentially messy emotional reactions and reduce the opportunities for employees to ask uncomfortable questions. But these "lean" media also signal a lack of engagement—an insensitivity to the human implications of negative messages. Most employees expect more from their leaders. In addition, written messages are unidirectional. They limit opportunities for the employee's point of view to be voiced and considered on its merits. This lack of consideration often breeds resentment ("He didn't even have the decency to tell me to my face."). In short, the impact of the negative message is amplified when senders make poor communicative choices.

All of these observations suggest that the signal-processing assumptions of the cybernetic feedback model are too simplistic. In response, researchers have turned their attention to uniquely human influences on feedback, including linguistic qualities of messages, relationship context, cultural variations, and worker identity. These are the factors that give feedback its meaning (Cusella, 1987), and the meanings that employees construct from feedback messages determine how they respond. The challenge for providers of negative feedback is to provide messages that are clear but also sensitive to relational and identity threats.

❖ WHY IS DELIVERING AND SEEKING FEEDBACK IMPORTANT?

Although it has been researched for decades, feedback remains a central topic of interest for both employees and management theorists. Here are some of the reasons.

Improving Performance

As most college students know, it is difficult to improve performance on class assignments if feedback from the instructor is limited, unreasonably delayed, or of poor quality. The same is true at work. In fact, employees frequently express concerns about a lack of useful feedback from supervisors.

Kaling was a young professor when she experienced the consequences of poor feedback practices.

> I had been working hard for more than 2 years, developing new classes and working closely with my students. In faculty meetings I received compliments from my colleagues, who appeared to appreciate my efforts to take on some of the department's student advising duties and community service obligations. My director was always pleasant, although she rarely commented on my work. I assumed she was pleased, because I had yet to hear otherwise. To my great surprise, my 2-year review went very poorly. She told me I was spending too much time on teaching and not enough on research. I shouldn't be doing the work of my senior colleagues, even if they asked me too, she said. What's more, if I didn't "shape up" in the next 12 months, I should start looking for another job. I was shocked to hear this news and felt betrayed. Why wasn't I told earlier so I could have changed my priorities?

It appears that the positive feedback Kaling received was unrelated to her organization's most important performance goals. Honest and early feedback may have helped Kaling adjust her task priorities and perhaps retain her position. Unfortunately, supervisors are often reluctant to provide such feedback, sometimes for legitimate reasons, sometimes not (see Textbox 2.1).

Textbox 2.1	**Six Reasons Supervisors Avoid Negative Feedback**

1. To avoid hurting the employee's feelings

2. Fear of an angry, blaming, or defensive response

3. Lack of skill in communicating feedback

4. Assumption that the employee will correct behavior without feedback

5. Desire to preserve a harmonious relationship with the employee

6. Political motives (e.g., undermining an employee's success)

Given its prominence in the management literature, it would be easy to assume that negative feedback always enhances performance. But the research yields a more nuanced conclusion. Negative feedback can actually depress performance when it is poorly communicated. In such circumstances, employees may feel personally attacked, hopeless, or demotivated. Table 2.1 offers guidelines for providing constructive feedback.

Table 2.1	Twelve Practical Guidelines for Constructive Feedback

Guidelines

1. Give negative feedback in private to avoid unnecessary embarrassment.

2. Positive feedback delivered in public can have strong motivational effects.

3. Informal feedback can be less threatening than formal feedback (performance evaluations).

4. Frequent feedback is more useful in correcting performance then occasional feedback.

5. Negative feedback should focus on work practices, not personal characteristics.

(Continued)

Table 2.1	*(Continued)*

6. Use feedback as an aid to employee development rather than as an evaluation tool.

7. Refer to concrete evidence when commenting on performance shortcomings.

8. Immediate feedback may be more useful than delayed feedback.

9. Specific instructions can be more useful than general admonitions (such as "work smarter!").

10. Acknowledge positive as well as negative contributions.

11. Identify and address problems early before they escalate.

12. Multisource feedback can be more useful than single-source feedback.

Adapting to Changing Conditions

As proponents of systems theory have long informed us, organizations are greatly influenced by the environments in which they reside. With the rapid pace of change in most industries, organizations that thrive are those that constantly scan the environment for new information about customers, competitors, and opportunities. In other words, they seek feedback constantly to help make adjustments in performance. The internal environment is also tapped for feedback, and employees are encouraged to ask questions, raise concerns, and make suggestions for improved work processes.

Honoring Those "Closest to the Work"

Workers often hold more task-relevant knowledge than those who manage them. Salespeople know their customers' needs. Assembly line workers know their machines. Teachers understand the learning challenges of their students. By seeking upward feedback from those closest to the task, managers honor their expertise and gain valuable information about how to improve work processes. Managers who fail to cultivate feedback find themselves with a dispirited staff and an unresponsive organization—the very situation faced by Dunder Mifflin, the fictional paper supply company featured in *The Office*, a popular television comedy (Textbox 2.2).

Textbox 2.2   **Dysfunctional Feedback Practices at *The Office***

The Office, a popular television comedy, depicts working life at Dunder Mifflin, a struggling company that delivers paper supplies to small businesses in Scranton, Pennsylvania. Audiences find the show funny because its fictional employees are oblivious to even the most basic principles of organizational communication, including those regarding effective feedback. Manager Michael Scott rarely asks for employee input, pointedly ignores the office suggestion box, and becomes defensive at the slightest hint of criticism. Wary of their supervisor's hypersensitivity, the largely dispirited members of the staff rarely offer suggestions for improving Dunder Mifflin's competitiveness. From past experience, they know that public embarrassment and other miseries await those who dare to "upstage" their chronically insecure supervisor. However, even in the fictional world of *The Office*, this lack of upward communication comes with a price. Stuck with an outdated business model, Dunder Mifflin is rapidly losing market share to more nimble competitors.

Managing Misunderstanding

A critical communication competency in today's relatively chaotic work environments is the capacity to be comfortable with uncertainty. Of course, ambiguity has always been an inevitable, even desirable, aspect of organizational communication. What if you were asked to perform a task that is complex, ill-defined, or creative, such as designing a new advertising campaign or writing a blog for your company's Web site? In this situation, it would be counterproductive, and maybe naive, to ask your boss for perfectly clear task instructions. Part of this task involves structuring the work yourself, drawing on your own knowledge and talent. Although some risk of misunderstanding must be accepted, employees can be more creative when managers avoid overspecifying job requirements.

In workplaces increasingly defined by technical dialects and cultural diversity, employees should simply expect misunderstandings to occur. Feedback then becomes a tool for processing multiple interpretations. Years ago, psychologist Karl Weick (1969) introduced the term *equivocality* to describe this potential for multiple interpretations (see Textbox 2.3). Equivocality is high when you are negotiating a brand-new contract with a business partner from another culture or when a normally supportive colleague angrily criticizes you at a team meeting. These situations require more deliberate communication ("Are we using these terms similarly?"), consideration of multiple interpretations ("Is the anger really directed at me, or is it a reaction to overwork and stress?"), and multiple feedback cycles ("Let's take another look at the contract details now that we have had time to share the basic principles with our colleagues."). In contrast, equivocality is low in routine situations, where the appropriate behavioral response is obvious. When a customer raises a familiar objection, the well-trained salesperson knows the right answer immediately, without much thought or consultation.

Textbox 2.3   Why Do Weick's Ideas Matter Now?

Weick's (1969) ideas remain highly relevant today given that high levels of equivocality are a given in the rapidly changing and globalizing economy. In adopting his perspective, workers recognize that organizations are not merely static structures with prefabricated roles that employees "step into." They assume instead that both leaders and members participate in an ongoing process of organizing. Communication practices help the organization make meaning from changing and uncertain conditions and continuously learn new ways of responding. How? Giving appropriate feedback, actively seeking it from internal and external sources, and designing feedback loops into your workplace decision making—these are competent communication practices in highly equivocal work environments.

Delivering feedback, particularly negative feedback, can be difficult because it gives rise to several levels of risk. In offering negative performance feedback to a teammate, for example, one can reduce the risk of continued poor performance. Feedback may help the recipient perform the work better and faster. But the feedback also potentially puts the recipient's identity at risk. He or she wants to be perceived as a competent employee. In addition, the feedback provider risks coming off as a pushy "know-it-all"—threatening his or her identity. Another result could be relational tension. How, then, do we preserve cohesive team relationships while criticizing members of the team?

Constructive upward communication may call attention to unexpected negative results or expose dysfunctional practices that remained hidden from view. In the long run, such feedback helps an organization make adjustments that ensures its continued success. When communicated skillfully and received gracefully, upward feedback allows employees to preserve their identities as competent and committed members of the organizational team. Yet these messages have the potential to threaten the identities of the recipients (who may feel responsible or criticized) and create tensions with supervisors, who sometimes don't want to acknowledge bad news. Needless to say, the delivery of unwanted feedback is a risky form of communication.

Fortunately, the research provides considerable insight on how to manage the risks.

❖ KEY RESEARCH STUDIES

Delivering Bad News at UPS

United Parcel Service (UPS) is an international delivery company with several hundred thousand employees and gross revenues in the billions of dollars. One of the authors directed a study of "bad news" delivery practices at the massive UPS Air Group hub in Louisville, Kentucky (Wagoner & Waldron, 1999). UPS is a successful company with a strong culture emphasizing loyalty, commitment, and conformity with exacting rules and safety procedures. In some ways similar to the military, the culture at UPS Air Group emphasizes clarity, structure, safety, and a "no surprises" ethic. In addition to extended interviews and site visits, the data included survey responses from more than 300 lower- and mid-level managers about the kinds of routine bad news they were called upon to communicate and the message delivery strategies that they used. The authors intentionally avoided catastrophic bad news situations, such as those involving aircraft crashes and layoffs, choosing to focus on the more common varieties encountered in the course of a normal workday.

Employees described a specific bad news incident, providing, as best they could, a verbatim account of what was said. The first question addressed by the study concerned the nature of naturally occurring bad news. At least at UPS, four types were most common, as reported in Table 2.2. These included poor performance, broken rules, denied requests, and negative external circumstances or events.

Wagoner and Waldron (1999) used politeness theory (Brown & Levinson, 1978) to address why negative feedback and other forms of bad news are so hard to deliver. The theory is predicated on the idea that all social actors possess a valued self-concept (or "face") that they wish others to accept. Bad news messages are face threatening because they put at risk one of two primary dimensions of face. These include the desire to be approved by others and the need to be unimpeded in one's actions (i.e., autonomy). Messages that criticize poor performance or call attention to broken rules obviously threaten the need for approval. Rejections, insults, or complaints may function similarly. When employees deny requests, give corrective feedback, or make threats, the recipient's autonomy is restricted; they perceive limited choices in the face of such messages. The

| Table 2.2 | Types of Routine Bad News at UPS Air Group |

Type of Bad News	Examples
Poor performance	Low annual evaluation
	Poor aircraft simulator results
	Too many errors in reports
Broken rules	Tardiness
	Absenteeism
	Failed to follow check-in procedures
Request denied	Day off rescinded
	Change in shift denied
	Rejection of promotion request
External circumstances	Regulatory change in training requirements
	Reduced role due to hiring of more experienced pilots
	News of a relative's death (delivered at work)

Source: Wagoner and Waldron (1999). Used by permission.

authors agued for a third face need based on earlier work (Lim & Bowers, 1991). Fellowship is the need for belonging or togetherness. Communication that conveys rejection, disqualification, or exclusion threatens fellowship.

The researchers wanted to know how these face threats were managed in workplace encounters. In other words, what message strategies allowed negative information to be communicated while protecting the identities of the parties? Drawing again from politeness theory and the data, they identified three strategies for delivering bad news.

- *Approbation:* These messages affirm an employee's sense of competence in some aspect of performance. For example, in offering corrective feedback to a teammate, an experienced employee might also genuinely praise his or her work ethic, commitment to the team, and track record of success.

- *Tact:* The approach minimizes the imposition of the feedback message by preserving options for the recipient—allowing him or her some freedom to control the conversation. A tactful team leader might begin a performance evaluation by allowing an underperforming member to define his or her own performance first, rather than simply responding to the supervisor's ratings. In another example, senior employees sometimes denied a coworker's request to exchange shifts, but they increased options by suggesting coworkers who might be available to do so.

- *Solidarity:* Solidarity mitigates face threat by communicating that the recipient should feel understood by others—affirming belonging to the workgroup. Solidarity is implied by phrases such as, "We are all in this together," "I have made that mistake before," and "You are an important part of the team."

The Wagoner and Waldron (1999) study offered some guidance on how experienced employees use these three strategies when delivering bad news. First, they often combined the strategies so as to address multiple kinds of face threat, as in this statement: "I can't approve your request to attend the new software training (potential autonomy threat) but I appreciate your commitment to improving your skills (approbation) and hope you will consider attending next month (tact)." Second, unmitigated threats, including "bald" criticisms, such as, "You just failed to perform today," were used judiciously. Bald face threats can reduce motivation and focus the employee's attention on face protection rather than task improvement. Third, some evidence suggested that face-saving strategies were adapted to the type of bad news. For example, tact was used extensively in all situations, but it was particularly common when denying requests. Solidarity was more likely to be invoked when correcting a rule violation ("We all value our safety here, and that is why we expect you to follow the procedures."). Finally, bad news was often delivered in person rather than electronically or in written statements. This interpersonal approach communicated solidarity and displayed consideration for the recipient.

Cultivating Multisource Feedback

Performance feedback is often assumed to involve two persons in the traditional roles of sender and receiver. However, in recent years, the value of receiving feedback from multiple sources has been recognized as an important element in the employee development process.

Multisource feedback (MSF), sometimes referred to as 360-degree feed-back, incorporates information from peers, bosses, subordinates, and even customers. The process has received considerable research atten-tion in recent years and has been adopted by numerous organizations. Management researcher Leanne Atwater and peers recently summa-rized the MSF literature and reported results of a 3-year study (Atwater, Brett, & Atira, 2007). They observed 145 leaders in two different work settings, a retail organization and a school district. Leaders were rated by peers, subordinates, and managers at multiple points in time. Leaders also rated their own performance and reported on their per-ceptions of the MSF process.

MSF is more complicated than traditional feedback methods, and because it increases the number of evaluating parties, the potential for face threat certainly can be magnified. Indeed, MSF programs sometimes falter due to a lack of procedural safeguards. Atwater et al. (2007) make a series of helpful recommendations for making MSF both safe and effective. We summarize some of those below, with an emphasis on the communication factors that will matter most if you participate in an MSF process.

The first consideration involves the characteristics of the message receiver—the employee who is the target of the multisource feedback. The research indicates that employees respond more positively to MSF if they are (a) open to new experiences, (b) possess a learning orienta-tion, and (c) see that the feedback can advance their career goals. Furthermore, those who overrate themselves compared to other feed-back sources may be more motivated to make improvements in per-formance. On the other hand, employees who have become cynical tend to react unfavorably to MSF, as do those who report negative emotional reactions upon receiving feedback. Regarding this last observation, Kluger and DeNisi (1996) proposed feedback intervention theory (FIT). According to these authors, feedback should focus the recipient's atten-tion on the tasks identified for improvement rather than peripheral concerns, such as one's self-perception or how one's performance com-pares to peers. Feedback about these nontask concerns can result in emotional reactions such as despair or pride, which in turn interfere with task performance. All of this suggests that an employee's personal reaction to receiving feedback can facilitate or hamper the success of an MSF program.

A second consideration involves the qualities of feedback mes-sages and the channels used to deliver them. Although some contro-versy remains regarding the issue, employees may prefer numeric ratings over qualitative (textual) feedback, particularly when they can compare their ratings to the performance of others in similar positions (normative data). Providing both kinds of feedback is recommended. With regard to feedback valence, those who receive negative feedback tend to set more self-improvement goals. Not surprising is the finding that employees who receive positive feedback tend to be happier with the process. Anonymity is another important consideration. In particular, feedback providers must be assured that they will remain anonymous if their feedback is to be honest and useful. This is particularly true for those who are rating someone with more power in the organization, like an immediate supervisor. Just as important, MSF is more effective when recipients know the ratings are confidential—seen only by them and used only to aid their self-development efforts. The MSF process must feel safe to all participants if it is to be effective.

A third set of variables concerns outcomes of MSF. In general, it appears that a well-designed MSF program helps employees recognize discrepancies between self and other perceptions. It helps feedback recipients become aware of the need for change and spurs meaningful consideration of self-development goals. In reality, MSF recipients tend to show only modest improvement in ratings from year to year, but Atwater et al. (2007) argue that substantive long-term change is likely, particularly when recipients receive appropriate coaching and mentoring to supplement the feedback.

The logistics of MSF programs can be daunting. Obtaining ratings from external sources (customers, suppliers) can be time-consuming. For that reason, many organizations use only internal raters. Supervisors tend to be responsive to feedback provided by subordinates, but power differences discourage honest reporting. In addition, employees must perceive a meaningful connection between MSF and other human resource programs, including training, promotion, and reward systems. MSF requires a climate of trust. Employees won't take it seriously if they think management will exploit the system or if they feel their careers are at risk due to downsizing and layoffs. Although the process might prove useful as an evaluative tool in organizations with long MSF track records, it is more useful as an employee development process. Finally, the efficiency of MSF can be improved by the use of online systems for collecting and synthesizing feedback.

Feedback-Seeking Behavior

Another communication strategy for improving performance is actively seeking feedback from peers and supervisors. Feedback seeking is a preemptive approach. It allows employees to gather assessments of their work prior to formal performance reviews and to head off serious performance failures through early detection and correction. Employees who seek feedback are more likely to be successful within their workgroups, and their teams tend to be higher performing (Barr & Conlon, 1994). Feedback seeking is risky in the sense that it makes the employee vulnerable to criticism. Of course, feedback may be ego affirming, which is why some coworkers sometimes fish for compliments.

Due to it being risky, some employees fail to seek feedback when it would be wise to do so. Status differences, cultural norms, and ego protection are among the factors that inhibit feedback seeking. In an interesting laboratory study of team behavior, researchers determined that gender is another consideration (Miller & Karakowsky, 2005). The researchers randomly assigned 286 business students to teams that were tasked with developing a negotiation strategy in response to one of two case studies. The cases were designed to be gendered, with the "male" task involving negotiations over a used car and the "female" task involving negotiations of relationship boundaries. It was expected that the gender of the member, the gender composition of the group, and the nature of the tasks would influence a member's willingness to seek feedback from fellow members.

In fact, the researchers did find that gender mattered. Males were most likely to seek feedback when performing the "male-oriented" negotiation tasks in a team comprising mostly male members. Women seemed less reluctant to seek feedback from opposite-sex members, particularly when performing the male-oriented negotiation task. The results suggest that feedback seeking in men is inhibited by ego exposure (the possibility of embarrassment in front of female members) and task expertise. Females seemed most concerned with task expertise. If male experts were available, females were willing to seek feedback from them. Taken together, these results suggest that, at least for males, societal assumptions about gender may be inhibiting an important form of performance-enhancing communication. Because teams are common in the workplace, the results may have broad application.

Before moving to a discussion of the risk negotiation cycle, we cue you to an important textbox summary that appears in each chapter (see Textbox 2.4). These textboxes highlight the communication options relevant to the topic of the given chapter—in this case, the communication options relevant to delivering and seeking feedback.

Textbox 2.4   Communication Options

Delivering Criticism and Bad News (Wagoner & Waldron, 1999)

Silence (the "mum effect")
Face-to-face vs. written/e-mail
"Bald" approaches (ignore face threat)
Tact (gives choices, preserves options)
Approbation (compliments, affirmations)
Solidarity (acknowledging belonging, showing empathy)
"Preemptive" bad news

Multisource Feedback (Atwater et al., 2007)

Task-focused feedback vs. individual-focused feedback
Numeric ratings vs. qualitative comments
Normative (comparative) feedback
Anonymous feedback
External vs. internal sources of feedback
Facilitated group discussion of feedback

Feedback-Seeking Behavior

Feedback seeking from peers
Feedback seeking from supervisors

❖ NEGATIVE FEEDBACK AND THE RISK NEGOTIATION CYCLE

We have established that the communication of negative feedback can be a risky endeavor. And we know that both leaders and members sometimes choose to be "mum" rather than deliver bad news. Yet, it is clear that successful communication of negative information is crucial both to organizational performance and personal development. In this section, we apply the risk negotiation cycle (see Figure 2.1) to the task of communicating negative feedback.

Attending

In feedback situations, employees confront risk at the individual, relational, organizational, and cultural levels. An honest self-assessment of your own feedback receptivity may be the first order of business. Are you receptive to change? Do you approach feedback situations with a

Figure 2.1 Delivering and Seeking Feedback and the Risk Negotiation Cycle

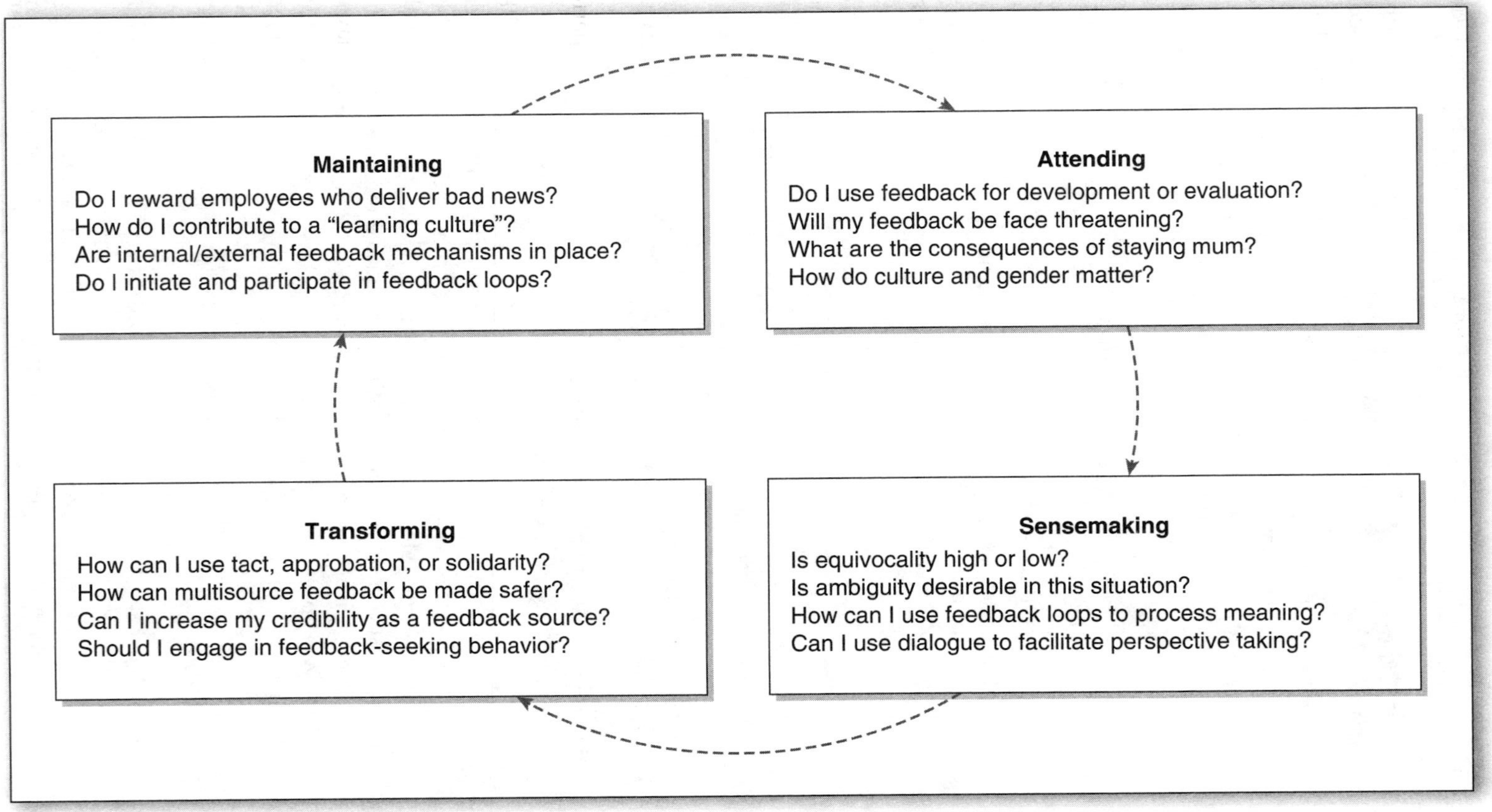

Attending

Do I use feedback for development or evaluation?
Will my feedback be face threatening?
What are the consequences of staying mum?
How do culture and gender matter?

Sensemaking

Is equivocality high or low?
Is ambiguity desirable in this situation?
How can I use feedback loops to process meaning?
Can I use dialogue to facilitate perspective taking?

Maintaining

Do I reward employees who deliver bad news?
How do I contribute to a "learning culture"?
Are internal/external feedback mechanisms in place?
Do I initiate and participate in feedback loops?

Transforming

How can I use tact, approbation, or solidarity?
How can multisource feedback be made safer?
Can I increase my credibility as a feedback source?
Should I engage in feedback-seeking behavior?

learning orientation? If not, you are likely to find negative feedback threatening rather than motivating. Your reaction may be focused on your own emotions as opposed to improving task performance. Attending to these personal reactions is an important step in becoming a more competent feedback receiver and, perhaps, accelerating your development as an employee.

As a deliverer of bad news, it is important to attend to the potential face risks inherent in negative performance feedback and denied requests. Will these messages threaten the receiver's autonomy, competence, or sense of belonging? Is the target of your feedback cynical, defensive, or unreceptive to change? How substantial is the relational risk? Consider factors such as relational history and power differences. Have you developed a trusting relationship with this coworker? Do power differences make the message more intimidating or emotionally impactful? Is the recipient likely to view your message as evaluative or developmental? How do you intend it?

At the organizational level, businesses are at risk when they fail to encourage the reporting of negative feedback, particularly from those employees who are closest to changing environmental conditions. What would be the consequences if you reported bad news (like declining customer enthusiasm) to your boss? Would he or she "blame the messenger" or reward your willingness to speak up? Do you have the credibility to make your feedback convincing? As a supervisor, have you helped your employees recognize potential problems? Are they aware of warning signs, and will they recognize when performance is falling short of organizational goals?

Finally, are you aware of cultural or gender differences that might influence feedback? For example, the importance of face can be magnified in collectivist cultures, like that of the Chinese. Workers in collectivist cultures honor the group over the individual, and they value harmony over conflict. The tendency to suppress bad news may be accentuated in collectivist cultures, as will efforts to avoid behaviors (e.g., direct criticism) that threaten an employee's social standing (for additional information, see Chapter 7). Earlier, we noted that the gender of an individual worker and the gender composition of a work team may inhibit feedback-seeking behavior. Are gender differences a factor in your own approach to performance improvement?

Sensemaking

Feedback is an integral part of the process of making meaning. As we mentioned earlier, a key issue is the degree of equivocality present in a given organizational situation. How much ambiguity is desirable in this situation? Are multiple interpretations possible? How can you initiate feedback cycles to help your coworkers make sense of conflicting messages, sift through potential causes of a problem, and choose from multiple courses of action? What kinds of communication practices will aid sensemaking? Consider asking questions, consulting with colleagues, scanning the external environment, and engaging in structured group discussions. Multisource feedback programs offer an opportunity to check self-perceptions against those of your peers, subordinates, and managers. Your goal should be to develop a capacity to observe situations from multiple points of view, the skill of perspective taking.

Finally, we recommend that your sensemaking efforts be guided by principles of dialogue (see Textbox 2.5). The goal of dialogue is to enhance understanding through interactions with coworkers. Its purpose is not to persuade, win, or impose your personal understanding (for a discussion of dialogue in organizational settings, see Deetz, Tracy, & Simpson, 1999).

Textbox 2.5   Some Principles of Dialogue

- Work cooperatively to improve understanding of issues and problems

- Uncover and explore hidden assumptions

- Construct potential alternates to familiar meanings

- Discover areas of agreement

- Question areas of superficial or false agreement

- Suspend the tendencies to evaluate, compete, and debate

Transforming

Face management strategies such as approbation, tact, and solidarity can transform the identity risk inherent in criticism. In contrast, bald feedback exacerbates risk; it fails to provide identity support for the hearer. The result may be an employee who is more concerned with identity defense than task performance. Keeping mum protects the self but suppresses potentially valuable information—information that could help others improve their performance or help your organization make important adjustments.

Earlier, we distilled guidelines for making feedback both effective and safe. These included focusing on tasks and not persons, giving negative feedback in private, and providing concrete instructions rather than generalized admonitions. Some of these guidelines will be particularly helpful with the sometimes intimidating task of upward feedback. Employee credibility is important in such situations, and it will be enhanced if you use concrete evidence to support your personal observations. What kinds of evidence would help your boss focus on the problem and not on you? In addition, your efforts to exchange frequent and informal communication with your boss can make feedback part of your communication routine. In that context, bad news is less negatively surprising to your boss and less threatening to both of you. As a manager, how would you reward employees who choose not to stay mum? Are your employees comfortable with the prospect of reporting negative feedback to you? If not, what can you do to make them so?

Multisource feedback systems have the potential to be transformative, but they can be risky. Organizations make them safer by preserving the anonymity of raters, ensuring that only the recipient (not his or her bosses) view the feedback, and conceptualizing MSF as a development activity, not an evaluation system. When employees mistrust management's intention or feel insecure in their jobs, MSF becomes more threatening and fails to improve performance.

Maintaining

Once delivering negative feedback becomes a safe process, that sense of safety must be maintained. This can be achieved by recognizing and rewarding employees who display competent feedback practices, including those courageous enough to report ethical lapses and those who question prevailing wisdom. Managers can encourage employees to engage in feedback-seeking behavior, rather than passively waiting for guidance. This way, employees can take responsibility for gathering assessment information at the time it is needed, rather than later, when the information is too late. Structural help may be necessary. For example, teams may need mechanisms for accessing external feedback (from potential customers or experts). They may need extra time to engage in multiple feedback cycles when equivocality is high. Indeed, when organizations strive for a learning culture, when employees adopt a learning orientation, the competent communication of negative feedback becomes a valued practice rather than a risky one.

❖ CONCLUSION

In conclusion, we present you with a case study, *The Trouble With Marty,* based on the consulting experiences of one of the authors. Imagine yourself to be Marty's irritated coworker or his boss. Then think about how Marty's "customers" view the situation. What about Marty himself? How does he see things? Try to apply the risk negotiation cycle discussed earlier in the chapter, with its emphasis on processes of attending, sensemaking, transforming, and maintaining.

You are a technical support staffer in the computer services department of a major corporation. The department purchases, installs, and maintains software and hardware for all computer users within the company. Marty Jones joined the department 3 months ago after your team got "dinged" in the last employee survey for not being customer oriented enough. Your boss needed someone who could respond to an increasing number of staff requests for technical assistance. Marty loves visiting the various offices to help people with their computer problems. He thinks this is the perfect job for someone with his computer knowledge and training skills.

You know Marty is proficient technically. But, in your view, Marty has been a problem since the day he arrived. He seems a little too pleased to display technical know-how. He gets carried away. This is most obvious when Marty leaves his office to go out on a call. He usually spends way too much time on each call, providing more help and advice than the caller originally requested. Sometimes Marty provides more than an hour of individual instruction to a single secretary or manager! That's not his job! Marty needs to solve the problem quickly and then get back to the office to assist with the next help request. The training department is supposed to provide extended instruction.

You tried to correct Marty's behavior by pointing out these obvious shortcomings and encouraging him to be more professional. He just shrugged and said he was just trying to help each client as best he could. "They always seem to come up with more questions," Marty observed. So how could he just ignore them and return to the office? But you know that Marty doesn't just answer questions; he brings up new ideas for using the software and then shows the client how to implement them. And you heard from a colleague that Marty sometimes roams the halls gathering an audience of staff assistants to watch him display a new piece of software!

Marty's showboating is creating problems in the department because other technicians are covering requests that Marty should handle. Morale is sinking and response time is lengthening. In the meantime, Marty has become so popular with users that some call and ask for him by name! They won't accept help from anyone else. To make things worse, your boss seems thrilled with all the compliments Marty is garnering for her department!

Attend to the kinds of risks evident in this scenario. Are identities or relationships in danger? Are face threats present? Think about the feedback Marty is receiving (or not receiving) and how it is affecting his task performance and that of his unit. Do Marty's perceptions of his performance align with those of his coworkers? Consider how positive and negative feedback is motivating Marty.

Consider the sensemaking efforts of Marty and his coworkers. Does the concept of equivocality apply here? Are multiple interpretations possible? Think of feedback practices that could help Marty and his coworkers make sense of this situation. What kinds of information exchange are being used currently by Marty and his boss? Are more robust feedback cycles needed? Consider the role of multisource feedback in this scenario and how it might help the parties increase their perspective-taking capacity.

Could risk be transformed through the use of tact, approbation, or solidarity? The case study is written from the perspective of Marty's coworker, who is contemplating the delivery of bad news to Marty and the boss. Which communication strategies would exacerbate the risk, and what kinds would make the situation safer? If you were Marty's coworker, which of the 12 guidelines for constructive feedback would be helpful to you in this situation?

Maintaining a safe communication environment should be a concern of Marty's supervisor. What changes in reporting structures and reward systems would make the delivery of feedback less risky? What procedural changes would permanently improve the quality of feedback in this organization? Could Marty be encouraged to use feedback-seeking behavior with his peers as a way to monitor his performance? Design a multisource feedback process that could be used to help Marty, his coworkers, and the supervisor become more effective.

❖ REFERENCES

Atwater, L. E., Brett, J. F., & Atira, C. C. (2007). Multisource feedback: Lessons learned and implications for practice. *Human Resource Management, 46,* 285–307.

Barr, S. H., & Conlon, E. J. (1994). Effects of distribution of feedback in work groups. *Academy of Management Journal, 37,* 641–655.

Brown, P., & Levinson, S. (1978). Universals in language use: Politeness phenomena. In E. Goody (Ed.), *Questions and politeness: Strategies in social interaction* (pp. 56–289). Cambridge, UK: Cambridge University Press.

Cusella, L. P. (1987). Feedback, motivation, and performance. In F. M. Jablin, L. L. Putnam, K. H. Roberts, & L. W. Porter (Eds.), *Handbook of organizational communication: An interdisciplinary perspective* (pp. 624–628). Thousand Oaks, CA: Sage.

Deetz, S. A., Tracy, S. J., & Simpson, J. L. (1999). *Leading organizations through transition: Communication and culture change.* Newbury Park, CA: Sage.

Kluger, A. N., & DeNisi, A. (1996). The effects of feedback intervention on performance: A historical review, meta-analysis, and a preliminary feedback intervention theory. *Psychological Bulletin, 119,* 254–284.

Larson, J. R. (1989). The dynamic interplay between employee's feedback-seeking strategies and supervisor's delivery of performance feedback. *Academy of Management Review, 14,* 408–422.

Lim, T., & Bowers, J. H. (1991). Facework: Solidarity, approbation, and tact. *Human Communication Research, 17,* 415–450.

Miller, D., & Karakowsky, L. (2005). Gender influences as an impediment to knowledge sharing: When men and women fail to seek peer feedback. *Journal of Psychology, 139,* 101–119.

Rosen, S. M., & Tesser, A. (1970). On reluctance to communicate undesirable information: The MUM effect. *Sociometry, 33,* 253–263.

Tesser, A., & Rosen, S. (1972). Similarity of objective fate as a determinant of the reluctance to transmit unpleasant information: The MUM effect. *Journal of Personality and Social Psychology, 23,* 46–53.

Timmerman, P. D., & Harrison, W. (2005). The discretionary use of electronic media: Four considerations for bad news bearers. *Journal of Business Communication, 42,* 279–389.

Wagoner, R., & Waldron, V. R. (1999). How supervisors convey routine bad news: Facework at UPS. *The Southern Communication Journal, 64,* 193–210.

Waldron, V. R. (2008). Feedback processes in organizations. In W. Donsbach (Ed.), *The international encyclopedia of communication* (Vol. 4, pp. 1755–1759). Malden, MA: Wiley Blackwell.

Weick, K. E. (1969). *The psychology of organizing.* Reading, MA: Addison-Wesley.

Weiner, N. (1948). *Cybernetics: On control and communication in the animal and the machine.* New York: John Wiley.

3

Managing Emotion

I was working in customer service at a loan company. My job was to handle customer complaints, calm down the angry ones, make them feel more satisfied with our services. I'm not trying to brag, but I was good at my job and even had awards to show for it. All of us service reps got along pretty well and usually had some laughs on our breaks. Then this new manager was hired and he wanted to crack down on things. Nobody liked him. He would intimidate by spying on us and shouting stuff like, "You were late from break!" We weren't. He made me go to some basic training as a way to humiliate me. As angry as I felt, I couldn't say anything because that would be an excuse for him to fire me. Throughout the training I was written up for not being enthusiastic enough. Long story short, unfortunately the new manager drove my decision to quit.

Sanji, age 23

Cultural norms encourage us to keep our emotions out of the workplace. In fact, derogative terms are sometimes used to label an overly emotional coworker—labels like "unprofessional," "high maintenance," or even "out of control." At least in our imaginations, work is the place for analysis, planning, and cool heads—terms we often set in opposition to emotion. But Sanji reminds us of the many ways that the communication of emotion is an intrinsic and important part of so many jobs. As a customer service representative, he was required to calm down angry customers and make them feel satisfied. This kind of communication, the kind that manages our emotions and those of others, is so important in service jobs that researchers long ago gave it a name—*emotional labor* (Hochschild, 1983).

Emotion surfaces in many other ways for Sanji. He liked his job because of the "laughs" he and his coworkers sometimes shared, a suggestion that positive emotions make work more appealing. By "not trying to brag," Sanji was regulating the emotion of pride. Organizational norms teach us to distinguish between felt emotions and expressed emotions. Even when workers feel pride, they may hesitate to express it for fear of being boastful. Coworkers might greet such displays with disdain or envy. Sanji also struggles to suppress his anger at a supervisor, who seems bent on cultivating the emotions of fear and humiliation. Sanji is eventually written up for his unwillingness to demonstrate the correct emotions in training—for "not being enthusiastic enough."

This chapter addresses emotion management—the communication processes associated with feeling, eliciting, regulating, expressing, and fabricating our emotions and interpreting those expressed by others. The communication of emotion is an underappreciated but common (and necessary) form of organizational communication. And it can indeed be risky. Sanji left a job that had given him pleasure and financial reward, in part due to the emotional upset associated with his new supervisory relationship. His organization lost a productive employee. Other workers find that the emotional demands of their jobs put them at risk of stress, burnout, strained relationships, and even emotional numbness. Frequent demands to throttle back emotion, the pressure to fabricate emotions we don't feel—these demands could eventually change the way we see ourselves at work and at home. In other words, our identity is placed at risk. Of course, emotion management is a necessary skill and often a positive one. We use it to maintain harmonious relationships, improve our performance on stressful tasks, and make work a satisfying (and fun) social experience for ourselves and our peers.

❖ WHY IS MANAGING EMOTION IMPORTANT?

Researchers report that the management of emotion is an integral and sometimes taken-for-granted part of most jobs (see Miller, Considine, & Garner, 2007). Consider its functions.

Improving Task Performance

As Marie Hochschild (1983) made clear years ago in her study of airline flight attendants, service workers don't just get emotional *about* their work. Instead, emotion *is* work. The very tasks they perform are emotional, and their success, even their compensation, hinges on the ability to manage their feelings and those of others. The attendants in Hochschild's study were asked to appear cheerful at all times, even when agitated passengers made obnoxious demands at 30,000 feet. Ignoring their own fear, attendants were required to calm passengers frightened by the bucking and shuddering of an airliner negotiating turbulent skies.

Closer to home, college students frequently take part-time jobs as restaurant servers, paying their bills from meager wages and tips. But as any server knows, income from tips is linked to emotional control. Those who are resolutely cheerful, calm under fire, and able to "take it" when customers vent their frustrations generally make more money. Of course, emotion management has life-threatening consequences in some jobs. It is especially important for 911 operators who sometimes deal with hysterical callers (see Tracy & Tracy, 1998) but also for police officers, emergency room nurses, and many others. Most manage emotion skillfully, but Textbox 3.1 presents the one author's recollections of an instance when emotion was managed ineffectively.

Textbox 3.1 The Cost of Mismanaged Emotion

In Arizona, a 911 operator reportedly received a call from an agitated citizen reporting that his son was experiencing distress. When asked to calm down, the caller simply became more upset, demanding in profanity-laced language that an ambulance be dispatched immediately. The operator reacted indignantly to the profanity and refused to provide assistance until the caller stopped his tirade. While the emotions boiled, precious seconds ticked away. Help eventually arrived, but sadly, it was much too late.

As we saw in Sanji's account, skillful detection, regulation, and production of emotion is a routine but critical part of less dramatic forms of work. The job success of salespersons, teachers, managers, and countless service professionals depends on this communication skill.

Enhancing Climate

Another positive function of emotional management is its capacity to make the workplace more hospitable. By agreeing to edit out feelings such as hostility, envy, and fear, employees create a relatively tranquil climate, one that allows fellow employees to focus on the less emotional aspects of their work. The climate might also be enhanced when workers share feelings of excitement, amusement, and cheerfulness. When employees recognize sadness and express sympathy for a coworker's disappointment, they are creating a climate that "feels" more personal and humane. Of course, efforts to create an emotionally harmonious workplace can be exhausting, particularly if they are inauthentic. Moreover, manipulative uses of emotion may create false perceptions of calm, which may eventually crumble under the weight of unexpressed negative emotion.

Forging Relationships

Due to shared circumstances and interdependent tasks, coworkers often become friends—and sometimes enemies. These "blended relationships" have caught the attention of communication researchers (Bridge & Baxter, 1992). Some work relationships, but certainly not all, become important sources of emotional support. Competent communication involves learning how and when to disclose personal feelings, recognizing the signs of emotional distress, and providing appropriate kinds of emotional support for distressed peers and subordinates. It involves adept management of relational boundaries, knowing when it is OK to "lay it on the table" and when to be circumspect.

Signaling Moral Failure

Some emotions serve a cautionary function by marking violations of the moral codes that govern interactions at work. This has been called the signal function of organizational emotion (Waldron, 1994). For example, guilt, when detected in ourselves or revealed through conversations with others, signals that personal or organizational values have been flouted. The communication of other emotions, such as fear, indignation, or regret, also serves moral purposes (see Table 3.1 for a list of the moral emotions). Employees monitor the moral health of the workplace by learning to recognize these emotions, and by communicating them appropriately, they may resist ethical abuses and prompt organizational reflection about moral concerns. Of course, norms and reward systems need to encourage employees to communicate these feelings or they will be ignored or forced underground. The result? Wayward employees are allowed free reign until the situation is too serious to be ignored. By then, the organization may face legal and financial trouble.

The widely publicized and rapid meltdown at Enron, a high-flying energy trading company, is a classic case from earlier this decade, while the implosions of financial companies such as Bear Sterns, AIG, and Lehman Brothers stand as contemporary cases from recent years.

| Table 3.1 | Moral Emotions and Their Social Referents |

Emotion	Social Referents
Admiration	Success of deserving others
Anger	Hurtful or immoral behavior committed by others
Embarrassment	Acts that reveal moral failures or create an appearance of moral failure
Envy	Desire for the qualities, possessions, or accolades possessed by others
Guilt	Responsibility for wrongdoing
Humiliation	Threats to dignity; dehumanizing behaviors
Humility	Exposure to transcendent moral forces
Indignation	Ire at the unfairness of a social situation or system
Jealousy	One's rightful role in a relationships is threatened by rivals
Outrage	Fury aroused by the offensive acts of others
Pride	Personal or group accomplishments; recognition by valued others
Regret	Having hurt others or made a serious mistake
Resentment	Sustained or acute ill-treatment of others
Scorn	Someone or something held in contempt
Schadenfreude	Shame experienced by another brings joy to the self
Shame	Disgraceful, unworthy, or dishonorable behavior
Shock/surprise	Unexpected moral violations by others
Sympathy	Pain or distress of another brings feelings of pity or sorrow

Source: Waldron (2009). Used by permission.

When emotional communication fails, organizations risk the loss of its positive contributions. Customer service suffers when employees on the front lines lose their enthusiasm. The signal function of emotions is dulled when organizations and employees ignore them. But emotion is risky in other ways because it can lead to the restriction of identity, the practice of emotional tyranny, burnout, and what we call emotional spillover.

Identity Restriction

When employees spend long days faking emotion, they may lose touch with the emotional traits that previously defined their identity. These new emotional responses may be effective at work but may lead to identity confusion and a sense of artificialness in nonwork contexts. For example, professors are trained to develop an emotionally detached and highly analytic persona; it helps them keep intellectual arguments from becoming personal. This forced coolness may be restrictive in family conflicts, where emotional detachment could be interpreted as a lack of compassion.

Yet emotional training is common in some kinds of work. Extreme approaches to sales training compel new hires to repress certain negative emotions while substituting other more acceptable ones. Because emotions are important components of identity, this training may change self-perceptions and the perceptions of others who know us. Certainly, these changes could be for the better. Learning to replace extreme anger with other emotions would be a productive move for a person prone to violence. But emotional tinkering can restrict the range of feelings people allow themselves to experience and express. This kind of identity restriction could be harmful. This seems perhaps to have been the case with the bible salesman profiled in Textbox 3.2.

Textbox 3.2   The Emotional Education of a Book Salesman

Dan was fairly typical of students at his rural state university. While browsing for summer jobs at the Career Center, Dan's eye settled on an eye-popping advertisement for a lucrative summer job selling bibles and encyclopedias. Dan applied for and got the job.

After classes ended in May, Dan found himself driving to a remote location where he and thousands of other students would attend sales boot camp—intensive training in the emotional art of door-to-door book selling. For days, Dan and his colleagues were subjected to highly emotional speeches by legendary salespeople, all of whom exhorted the students to embrace a positive attitude. Trainees showed they were "fired up" by participating in chants, cheers, and positive self-affirmations. Students were taught that sales success turned on the power of an unending smile and the charm of a cheerful demeanor. After a week of nearly around-the-clock expo-sure to this barrage of positivity, Dan's easygoing personality, natural caution, and nagging doubts about his promise as a salesperson were transformed into a sunny sense of self-confidence and an unswerving commitment to eliminate doubt and negativity from not just his work but his relationships with other people.

Dan spent a trying summer slogging with two other young men across the humid Midwest, making barely enough money to cover their expenses. Despite facing rejec-tion at nearly every front door, Dan's cheerful outlook never failed. He simply hadn't learned to be positive enough—that was the explanation for the poor sales results.

Dan's family and his girlfriend noticed a change in him that fall. He was res-olutely positive at even the most trying times. He offered a hearty handshake to anyone he encountered. Dan refused to socialize with "negative people" and pre-ferred not to share feelings like frustration and anger. Amazed at his new confi-dence and outgoing personality, family members couldn't help but wonder if it all was "real." Had they gained a salesman at the cost of the son and sibling they knew so well? Years later, Dan is a highly successful sales agent. His many acquaintances enjoy Dan's sunny demeanor and unfailingly positive outlook. He never loses his cool or brings them down.

Burnout

Workers who must constantly draw on their capacity for emotional communication may be subject to burnout and emotional exhaustion, particularly if they receive limited emotional support from their organi-zations and peers. Research on social workers, nurses, and other human service professionals indicates that emotional fatigue is one reason peo-ple leave their profession (Miller, Birkholt, Scott, & Stage, 1995). Similarly, elementary school teachers who tend to the emotional needs of children may find their resources exhausted when confronted by the needs of their own family members. When faced with danger, humans experience a surge of energy and a heightened state of awareness. This *fight or flight* response is essential in crisis situations. But when workers experience it constantly due to work demands or dysfunctional interac-tions, the result is physical and mental stress and, eventually, burnout.

❖ KEY RESEARCH STUDIES

The communication of emotion at work has received growing atten-tion from researchers. Here we briefly consider two key studies: the seminal ethnographic work of Marie Hochschild, whose influential book *The Managed Heart* (1983) reported her observations of the emotional labor performed by airline attendants. We also present a summary of Waldron's work on the role of emotions in work relationships (Waldron, 2000, 2009; Waldron & Krone, 1991).

Emotion as the Work

Hochschild's (1983) ethnographic study involved an intensive field investigation of the hiring practices, training regimes, and workplace behaviors of service work, with a particular focus on airline attendants. She found that airline attendants were selected in part based on their emotional communication. Those who were relentlessly cheerful in their manner were favored. Training involved a kind of emotional brainwashing in which trainees were taught to suppress emotions such as fear and annoyance at passengers. In-flight emergencies, drunken male passengers with groping hands, personal problems at home—none of these should crack the calm and cheerful façade. Hochschild introduced a variety of important terms into the research literature, including the contrast between surface and deep acting. *Surface acting* is evident when employees, including airline attendants, perform emotions but don't really feel them. It is a kind of emotional faking. *Deep acting* involves the internalization of required emotions. Employees actually learn to feel the emotions they are asked to perform on the job. Dan, the salesperson profiled previously, developed a deep enthusiasm for his products. He doesn't need to fake it. In other examples, teachers may learn to feel genuine pride in the accomplishments of their students, church workers may develop a feeling of genuine humility before God, and athletes develop a love of competition. Hochschild also described a kind of emotional transmutation—the conversion of one felt emotion into another, more acceptable one. The airline attendant confronted by an agitated passenger may learn to convert feelings of annoyance into a sense of compassion by imagining that the agitation is due to a fear of flying or a separation from family. Hochschild worried that these emotional sleights of hand, when practiced habitually, could leave employees divorced from emotional reality.

Emotion in Work Relationships

In a series of studies, one of the authors observed the emotional communication tactics used in work relationships (see Waldron, 2000, 2009). Table 3.2 describes some of these and provides examples. This work is based on surveys, interviews, and observations with workers from numerous occupations—parole officers, factory workers, school cafeteria workers, government staffers, lawyers, and judges. In an early survey study of the emotional lives of parole officers, many of whom spent their days supervising felons, it became obvious that the most intensely emotional experiences involved not the rather daunting tasks they performed but relational incidents with coworkers (Waldron & Krone, 1991). On anonymous surveys, officers shared narratives of betrayal, public humiliation, and injustice as well as moments of intense joy and pride. The tactics used to communicate emotion were important as these workers managed problematic work relationships.

Table 3.2   Emotional Communication Tactics

Tactic	Description and Example
Venting	Unedited expression of feelings After work at a local bar, service employees hold an unrestrained "bitch session" about their demanding customers.
Editing	The emotion is expressed but some elements removed or altered to make the message more effective or organizationally appropriate A boss verbally conveys disappointment in an employee's poor performance but edits anger from his or her tone of voice.
Suppression	Preventing the expression of an undesired emotion You refuse to express anger at a coworker who is attempting to get under your skin through rude and annoying behavior.
Fabrication	Expressing an emotion when you feel none A salesperson learns to be cheerful at all times.
Substitution	Felt emotions that are transformed into approved emotions You are irritated by a new work policy, but you profess to be excited by the challenge.
Elicitation	Using communication to create emotions in others A team member is "guilted" into accepting extra work.

Source: Waldron and Krone (1991); Waldron (1994).

Waldron (1994) later articulated these tactics in some detail. Parole officers *vented* emotion, as a way to "let off steam"—to unload or express internal feelings in an unrestrained way. Quite often workers *edited* emotional displays, sometimes by softening or removing the elements that they considered too intense or unprofessional. Some emotional experiences were completely *suppressed*. That is, the employee refused to display any aspect of the emotion, often because coworkers' reactions were expected to be negative or unpredictable. As noted in Table 3.2, to preserve a professional demeanor, employees also *fabricated* or *substituted* emotions. Finally, Waldron observed that emotion was often *elicited* by workers or their peers, as when threats were used to induce fear or compliments were offered to instill a sense of pride.

Later, Waldron (2000, 2009) identified several ways in which emotional communication defines and redefines work relationships. First, emotional communication *regulates interactions* among coworkers, enforcing a system of rights, obligations, and values. For example, a story told by factory workers related their efforts to humiliate a rookie floor boss who had abused his newfound power by embarrassing less productive workers, taunting them, and issuing hollow threats (Waldron, Foreman, & Miller, 1993). This former peer had gotten "too big for his breeches," so he was subjected to a series of anonymous and embarrassing practical jokes. The supervisor was further embarrassed when work crews intentionally slowed production, subjecting their boss to the displeasure of higher-level factory management. In short, the humiliation suffered by the faculty workers was interpreted as a grave form of relational injustice. They sought to restore justice by manipulating the emotional experiences of their abusive boss.

Emotional communication sustains work relationships in a second way. In observing the interactions of workers at a beleaguered and underfunded state agency, Waldron (2000) saw that emotion was used as a *relational resource.* When management announced that layoffs were likely, workers cheered each other up with black humor and funny stories. In this way, the elicitation of emotion promoted resilience and cohesion. The language of emotion was also a useful resource at this agency, particularly when defining relationships with disliked coworkers and managers. They were described as "pouty," "needy," "bitchy," "out of control," "edgy," and "mercurial." In this sense, emotion words are used to define workplace interactions and personalities.

Finally, on the basis of his observation of lawyers, judges, and defendants in a common pleas court, Waldron (2000) argued that emotion is a *collective performance.* He reported that defending and prosecuting attorneys appeared to coordinate their "on-stage" performances to ensure that the accused (and their observing family members) experienced certain emotions (see Textbox 3.3). For example, with the presiding judge, the attorneys collaborated to create an aura of grim formality to ensure that the young (and often poor) defendants were sufficiently afraid of the potential consequences of their alleged crimes. The attorneys conveyed a false hostility to the other side's case, perhaps to create the impression of a truly adversarial proceeding (when, prior to the trial, the attorneys were observed joking about the poor quality of the defendant's case). Finally, after the sentencing, the attorneys worked to convince defendants to feel relief at the relatively mild punishment rather than disappointment at the failure to obtain an acquittal.

Textbox 3.3 **Collective Emotional Performances in Court**

Grim formality: Communicated through somber dress, formal discourse, and ritualistic communication.

Elaborate concern: Communicated by concerned facial expressions, patting the defendant, and voicing concern for the future of family and defendant.

Adversarial posturing: Conveyed through presentation of arguments, hostile questioning, and nonverbal indicators of disagreement.

Cooling the mark: Attorneys create fear by emphasizing serious consequences and relief by cooperating to reduce the charges.

Source: Waldron (2000).

Emotional Tyranny

In a recent reanalysis of narratives reported by workers from a variety of organizations, Waldron (2009) argued that emotional communication can be used to promote unethical conduct. Powerful people enjoy more freedom to express their emotions. Some even express unedited negative emotion in a manner that harms others, a practice Waldron called *emotional tyranny*. Sharon, a secretary at a large university, for example, had this to say:

> My boss would rant and rave, like a nutcase, really. Then he would be nice as can be for a few days. Then out of the blue he would be embarrassing me or saying hurtful things. I never knew what to expect so I would come to work on pins and needles. Everyone else was that way too. Never quite sure of what to say or do.

Sharon's work life was made miserable by an emotionally mercurial boss. But as noted in Table 3.3, the emotional weaponry of workplace

| Table 3.3 | Manipulative Emotional Practices With Discourse Examples |

Tactic	Exemplar
Betrayal	"I put my heart into the job because my boss liked me and believed in me. But after he got promoted, I got nothing but coldness. He stabbed me in the heart."
Blackmail	"I (stupidly) told my boss about a crush I had on a coworker. He threatened to tell if I didn't show a good attitude. Maybe joking . . . but he enjoyed the threat."
Deflecting	"He basically told us it was not his fault [that people haven't been paid on time]. We all should be mad at the contractor. He dodged responsibility."
Discounting	The dean asked, "Why did you care so much about the staff evaluations? All I care about is the faculty. We really don't need to be so emotional."
Embarrassing	"She criticized me right on the floor, in front of my customers (two were my friends)! My face went red and I ran for the bathroom."
Exhorting	"[My boss] was like a preacher at church, getting us all whooped up and excited about the company and our sales. But we found out it was all BS. The company didn't care about us and the bosses made all of the money. We were used."
Faking	"The HR person could really pretend like she was sincere when we brought up a grievance. Like she cared and was all worried. But it was an act, a joke really."
Grinding	"After a while I got tired of the everyday anger control issues. She snipped and yelled and wore me down over time. I finally left (which is what she wanted)."
Guilting	"Because I was super-dedicated back then, they could guilt me into anything. I'd stay late because they would make feel disloyal or selfish for going home."
Intimidating	"I was told I would pay a huge price if I went public with the problem. Basically, they scared me into conformity."
Orchestrating	"This guy (team leader) was threatened by me. So he went around spreading rumors that I wasn't working hard and thought I was too good to work. Before I knew it people resented me."
Reframing	"You think poor sales are no big deal? This is an embarrassment to me."

Tactic	Exemplar
Ridiculing	"When I see my servers cry, I know they aren't ready for prime time. Crying doesn't make customers happy and babies don't get tips. I say, buck-up!"
Shaming	"After I complained, they made me feel like I was being selfish, like I was more important than everybody. Just because I wanted them to follow the [curriculum development] process rather than just rush it through."
Silencing	A college professor told me, "Sure I am disgusted . . . and I think the policy is stupid. But keep my name out of it. I have already had my head chewed off in too many meetings (by university administrators)."
Vanquishing	"Wipe that smile off your face and don't let me see it again!"

Source: Waldron (2009).

tyrants takes many forms. Employees should recognize the emotional communication practices that are commonly used by bosses and peers for manipulative purposes. This awareness helps us better understand the feelings we experience in the presence of certain coworkers, and it may help us avoid work relationships that are emotionally unhealthy.

The research reviewed thus far documents that emotional communication is a rich and important aspect of work life. Competent employees recognize their communicative options and use this knowledge to manage risks to themselves and to others. As with the other chapters, we summarize these communication options in a textbox (see Textbox 3.4).

Textbox 3.4   Communication Options

Emotional Acting (Hochschild, 1983)

Surface acting
Deep acting

Emotional Communication Tactics (Waldron, 1994; Waldron & Krone, 1991)

Venting
Editing

(Continued)

Textbox 3.4   *(Continued)*

Suppression
Fabrication
Substitution
Elicitation

Using Emotion to Define Work Relationships (Waldron, 2000)

Regulating relationships
Relational resources
Collective performances

Practices of Emotional Tyrants (Waldron, 2009)

Betraying	Blackmailing
Deflecting	Discounting
Embarrassing	Faking
Grinding	Guilting
Intimidating	Exhorting
Orchestrating	Reframing
Ridiculing	Shaming
Silencing	Vanquishing

❖ COPING WITH EMOTION AND THE RISK NEGOTIATION CYCLE

We have established that the communication of emotion is pervasive, important, and sometimes risky. But how can the risk be managed? Recall that the Risk Negotiation Framework from Chapter 1 proposes that risky situations are shaped through a cycle of communication behaviors. As potentially risky situations unfold, risk is managed through the joint behavior of the participants, ultimately leading to an enhanced sense of safety or a more acute sense of endangerment. In the case of emotion, we see the process working this way (see Figure 3.1).

Attending

The first element of the communicative task is attending to emotional cues. This process includes self-monitoring, as employees examine their feelings about work, including the moral emotions identified

Figure 3.1 Managing Emotion and the Risk Negotiation Cycle

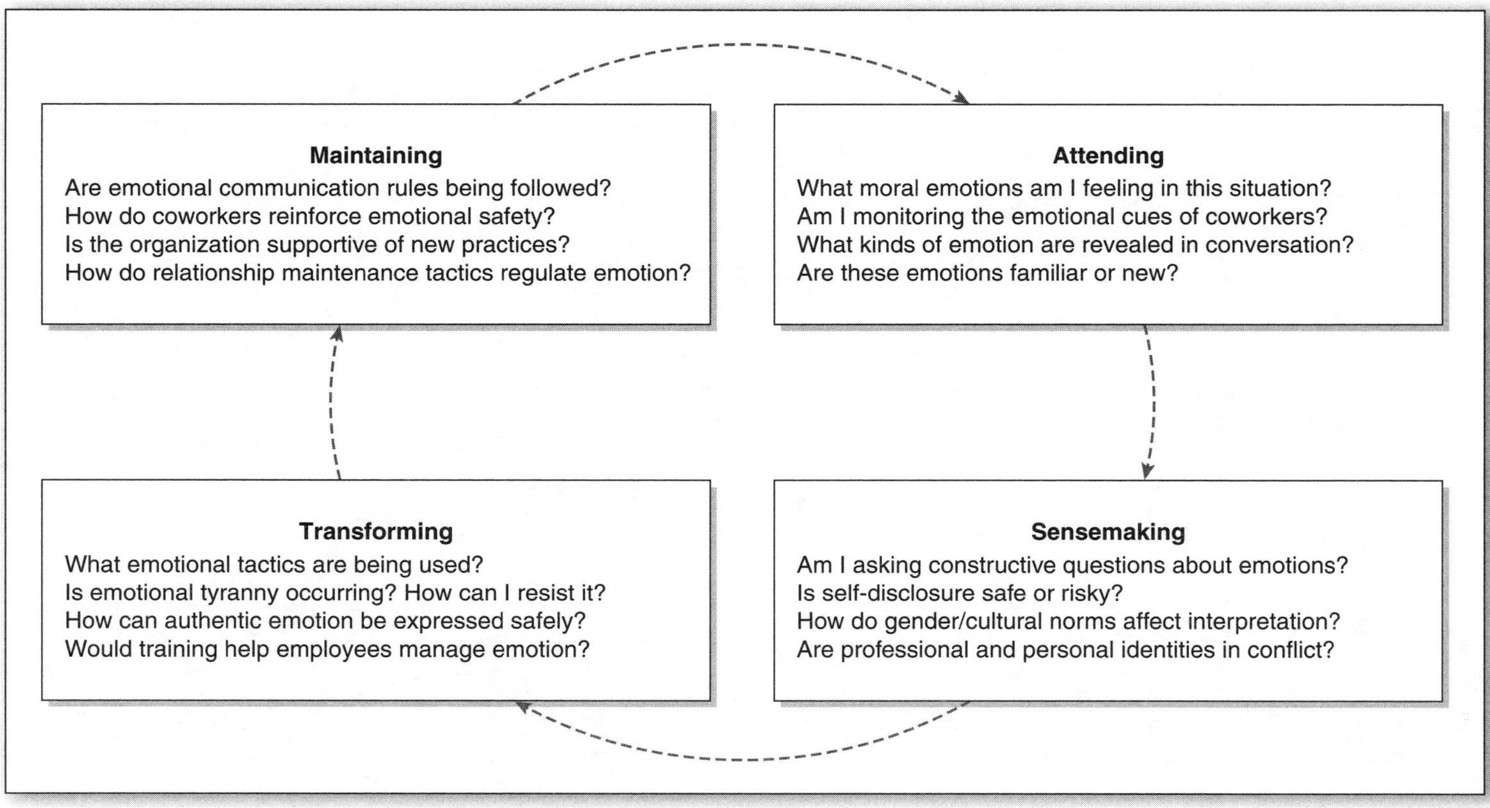

Attending

What moral emotions am I feeling in this situation?
Am I monitoring the emotional cues of coworkers?
What kinds of emotion are revealed in conversation?
Are these emotions familiar or new?

Sensemaking

Am I asking constructive questions about emotions?
Is self-disclosure safe or risky?
How do gender/cultural norms affect interpretation?
Are professional and personal identities in conflict?

Maintaining

Are emotional communication rules being followed?
How do coworkers reinforce emotional safety?
Is the organization supportive of new practices?
How do relationship maintenance tactics regulate emotion?

Transforming

What emotional tactics are being used?
Is emotional tyranny occurring? How can I resist it?
How can authentic emotion be expressed safely?
Would training help employees manage emotion?

previously. Are they feeling agitated, guilty, fearful, frustrated, or burned out? Other-monitoring is the process of perceiving emotions through the nonverbal cues displayed by peers, supervisors, and others. For example, a leader might note hesitancy in a member's tone of voice; perhaps this is an indication that he or she feels some trepidation at the prospect of delivering bad news (see Chapter 2). Through facial expressions and tense posture, team members may signal impatience or frustration. Interaction-monitoring involves observing and listening to the emotional tone of conversation. Emotions may be communicated implicitly in messages that are notably brief, abrupt, defensive, loud, despairing, accusatory, or sullen. In addition to these nonverbal indicators, interaction often includes verbal characterizations of emotional behavior. These often mark perceived violations (or misperceptions) of the organizational norms that regulate emotion, as when a coworker is described as unprofessional or the weekly staff meeting is described as a "bitch-fest."

Attending also means awareness of historical factors that shape current experiences. Examples include the fears that have been building in distressed coworkers, the communication patterns that sustain a chilly or warm supervisory relationship, and memories of the organizational past that stir employee emotions of pride or resentment. The enduring dispositions of participants can shape perceptions of workplace encounters. For example, some employees are inclined to be more attuned to the different kinds of emotional states experienced by themselves and others. When emotionally observant supervisors recognize that employees are fearful (or frustrated or indignant), they can better adapt the emotional tone of their communications. One adaptive approach is to acknowledge the emotion before proceeding to the task at hand ("You seem a bit nervous. Is everything OK?"). Another common tactic is to provide a rationale before issuing a directive or to make a request when you anticipate a defensive emotional reaction ("Customer service is especially busy this month, which is why I'd like you to spend 2 hours a day working in that office."). Being emotionally observant is particularly relevant when dealing with people who experience unusually high levels of anxiety in public speaking or group settings (McCroskey, 1982). Perceptive supervisors can make these tasks feel less risky for apprehensive communicators (Richmond & McCroskey, 1992). For example, apprehensive workers may perform better when asked to speak informally at team meetings rather than formally in front of large groups. For other suggestions, see Textbox 3.5.

| Textbox 3.5 | Attending to Communication Apprehension at Work |

- Recognize that differences in apprehension exist among workers and assign tasks accordingly.

- Look for nonverbal cues that signal apprehension.

- Practice presentations and conversations in nonthreatening settings.

- Use communication technologies in place of face-to-face interaction.

- Use remediation methods, such as desensitization or cognitive restructuring.

Sensemaking

Emotional cues are inherently ambiguous, and they often are merely a signal that something larger is happening in the organization or work relationship. Sensemaking behavior helps decipher the possible meanings of emotion. Constructive questioning is one such behavior. Some emotions are reactions to breaches of the expectations that define role identities and work relationships. Constructive questioning is the process of inquiring about the underlying sources of emotion. What could explain the feelings of anger workers feel toward their organization? What did they expect and how have those expectations been violated? What are the (sometimes unexpressed) communication rules that govern a work team's interactions? Does the collective frustration experienced by team members suggest that the rules need to be renegotiated? Why do employees feel shame or guilt at the actions they have taken on behalf of themselves or their employer?

Self-disclosure is another behavior associated with sensemaking. Because the meanings of emotion are ambivalent, employees often test their interpretations against those of other employees. This kind of reality checking can be a good thing if a peer can be trusted to keep disclosures confidential. For example, if an employee feels annoyed at the continual complaints of a team member, he might reveal these feelings cautiously ("Has Rodney been a little cranky lately? I have been feeling annoyed by his argumentative style in our meetings."). He may find that others share this emotional reaction—an indication that team norms are in fact being flouted by Rodney's behavior. He may also learn that Rodney's emotional displays should be reinterpreted in light of new information (perhaps Rodney is under considerable personal stress). Or, yet another possibility, maybe the employee is being too emotionally vigilant in team meetings in reaction to past conflicts. The reasons for this employee's hypervigilance may be worth exploring as part of the sensemaking process.

Sensemaking is particularly susceptible to cultural context. What appears to be "normal" emotional behavior at work is in part shaped by cultural expectations communicated through family socialization, popular media, and religious training. One example involves gender differences in emotional displays (see Martin, Knopoff, & Beckman, 2000). In the United States at least, men are expected to be largely unemotional in the workplace and cool under fire. Powerful males are allowed to be angry, particularly when incompetent subordinates are involved, but signs of fear or tears of sadness are generally taboo. (see Textbox 3.6). Boys (and girls) learn these expectations from parents and coaches at youth sporting events (see Meân & Kassing, 2008), from the leading men in action-adventure films, and from television shows that feature emotionally demanding work in such places as police stations or emergency rooms. On the other hand, American females are expected to be compassionate and emotionally engaged. Somehow powerful women are expected to be both composed and decisive (like males), but they shouldn't appear icy, bitchy, or distant. Of course, cultural norms are always evolving, but, needless to say, emotional communication can be particularly risky for women as they negotiate these conflicting cultural expectations.

The perplexing emotional restrictions on the behavior of powerful women surfaced in the Democratic primary race of 2008, as news media across the nation covered the candidacy of Hillary Clinton, the first female to mount a major run for the presidency of the United States. Persistently criticized for seeming emotionally distant in speeches, Clinton shed several tears in a confessional talk with a group of New Hampshire voters. This emotional display prompted a flurry of editorializing from nearly every U.S. newspaper.

Textbox 3.6   Crying in Public: The Politics of Emotion

An article in the *Washington Times* (Bellantoni, 2008) dubbed it the "Comeback Cry." Few displays of emotion have so incited so much speculation from voters and the press. It was reported that the New York senator and presidential candidate teared up when a voter in Portsmouth, New Hampshire, inquired about the rigors of the campaign trail. The next day, Clinton pulled off a surprise win in the state's Democratic primary.

The *Times* quoted Senator Dianne Feinstein, a California Democrat and a Clinton backer, who offered that Clinton's tears displayed "humanity and real warmth . . . an emotional connection" with female voters. In the news story, Clinton campaign chairman Terry McAuliffe lauded Clinton for showing the compassion that voters needed to see for themselves. But other commentators questioned the authenticity of Clinton's emotional moment, noting that she had rarely been emotional in public during her many years in the public eye.

In television interviews, Mrs. Clinton acknowledged the impact of her emotional connection with New Hampshire voters. She suggested that emotional displays help voters appreciate the humanity of candidates. The complicating role of gender expectations was evident in Clinton's comments during a FOX News interview, which also were included in the *Times*'s story. "Maybe it's a little more challenging for a woman in this position because, obviously, we know what people will say, but maybe I have liberated us to actually let women be human beings in public life" (Bellantoni, 2008, p. A01).

American culture encourages workers to build emotional barriers between professional and private life, to accept that "business is business" and domestic and spiritual lives are something else entirely. This can be a good thing. After all, home should offer some relief from the emotional demands of labor as few employees enjoy workplaces that share completely our personal preferences and values. But this demarcation is probably unrealistic, and it can be problematic, particularly when it comes to the moral functions of emotion. Consider the case of Felipe, who managed a branch location of a large restaurant chain. Felipe was informed by his superiors that the location would be closed in several weeks, although he was assured of a job at another branch. Felipe was asked not to inform his local staff of the imminent closure. Management wanted the store to close in an orderly way and feared the employees would quit en masse if they discovered the truth. A religious person who valued forthrightness in his personal affairs, Felipe felt guilt at the prospect of this deception. The emotion of guilt prompts employees to apply moral standards when making sense of their behavior. Should Felipe separate his personal ethical standards from those he practiced at work? What should be more important, serving the interest of the organization that supports his livelihood or preserving his personal identity as an honest person? Felipe's case illustrates the danger, and even the folly, of assuming that private and workplace emotions can be cleanly divided. He sided with his employer, but nagging feelings of guilt persist to this day.

Transforming

Earlier we described the emotional communication practices, such as venting or editing, that transform work relationships. We also introduced the destructive communication practices of emotional tyrants. The use of fear tactics to gain the compliance of workers is just one example. Fear is an unpleasant emotion in nearly all circumstances, and its use can harm not just the targeted employees but also the larger interests of an organization. Fear has a tendency to paralyze thinking, so fearful employees may do just what they are told to do—and nothing else. Fear tactics can discourage independent thinking while encouraging defensive behavior and resentment. This is true of those who are victimized, as well as those who observe these tactics in use.

More positively, transformative communication reduces risk and increases safety. Individuals or work teams may decide to place new restrictions on harmful emotional practices. These might include gloating, expressions of envy, public embarrassment, and unedited displays of anger. For instance, the venting of frustration felt toward the larger organization may serve a useful cathartic purpose, and it can forge emotional connections between team members. However, it may be wise to restrict "group bitching" to certain times (e.g., after work) and venues (off-site) and subject it to certain communication rules (e.g., no personal attacks on other team members). In this way, employees vent their authentic emotions in a safe manner that minimizes risk to team relationships and preserves productivity on the job. Similarly, other emotional practices promote safety in teams. These might include displays of camaraderie or public expressions of encouragement.

At the organizational level, safety is enhanced when emotion is recognized as a common, legitimate, and potentially valuable part of working life. Safe organizations monitor abusive emotional practices such as public humiliation and unchecked displays of anger. They train employees in more constructive forms of interaction. In contrast, organizations that simply repress employee frustration, anger, or indignation may be missing important warning signs. When unaddressed, these emotions may lead to turnover, burnout, and, in extreme cases, sabotage of the organization or workplace violence. Yet organizations can only do so much to help employees manage intense emotional experiences. Employees may need help from therapists, religious leaders, and other consultants outside the organization.

Maintaining

With the tasks of attending, sensemaking, and transforming completed, the final element of the risk negotiation cycle remains—maintaining safe levels of risk. In the case of emotional communication, this task often involves continued compliance with new communication rules. Maintenance requires practice, self-reminding, the support of coworkers, and positive recognition. A worker who pledges to overcome a fear of speaking in meetings will need encouragement when resolve falters. A supervisor seeking to curb angry outbursts may need to avoid situations that trigger anger. A team member who demotivates the group with continual complaints will need to be reminded of the team's positive accomplishments. Safe emotional communication practices must be reinforced by the organization. For example, a member who has decided to no longer be intimidated by an abusive boss will need the continued support of the human resources office and, quite possibly, powerful allies in management.

Relationship maintenance behavior shapes the emotional tenor of workplace interactions. For example, some members use regulative behavior to maintain supervisory relationships. They hide bad news and severely limit their emotional displays. Employees often cite compelling reasons for using this defensive approach, but ironically, regulative behavior can heighten the intensity of the negative emotions an employee feels during encounters with a supervisor. Why? These employees limit their communication to high-stakes formal contacts, such as monthly status reports or required performance reviews. Consequently, the parties operate from limited personal understanding. Power differences may be more salient. The consequences associated with any one encounter are high. For all of these reasons, when compared to other relationship maintenance approaches (informal, contractual, direct), regulative communication leads to emotional vulnerability and heightened perceptions of risk. Thus, it may be that ordinary relational communication practices are most important in maintaining a sense of emotional safety.

❖ CONCLUSION

In conclusion, we introduce Maria, a highly motivated new employee, one who was genuinely excited about her future with the medium-sized advertising firm that had hired her right out of college. Use the four phases of the risk negotiation cycle to examine how Maria managed her emotions in this work situation.

> As a relatively new member of the staff, Maria was pleased to be working with a small team of creative people—all laboring feverishly to design a new advertising look for a local health food chain that hoped to go national in the next 12 months. The work was demanding and the deadline was tight, but the client seemed pleased with designs the group had produced thus far. But Maria had a problem, and his name was Phil. A longtime employee and friend of the agency's owner, Phil seemed threatened by Maria. In creative meetings, he tended to call her by denigrating names, like "gee whiz kid" and "Miss Eager Beaver." He often criticized Maria's ideas in brainstorming sessions and generally seemed uncomfortable with her presence on the team. The senior team members sometimes laughed at Phil's teasing comments, but often they just looked uncomfortable and fell silent. Nevertheless, these coworkers found merit in Maria's work, and they told her so privately. Maria possessed a sense of humor and she could take the teasing. But after several months of Phil's unrelenting negative attention, she felt both humiliated and angry. Maria needed to do something about Phil or she would soon lose her cool.
>
> Maria considered reporting Phil's behavior to the agency's owner. Fueled by indignation, she reviewed her argument. Upon reflection, she determined that Phil's behavior was a form of harassment. Before reporting him, Maria confided in Nolani, a coworker with 4 years of experience at the agency. Nolani confided that Phil treated all new employees this way. The owner actually was well aware of these antics and excused Phil's behavior as a playful form of new employee initiation. Nolani thought Phil was an insecure bully, and she suggested that Maria "call him on it." In fact, as the two women discussed the matter, they decided to place "process issues" on the agenda for the next team meeting. As it turned out, Nolani and the other members supported Maria's concerns and added their own. Phil backed down without a fight.

How successful was Maria in attending to the emotional dimensions of this situation? Did she engage in self-monitoring? Which emotions did Maria feel? Were they moral emotions? What did these emotions tell her about herself and the situation she faced at work? Did the emotional cues provided by coworkers reveal useful information in this situation? What were they? We mentioned that past events can make situations more or less emotional for organizational members. Were past events important in this case? What other aspects of the organizational context shaped the emotions felt by Maria? Was it risky for Maria to take action on her feelings?

Consider Maria's sensemaking activities. In response to her emotions, did Maria engage in constructive questioning? Were coworkers helpful as Maria tried to interpret Phil's behavior? Was it safe for Maria to disclose her feelings to coworkers? Why or why not? Consider the culture of this particular organization. How was Maria advantaged or disadvantaged by informal rules and norms? Are these unique to the organization, or are they drawn from the larger society? Did Maria engage in sufficient sensemaking before deciding on a course of action? Did she take advantage of multiple and varied sources of information to develop an informed understanding of the situation?

Transforming behavior can increase safety or exacerbate risk. Was Maria subjected to emotional tyranny? Did she resist it? Was she successful? Which kinds of emotional communication tactics did Maria use in this case? Consider that emotional communication can define the relationships of coworkers. Did you see evidence that the emotional behaviors of Maria or her coworkers defined or redefined their relationships? We argued earlier that some kinds of emotional experiences are collective performances. By coordinating their communication behaviors, Maria's coworkers created emotions in their work team. Which emotions were created, and which kinds of interaction created them?

Emotional communication practices can be used to maintain a safe environment for employees. How are the ongoing communication practices of this organization increasing or decreasing risk? Were Maria and her colleagues able to establish communication procedures that managed risk in their work team? What might they do in the future? Which relationship maintenance practices would help Maria sustain relatively safe relationships with her peers? With Phil? With the company's owner?

❖ REFERENCES

Bellantoni, C. (2008, January 10). Did Hillary win N.H. crying game? *The Washington Times*, p. A01.

Bridge, K., & Baxter, L. A. (1992). Blended relationships: Friends as work associates. *Western Journal of Communication, 56,* 200–225.

Hochschild, M. (1983). *The managed heart.* Berkeley: University of California Press.

Martin, J., Knopoff, K., & Beckman, C. (2000). Bounded emotionality at The Body Shop. In S. Fineman (Ed.), *Emotion in organizations* (2nd ed., pp. 115–139). London: Sage.

McCroskey, J. C. (1982). *An introduction to rhetorical communication* (4th ed.). Englewood Cliffs, NJ: Prentice Hall.

Meân, L. J., & Kassing, J. W. (2008). Identities at youth sporting events: A critical discourse analysis. *International Journal of Sport Communication, 1*(1), 42–66.

Miller, K. I., Birkholt, M., Scott, C., & Stage, C. (1995). Empathy and burnout in human service work: An extension of the communication model. *Communication Research, 22,* 123–147.

Miller, K., Considine, J., & Garner, J. (2007). "Let me tell you about my job": Exploring the terrain of emotion in the workplace. *Management Communication Quarterly, 20,* 231–271.

Richmond, V. P., & McCroskey, J. C. (1992). *Organizational communication for survival.* Englewood Cliffs, NJ: Prentice Hall.

Tracy, S. J., & Tracy, K. (1998). Emotion labor at 911: A case study and theoretical critique. *Journal of Applied Communication Research, 26,* 390–411.

Waldron, V. (1994). Once more, with feeling: Reconsidering the role of emotion in work. In S. Deetz (Ed.), *Communication yearbook 17* (pp. 388–416). New York: Lawrence Erlbaum.

Waldron, V. (2000). Relational experiences and emotion at work. In S. Fineman (Ed.), *Emotion in organizations* (2nd ed., pp. 64–82). London: Sage.

Waldron, V. (2009). Emotional tyranny: Suppressing the moral emotions at work. In P. Lutgen-Sandvik & B. Sypher (Eds.), *Destructive organizational communication.* New York: Routledge.

Waldron, V., Foreman, C., & Miller, R. (1993). Managing gender conflicts in the supervisory relationship: Relationship definition strategies used by women and men. In G. Kreps (Ed.), *Sexual harassment: Communication implications* (pp. 234–256). Cresskill, NJ: Hammond.

Waldron, V., & Krone, K. J. (1991). The experience and expression of emotion in the workplace: A study of a corrections organization. *Management Communication Quarterly, 4,* 287–309.

4

Resisting Bullying
and Harassment

I had a very passive boss who wouldn't handle a confrontational, bullying employee. This employee bullied many people at work, including me. I asked if he [the direct supervisor] would involve the principal or director as a buffer. He said he would and didn't. The bullying continued. I went to the principal and asked for help and was pretty emotional by then. The principal asked if I wanted a mediation meeting with the bully. Imagine that! I said no. I didn't want to be in a room—talking with this person.

Brenda, age 37

I n this scenario, Brenda faces a workplace bully who perpetrates abusive behavior unchecked by her school's leadership. Her direct supervisor not only fails to intervene to disrupt the bullying but also fails to bring upper management's attention to the issue. In fact, Brenda took it upon herself to go to the principal directly. By this point, she is emotional—the bullying has taken a personal toll. Her frustration with management's inattentiveness is compounded when her direct supervisor, who promised to act, failed to do so. Adding insult to injury, the principal's reaction underestimates the severity of her concerns, implying that mere personality differences are at work and that these could be resolved through "mediation." The principal apparently hopes for an easy resolution. However, workplace bullying is a complex issue. It often unfolds over a long period of time, goes unchecked, and causes great personal duress for the victim.

Unfortunately, Brenda's experience is not as unusual as we might wish. Bullying is no longer limited to grade school kids on a playground but has in fact become somewhat commonplace in contemporary organizations (Lutgen-Sandvik, Tracy, & Alberts, 2007). Due to its prevalence in the workplace, we view bullying as a kind of risk, one that potentially threatens an employee's well-being, self-esteem, livelihood, and career. To avoid these detrimental effects, employees should prepare strategies for defending their interests while minimizing risk. Brenda's experience demonstrates that managers will not always intervene and, if they do, may or may not be effective. By better understanding the dynamics and repercussions of workplace bullying, employees can marshal the social and organizational resources they will need.

Existing definitions of workplace bullying (Moayed, Daraiseh, Shell, & Salem, 2006) highlight features that distinguish it from other acts of aggression. These include intensity, repetition, duration, and power disparity (Lutgen-Sandvik et al., 2007). Intensity refers to the number of different types of attacks to which victims are subjected by bullies, whereas frequency refers to how often the attacks occur (e.g., weekly, daily). To be considered bullying, the attacks must persist over time (i.e., duration) and not simply be isolated one-time incidents. The final feature of bullying, power disparity, concerns the target's feeling that he or she is unable to prevent continued abuse. This may be due to an initial power disparity (e.g., subordinate status), or it may be a product of the bullying process. Bullying, therefore, does not occur in isolation, nor is it limited to a single type of action. Rather, bullying is a manifestation of power disparity played out in the interaction between employees over time.

What is workplace bullying? Textbox 4.1 provides a considerable list of behaviors that, when combined and used consistently across time, constitute workplace bullying. These range from overt acts such as outright intimidation and shouting to more covert behaviors such as withholding information and manipulating the workload of the target. Workplace bullying can take the form of aggressive acts (e.g., shouting at, shoving, or physically intimidating a coworker), attacks on self-esteem or self-confidence (e.g., spreading malicious rumors, making belittling remarks, and ridiculing coworkers), manipulation of work

Textbox 4.1	Typology of Workplace Bullying Behaviors

Aggressive Behavior / Physical Aggression	
Hostile reactions	Verbal abuse/shouting
Shoving	Blocking/barring access
Invasion of personal space	Acts of physical intimidation
Self-Esteem / Confidence Attacks	
Spreading malicious rumors	Highlighting mistakes
Belittling remarks	Leveling inaccurate accusations
Persistent criticism	Humiliation/ridicule
Stigmatizing	Making a scapegoat
Manipulation of Work / Capacity to Perform	
Setting up to fail	Assigning excessive workload
Withholding information	Removing responsibilities
Setting unrealistic targets/goals	Assigning meaningless tasks
Excessive monitoring	Destabilization/failure to credit
Pressuring to forego entitlements	Hints to quit
Ostracizing / Isolating	
Ignoring	Excluding
Subjecting to practical jokes	
Threats	
Threats to personal status	Physical threats
Threats to professional status	

Source: Harvey, Heames, Richey, and Leonard (2006); Lutgen-Sandvik et al. (2007); Moayed et al. (2006).

assignments (e.g., assigning excessive amounts of work, removing responsibilities, or unnecessary monitoring), ostracizing/isolating behavior (e.g., ignoring, excluding, and making the subject of practical jokes), and threatening behavior (e.g., physical threats, threats to professional or personal status).

Two other forms of aggression in the workplace often associated with bullying are mobbing and sexual harassment. Bullying behavior perpetrated by groups, rather than a single individual, is known as mobbing. It is very similar in nature to bullying but has the added intensity of being accomplished by a group or gang of fellow employees. Textbox 4.2 provides additional background on mobbing.

Textbox 4.2   Mobbing

Duffy and Sperry (2007) defined *mobbing* as "the nonsexual harassment of a coworker by a group of other workers of an organization designed to secure the removal from the organization of the one who is targeted" (p. 398). The notion of mobbing was only recognized in the research literature in the early 1990s. The term derives from the study of animal behavior and refers to the practice of animals singling out and ganging up on a specifically targeted animal with the intention of removing it from the group. Interestingly, the targets of mobbing behavior often are "individuals who have demonstrated exceptional accomplishment, commitment to work, integrity, innovation, and intelligence and competence" (p. 398). Thus, they are those who appear as a threat, rather than as a liability or weakness. Mobbing differs from bullying in that a group perpetuates the harassment versus a single person or individual bully. Yet the consequences of mobbing are similar, leading to senses of powerless and shame on the part of the victim as well as humiliation, loss of professional reputation, and degradation. As intended, mobbing can result in the removal of the victim from the organization, which implicates serious traumatic consequences for the victim (e.g., financial, career, health, and psychological concerns). Apparently, mobbing is more likely to occur in organizations that focus on achievement and profits yet provide little input to employees with regard to how to achieve these outcomes. Employees in such organizations feel the strain of having high expectations with little control over how they perform their respective jobs. It is also likely to be seen in highly bureaucratic, rule-oriented organizations (e.g., educational and government institutions) that may have codes of conduct but do not include mobbing in these protections. In such workplaces, concern for employees is secondary to meeting annual indices and/or accreditation standards.

Workplace aggression can also take the form of sexual harassment. There is no doubt that sexual harassment can be incredibly disruptive to one's career, health, and overall well-being. Chan, Lam, Chow, and Cheung (2008) conducted a comprehensive analysis of previous research related to sexual harassment. This involved examining the findings of 49 total studies that included more than 89,000 research participants. Their work revealed that victims of sexual harassment in comparison to coworkers who were not harassed reported (a) lower levels of job satisfaction, organizational commitment, and job performance; (b) higher levels of job stress and work/job withdrawal; and (c) higher levels of psychological distress and physical problems.

A recent review comparing employees' stories of harassment revealed that there are clear commonalities between workplace bullying and sexual harassment with regard to how each is perpetrated and in terms of the health and emotional outcomes of victims (Lopez, Hodson, & Roscigno, 2009). However, the authors of this study also noted that "these can be experienced as distinctly different forms of victimization" (p. 4). Whereas workplace bullying stems from struggles for power in the workplace, it does not involve targeting people merely due to their gender. In contrast, sexual harassment involves "behavior that violates, derogates, demeans, or humiliates an individual based on sex or gender" (p. 5). It is not rooted simply, then, in workplace power struggles but rather in fundamental societal gender dynamics. Sexual harassment surfaces when we consider the risk associated with managing workplace relationships (see Chapter 5) and monitoring organizational romance (see Chapter 6).

❖ WHY IS RESISTING BULLYING AND HARASSMENT IMPORTANT?

The Detrimental Effects of Workplace Bullying on Employees

The list of negative outcomes associated with workplace bullying is alarmingly long (Moayed et al., 2006). The most common outcome of workplace bullying is increased absenteeism, but other significant outcomes include increases in employee stress, health-related issues, turnover, and error rates. These are coupled with decreases in efficiency, work quality, and job satisfaction. Not surprisingly, these effects parlay into challenges and expenses for organizations.

Organizational Challenges That Accompany Workplace Bullying

Organizations that do not monitor and manage workplace bullying risk financial stability, general productivity, and corporate reputation (Harvey et al., 2006). The organizational costs include (a) lost workdays due to absenteeism, (b) increased health insurance and workers' compensation costs associated with chronic health and stress issues, (c) reductions in employee satisfaction and motivation that lead to lower quality work and reduced productivity, and (d) turnover that can lead to increased training and recruiting costs (Moayed et al., 2006). In addition, companies may face the added expense of litigation and compensation that accrue when victimized employees file grievances and pursue legal action (Harvey et al., 2006). Evidence suggests that workplace bullying also affects those who witness the bullying. Consistent observation of abusive and aggressive acts results in elevated levels of stress and negativity, as well as decreases in satisfaction (Lutgen-Sandvik et al., 2007). Thus, bullying does not affect targets alone but also workgroup members who observe abuse.

Workplace bullying can have a considerable impact on both employee and organizational performance. According to Harvey et al. (2006), workplace bullying affects organizational performance in four ways. First, it interferes with the daily task-specific abilities of employees. Second, bullying diminishes the spirit of organizational citizenship. Those who work with a bully are less likely to engage in behaviors that benefit the entire workgroup or organization. Third, bullying stifles organizational change and development, as bullied employees are less likely to bring innovative ideas forward. Finally, bullying compromises the overall veracity of an organization because it acts like an "organizational cancer" (p. 3), debilitating current members and repelling potential recruits. Given these major implications for employees and organizations, it is troubling that bullying appears to be on the rise.

A Notable Increase in Bullying Behavior

There are many factors contributing to the increase in workplace bullying. Harvey et al. (2006) deemed incompetence to be a significant factor. "Those that can, do; those who can't, bully!" (p. 3). They contended that employees ill-equipped to deal with contemporary organizational demands such as globalization, hyper-competition, consolidation, outsourcing, increased regulation, and unbridled technological advances react by bullying fellow employees. Furthermore, the authors argued that natural divisions may result when organizations actively pursue diversity initiatives, leaving room for bullies to single out victims based on difference. In addition, they contended that corporate downsizing has created not only high degrees of uncertainty for survivors but also opportunities for workplace bullies to chastise coworkers mired in uncertainty and inaction. Downsizing has reduced the number of middle managers as well, causing increased spans of control for individual managers who end up spending less time overseeing problem employees. This gap in oversight creates a space for bullying to occur and go unchecked. Finally, Harvey et al. stipulated that the absence of well-defined cultural norms regarding workplace bullying serves to tacitly endorse the behavior.

According to Lutgen-Sandvik et al. (2007), approximately 10% of American employees self-reported being bullied, whereas a notably higher proportion (28%) reported being subjected to acts that the researchers construed as bullying. This disparity raises interesting questions about the prevalence of bullying. Lutgen-Sandvik et al. speculated that employees "have naturalized bullying as a normal part of the job" and reasoned that employees in their study "associated the term with weakness or passivity and therefore avoided self-labeling" (p. 854). Regarding the prevalence of workplace bullying, they concluded "that approximately 35–50 percent of U.S. workers experience one negative act at least weekly in any 6–12 month period" (p. 854). Apparently, bullying affects a considerable population of the contemporary workforce to some degree.

❖ KEY RESEARCH STUDIES

Explanatory Models of Workplace Bullying

In their analysis of workplace bullying, Harvey et al. (2006) contended that three dimensions of the bullying event need to be considered: (a) the environmental characteristics that permit bullying, (b) the characteristics of the perpetrator, and (c) key characteristics of the target of bullying acts. In order for bullying to take place, the right combination of characteristics must be present. That is, someone predisposed to bullying must encounter a vulnerable target in a work setting that permits bullying.

According to Harvey et al. (2006), several factors contribute to an organization's susceptibility for tolerating workplace bullying. For example, all organizations possess standard operating procedures, norms of behavior, rules of conduct, heroes, or key personalities that determine organizational values and organizational climates that are more or less civil. Taken together, these factors shape an organization's tolerance for workplace bullying. When certain organizational conditions are set, bullying can occur and leave employees in a state of disbelief. Consider, for example, the employee who reported the following:

> I could never have believed that management would aid and abet a bully and liar because they knew that she was lying and in order to protect her they lied themselves. . . . It would have been much kinder

if they'd blindfolded me and shot me at dawn, cos they took away
everything that I ever morally believed in. Everything that I'd given.
(Lewis, 2006, p. 127)

In the absence of norms, rules, and values that restrict workplace
bullying, aggressive individuals will define their own standards of
conduct. In such circumstances, bullying behavior is more likely.
Organizations may implicitly condone bullying when they fail to implement appropriate checks and balances.

In addition, poor oversight and lack of training contribute to managers' inability to identify and manage bullying behavior. So too, do
deficiencies in the workplace design, such as poorly lit and isolated
workspaces that lack supervision. Socially isolated employees are
more likely to be targeted by workplace bullies. Finally, abusive
behavior is more frequent in workgroups characterized by lower
morale. Members may become sensitized to substandard treatment
and tolerant of bullying.

Research has revealed some key characteristics of bullies.
Bullies are socially and politically skilled and able to victimize others
while avoiding sanctions for doing so (Harvey et al., 2006). They may
be aggressive by nature and may have suffered at the hands of a bully
themselves during their formative years. Victims of bullying, on the
other hand, may report some degree of vulnerability with regard to
their self-esteem, are sometimes socially isolated in the organization,
tend toward negative affective states, and can suffer from learned
helplessness. Yet there are instances when vibrant and influential
organizational members fall prey because they have become rivals of
the bully.

On the basis of these considerations, Harvey et al. (2006) prescribed several strategies for discouraging workplace bullies. At the
organizational level, these include a thorough assessment of the workplace climate, standards of conduct, and potential sites for workplace
bullying. Other strategies include training for managers, reporting
mechanisms for employees, and monitoring processes for the organization. To reign in current and potential bullies, the authors suggested
bolstering selection and screening processes to prevent hiring potential
bullies, restructuring job requirements so bullies have less oversight
and contact with vulnerable employees, providing coaching and training for bullies to address previous transgressions, and creating mechanisms to facilitate the removal and termination of known bullies.
Finally, they stipulated that organizations could support targets of bullying by providing training that addresses victimization and responses

to bullying. Organizations should consider mechanisms for targets to report bullying without fear of retaliation, and physically moving victims to prevent future bullying.

Salin (2003) developed a model that examined the enabling, motivating, and precipitating factors related to workplace bullying (see Table 4.1). Accordingly, some combination of these factors, but not necessarily all

Table 4.1 Factors Explaining Workplace Bullying

Workplace Bullying Factors Include . . .	Workplace Bullying Occurs Because of . . .	Workplace Bullying Stems From . . .
Enabling factors	Perceived power differences	Hierarchical relationships
		Gender differences
		Minority status
		Organizational culture
	Low perceived costs	Lax formal sanctions
		Irregular enforcement
		Absence of formal policies
		Normalization of bullying
	Dissatisfaction and frustration	Dissatisfying roles
		Poor work conditions
		Job-related stress
Motivating factors	Internal competition	Limiting competition
		Punishing poor performers
		Forcing victims to exit
Precipitating factors	Attempts to regain control and power	Organizational changes
		Alterations to workgroup
		Downsizing

Source: Adapted from Salin (2003).

three, will be present for bullying to take place. Perceived power imbalances, low perceived costs for perpetrators, and general dissatisfaction and frustration serve as *enabling factors* for bullying behavior. Perceived power imbalances are fundamental to bullying. They can be attributed to hierarchical differences (e.g., a supervisor bullying a subordinate) but also emerge from other sources (e.g., minority status and gender differences). Power imbalances are embedded in certain organizational cultures where authority underpins most interactions (e.g., military or paramilitary organizations such as fire departments). Lax formal sanctions, which are irregularly enforced due to managerial oversight and abdication of responsibility to lower level managers, can encourage bullying. The absence of formal policies regarding workplace bullying and the normalization of the behavior in certain organizational cultures also factor into lower perceived costs for perpetrators.

General dissatisfaction and frustration among employees contribute to workplace bullying as well (Salin, 2003). Irritation derived from dissatisfaction with role responsibilities, role ambiguity and/or conflict, lack of control over job duties, and the like can encourage bullying behavior. Likewise, unsatisfactory work conditions such as crowding, noise, and uncomfortable temperatures can contribute to irritation and aggressive behavior. Stress is also an indicator of employee dissatisfaction and may predict bullying. Workplace bullying appears to increase with the stress of heavy workloads, hectic work environments, and time pressures.

The enabling structures discussed above are necessary but not likely sufficient for workplace bullying to occur (Salin, 2003). Bullying will be more likely when *motivating structures* that reward bullies are in place. These may be systems that prioritize internal competition and regularly rank and compare employees to one another on performance measures (e.g., sales numbers). In these situations, bullying a coworker may prove advantageous as it limits the internal competition not just with the target but also possibly with other coworkers who observe the bullying behavior. Furthermore, promotion of a workplace bully due to competitive performance measures condones the behavior as a viable means for getting ahead in the organization. Similarly, when performance measures and rewards are group or team based, bullying can be used to punish poor performers. As a result, bullying becomes a sanctioned form of eliciting better performance from lagging team members. Finally, bullying can serve as a mechanism for forcing employees to leave the organization when official mechanisms for firing or dismissing employees are inadequate. That is, poor performers can be pushed out by a bully when their performance is substandard but not to the degree necessary to be actionable.

Finally, in Salin's (2003) model, precipitating processes are the direct triggers of bullying. They often involve change in the status quo, which may be due to larger organizational changes, changes in the makeup of one's workgroup, or simply downsizing. These changes increase uncertainty and employees' senses of powerlessness. Bullying, in turn, can result as an attempt to regain control and power within the organization.

Spillover Effects of Workplace Bullying

Heames and Harvey (2004) provided a cross-level model of workplace bullying that considered the dyadic level, the group/meso level, and the organizational/macro level. Their model illustrates the spillover effects of workplace bullying from the dyad to the group and organization. At the *dyadic* level, negative outcomes experienced by the victim (e.g., reduced self-esteem, physical and mental health) spill over to the workgroup via negative relationships with other workgroup members. At the *group interaction/meso* level, spillover can be seen in the behavior of fellow coworkers. Coworkers may acquiesce to the bullying behavior out of fear that they, too, will be victimized, and they may engage in less supportive interaction with other group members because of the negative climate introduced by the abusive behavior. This appeared to be the case for one employee, who reported,

> As bad as it sounds, . . . I was glad when [a coworker] was cornered. Then at least I knew it wasn't me. . . . After that, [coworkers] would come to me and say, "Man, you were right, we should have believed you." (Lutgen-Sandvik, 2008, p. 109)

The proverbial "boy who cried wolf" is vindicated here as his account of being bullied only becomes verifiable when a coworker bullied in public view. The employee gains credibility in this instance, but at a cost; he implicitly endorses a workplace climate desensitized to bullying behavior. Thus, the spillover effects can be detrimental to victims as well as witnesses of bullying.

Spillover at the *organizational/macro* levels entails threats to corporate image and an organization's ability to attract and retain talented employees. Thus, organizations both directly and indirectly face the impact of workplace bullying as tensions created at the workgroup level feed a culture of negativity and a reputation for tolerance of bullying behavior. Spillover effects extend beyond the organization. The bully-victim interaction can have far-reaching consequences for employees' interpersonal relationships outside of work. Lewis and Orford (2005) identified what they called the "ripple effect" to denote the damage workplace bullying could have on previously healthy and socially supportive relationships with family and friends outside of work. By compromising these relationships, the ripple effect made victims even more vulnerable. In fact, people in their study reported that as workplace stress increased because of workplace bullying, so too did the difficulty of maintaining personal relationships. This was due in part to the frustration that relational partners experienced when victims continued to need support yet failed to take any action or advice from relational partners to put an end to the bullying behavior.

Phases of Bullying

Lutgen-Sandvik (2008) detailed phases of bullying and the type of identity work that people perform during these phases. In what she termed the *pre-bullying phase,* employees described unease but also uncertainty about whether they were being targeted or whether they misunderstood the aggressive behavior. In this phase, employees worked to protect their identities by engaging in first-level stabilizing and sensemaking. *First-level stabilizing* served to help employees "reduce discomfort, increase predictability and reclaim the relatively uneventful nature of day-to-day worklife" (p. 106), whereas *sensemaking* involved seeking the counsel of coworkers to confirm perceptions of abusive behavior. Although retrospectively it may be easy to determine that bullying has occurred, this is not always the case as it unfolds. Consider the example below taken from an account provided by Lewis (2006):

> One of the first things they said in the Industrial Tribunal: When you say that this started, why didn't you keep a diary about it? And that was their immediate thing. But when you first are in that situation, you don't think it's bullying, you think there's been a disagreement or a misunderstanding. And you wouldn't dream of immediately getting out a diary and writing a blow by blow account and dating it and signing it. (p. 129)

It takes time to recognize workplace bullying for what it is. The notion that one is being bullied begins to take shape during the pre-bullying phase through one's sensemaking about the experience.

Sensemaking is not unique to this phase, though. It occurs in later stages of bullying as well, but in those phases, it concerns why bullying occurred and what to do about it versus assessing whether certain behaviors constituted workplace bullying in the first place (see Table 4.2).

Table 4.2   Identity Work During Phases of Workplace Bullying

Pre-Bullying Phase	
First-level stabilizing	Reducing discomfort
	Increasing predictability
	Reclaiming nature of daily work life
Sensemaking	Seeking counsel of coworkers
	Confirming abusive behavior as bullying
Bullying Phase	
Reconciling	Aligning self-narratives and victimized behavior
	Regaining equilibrium
	Reducing dissonance
Repairing	Adjusting damaged professional reputations
	Authenticating the veracity of bullying claims
	Impugning the bully
Second-level stabilizing	Combating the undermining of beliefs
	Coming to grips with injustice
	Rebuilding identity narratives with altered beliefs
Post-Bullying Phase	
Grieving	Processing loss
	Revising self-narrative to include bullying episode
Restructuring	Reframing bullying as an impetus for learning
	Reframing bullying as transformational
	Reframing favored aspects of identity

Source: Adapted from Lutgen-Sandvik (2008).

In Lutgen-Sandvik's (2008) work, the *bullying phase* was marked by unmistakably abusive acts of an enduring nature, which transpired for 6 months to 8 years. In the bullying phase, employees clearly recognized and acknowledged that they were being bullied. To protect their self-identity, they used reconciling, repairing, and second-level stabilizing practices. *Reconciling* functioned to help employees bring their self-narratives and the way they behaved as victims of abuse into alignment. Reconciling was necessary to regain a sense of equilibrium that was ruptured when employees realized the mismatch between how they saw themselves and how they behaved (e.g., fearfully) in response to a workplace bully. It also served to reduce the dissonance produced in these instances. Lutgen-Sandvik provides a powerful narrative to demonstrate the reconciliation challenges faced by victims:

> I heard [the bully's] footsteps to the upstairs door, and I ran to my computer with my heart thumping. I remember thinking, "I am a highly educated, respected professional woman, and I am running to my desk like a child. What is wrong here?" I was physically sick at the thought that I'd be caught looking out a window. (p. 107)

In this instance, the victim's professional identity is unhinged by the bully and she reacts like a child. Such a dramatic rupture in identity warrants reconciliation for one to make sense of what has transpired.

Repairing was another strategy employees used to adjust their damaged professional reputations. Subjected to ongoing attacks on their character and competence from a bully, employees needed to engage in identity work that served to restore their reputation. They achieved this by convincing others of the veracity of their claims of abuse and by impugning the bully. The final form of identity work used by employees during the bullying phase was *second-level stabilizing*. At this point in the process, stabilizing was necessary to combat the powerful undermining of commonly held beliefs, such as "people will do the right thing," "companies will protect their employees," and "hard work will be rewarded." Targets of bullying were shaken by the realization that these beliefs were misguided. Second-level stabilizing therefore concerned "regaining equilibrium, coming to grips with injustice and rebuilding identity narratives with a set of altered beliefs" (Lutgen-Sandvik, 2008, p. 110).

In the *post-bullying phase*, targets were concerned with "re-storying one's damaged self-identity and weaving the experience into a long-term aspect of one's biography" (Lutgen-Sandvik, 2008, p. 110). They achieved this by practicing grieving and restructuring identity work. *Grieving* was essential for reconciling, processing, and accepting loss associated with professional reputation, organizational identity, self-confidence, and core beliefs in justice and fairness. It also was a necessary process that afforded employees the opportunity to craft a revised self-narrative that included the bullying episode. *Restructuring* built upon grieving by providing ways to reconceptualize bullying so that it fit comfortably into a new self-narrative. This could entail retrospectively viewing the event as something that spurred learning, that proved transformational, or that reaffirmed or expanded favored aspects of one's self-confidence.

Coping With Workplace Bullying

Lewis (2006) provided a sampling of some possible coping practices that people could use during different phases of workplace bullying. In early phases, people reported minimizing interpersonal difficulties. Accordingly, employees downplayed the seriousness of particular acts and failed to acknowledge an emergent pattern of abusive behavior. The bullying behaviors may have caused stress for the individual targeted but the victim dismissed them as isolated or trivial acts. Once targets began to identify a pattern of bullying behavior, they engaged in acts of self-preservation. These employees refused to draw attention to bullying behaviors because they believed doing so would call into question their competence. Thus, targets endured continued bullying with the expectation that they could resolve the situation themselves. Often this effort failed.

As workplace bullying endured, employees questioned their professional and organizational values (Lewis, 2006). Being bullied forced them to reevaluate their relationships with management and the power dynamics within their firms. Indeed, most employees reported feeling a loss of trust and identity. Another coping mechanism involved explanations for the mental and physical symptoms that accompany the stress created by the bully. These explanations located the problem within the individual bully rather than the social dynamics of the workplace. Finally, being able to recognize and name the pattern of behavior as "bullying" was a key turning point for many victims. It allowed them to assess problems, revitalize self-esteem, and begin recovering from the abuse.

Resisting Workplace Bullying

Lutgen-Sandvik (2006) considered the tactics that targets and witnesses used to resist and counter workplace bullies (see Textbox 4.3). *Exodus* involved "quitting, intentions/threats to quit, transfers/requests for transfers, and aiding others' exit" (p. 415). This entailed workers talking with one another about quitting, alternative job opportunities, and escaping.

Workers reported quitting on their own terms, sending messages to their former employers that made their anger, resentment, and disgust clear. Another tactic, *collective voice*, occurred when several employees joined forces to address abusive and bullying behavior. This was the case for Karla and her colleagues profiled in the following excerpt:

> Karla worked in an organization that, ironically, operated a battered women's shelter. She explained that four managers began talking in her office one afternoon about what they could do to stop the bullying director. Eventually, seven program managers secretly went to the home of a board member and explained the extent of the problem. They reportedly stated, "We just can't take it anymore" and were ready to find other jobs if the director was not removed. (The board had evidently sanctioned the director numerous times in the past without effect.) They each prepared written documentation for the board member, only to be used in case of a lawsuit. As much as possible, they all avoided contact and communication with the director, but reportedly spoke with many others about the director's abusive behavior. The board eventually fired the bully after a protracted, 7-month process in which the resisting workers were terrified of discovery. (Lutgen-Sandvik, 2006, p. 423)

As we can see from the experience of these employees, collective voice went beyond merely seeking the social support and comfort of coworkers sharing the same concerns. It started there but expanded to include an action orientation characterized by mutual advocacy (i.e., developing shared action plans, protecting coworkers and peers, and espousing an esprit de corps underpinned by connectedness, survival, and struggle) and contagious voice (i.e., the infectious desire to speak out in concert with others who had revealed comparable concerns about workplace bullying). Resistance in this case involved documenting the abuse and speaking directly to a member of the agency's board. Bullied employees were bolstered by contagious voice, which motivated them to share their concerns and their action plan (to resign if the bully was not removed) with the board member. Doing so proved risky but effective.

Reverse discourse occurred when employees assigned alternative meanings to repressive tactics and language. This involved embracing pejorative labels like "troublemaker" and accessing influential allies such as union representatives, trusted managers, and attorneys. Employees also located news and popular reports about workplace bullying to help workgroup members recognize and identify the abuse they were experiencing as abusive. Filing formal and informal grievances and documentation of interactions with workplace bullies were additional means of resistance. Together, these tactics served to empower targets and victims. They also provided employees with access to the mechanisms necessary for reconstituting their relationships with the bully and for repairing their standing within their respective organizations.

Textbox 4.3   Employee Resistance Strategies to Workplace Bullying

Exodus

    Quitting

    Intentions/threats to quit

    Transfers/requests for transfers

    Aiding others' exit

Reverse Discourse

    Embracing pejorative labels

    Accessing influential allies

    Accumulating expert knowledge

    Filing grievances

    Documentation

Confrontation

    Face-to-face conversations

    Public challenges

Collective Voice

    Sharing experiences

    Group consultation

    Mutual advocacy

    Contagious voice

Subversive (Dis)Obedience

    Manipulating labor

    Working to rule

    Avoiding

    Withholding information

    Retaliation

Source: Adapted from Lutgen-Sandvik (2006).

Employees practiced *subversive (dis)obedience* by manipulating labor efforts, by working to rule (i.e., doing just what was necessary and required), and by avoiding or withholding information (Lutgen-Sandvik, 2006). These reactions involved alteration of one's interaction with the bully. In contrast, retaliation involved directing hostile gossip and character assassinations at the bully during conversations with coworkers. Confrontation, distinguished by face-to-face conversations with or public challenges to the bully, occurred early in the process of abuse and generally appeared to cause additional difficulties. Considering these resistance practices, Lutgen-Sandvik (2006) concluded that employees used "multiple communicative tactics to (re)create a workplace environment marked by respect, dignity, and justice" (p. 422).

The following case illustrates how one particular employee used multiple resistance tactics when dealing with a workplace bully. Brad initially confronted his bully, but as that action led to additional bullying, he shifted to other strategies of resistance—mainly those characterized as subversive (dis)obedience.

> Brad described being shocked by the insulting, humiliating messages from the new agency director and immediately going to her and presenting his concerns. When she continued to criticize and micromanage his work, despite over 20 years' experience in the substance abuse treatment field, he again spoke with her. When the bully's insults allegedly escalated, her micromanagement became an unswerving response to his efforts, and she repeatedly altered his treatment programs and outreach plans, he spoke with a consulting board member. He reported that little changed so began documenting demeaning interactions, reducing work output, doing exactly what she asked, withholding information, and talking to community members about her. (Lutgen-Sandvik, 2006, p. 423)

We can see that after attempts to confront the bully failed to bring about the desired change in behavior and in fact made the situation worse, Brad opted to practice subversive (dis)obedience by reducing his output, working to rule, and withholding information. He also spoke to selected others about his supervisor. Brad adeptly mixed a host of resistance strategies to deal with this bully.

Workplace bullying is disruptive. It puts employees at risk, whether as a victim or a target (or, for that matter, a bully) as the effects spill over to the workgroup and organization. Thus, livelihoods, careers, job satisfaction, and the like are put at risk when workplace bullying occurs. Fortunately, as these key studies have revealed, there are communication options available that should help reduce the risk. These options are summarized in Textbox 4.4.

Textbox 4.4   **Communication Options**

(Organizational) Communicative Responses to Workplace Bullying (Harvey et al., 2006)
    Restructuring job/supervision responsibilities of a bully
    Providing coaching and training for bullies, targets, and witnesses
    Instituting nonretaliatory mechanisms for reporting workplace bullying
    Assessing workplace climate for tolerance of abuse and incivility

Communication During the Phases of Workplace Bullying (Lutgen-Sandvik, 2008)
        *Intra*personal communication to . . .
    Reduce discomfort
    Increase predictability
    Reconcile self-narratives to account for uncharacteristic behavior
    Regain equilibrium and reduce dissonance
    Rebuild identity narratives with altered beliefs
    Combat the undermining of beliefs
    Come to grips with injustice
    Revise self-narrative to include bullying episode
    Reaffirm favored aspects of identity
    *Inter*personal communication to . . .
    Seek the counsel of coworkers
    Confirm abusive behavior as bullying
    Adjust damaged professional reputations
    Authenticate the veracity of one's abuse claims
    Impugn the bully
    Reframe bullying as transformational and as an impetus for learning

Communicating Resistance to Workplace Bullying (Lutgen-Sandvik, 2006)
    Talking about quitting
    Collective sharing of experiences
    Practicing mutual advocacy
    Speaking out as a coalition
    Accessing influential allies
    Filing grievances
    Documentation of abusive acts
    Sharing hostile gossip about the perpetrator
    Engaging in character assassinations of the perpetrator
    Withholding information from the perpetrator
    Avoiding the perpetrator
    Confronting the perpetrator

❖ RESISTING WORKPLACE BULLYING
AND THE RISK NEGOTIATION CYCLE

Workplace bullying presents risks for targets, family members and friends of targets, witnesses, workgroups, and the organization as a whole. Employees and witnesses can suffer from added stress, mental and physical duress, and increased group tensions. Workgroups may function less civilly, more competitively, and generally more inefficiently when plagued by workplace bullying. Organizations can suffer with regard to their reputation and workforce, failing to attract and keep good people who want to avoid working in a hostile environment populated by workplace bullies and characterized by abusive behavior. The overt yet insidious nature of workplace bullying creates wide-reaching spillover effects that produce and reproduce risks at all levels of an organization's social structure. Nevertheless, communication can disrupt and derail abusive behavior in the workplace. It also can enable and facilitate bullying. We refer to the risk negotiation cycle (Figure 4.1) to examine how communication can work to manage the risks produced by workplace bullying.

Attending

In this part of the cycle, employees assess if in fact they are experiencing abuse. As the literature tells us, this is not always readily apparent but rather becomes evident over time as the pattern of behavior persists. Once employees recognize workplace bullying, they can and should begin to assess the factors that are contributing to abuse. Is it rooted in ethnic or racial differences? Gender? Or does it appear to be a product of a competitive work environment whereby a bully feels it is necessary to remove or neutralize the competition? In the former, targets may choose to seek action immediately by filing a grievance. In the latter case, victims may need to talk to a manager or coworkers about the organization's approach to internal competition. An employee's location in an organization can contribute to workplace bullying as well. Do they work in relative isolation? Are they an easy target in this respect? If so, risk may be mitigated by connecting socially with other workgroup members or by seeking a reassignment that places him or her more clearly in an interactive role in the company. The other major concern in detecting risk at this point is the severity of the abusive behavior and the effect it is having on the target. Is the abuse frequent and enduring? Or occasional and unusual? More severe bullying behavior will continue over time and occur regularly. In such cases, a

Figure 4.1 Resisting Workplace Bullying (WPB) and the Risk Negotiation Cycle

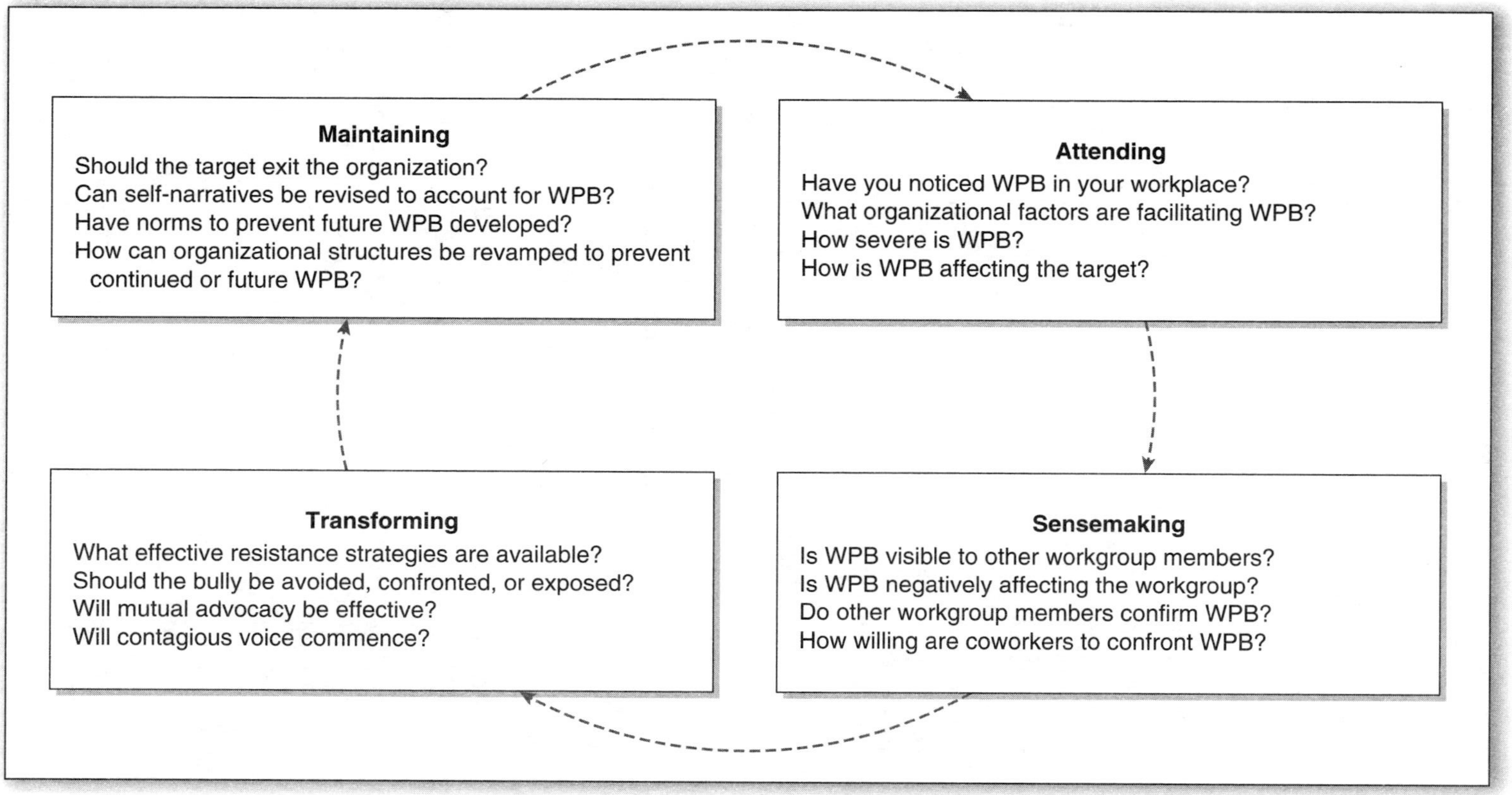

Attending

Have you noticed WPB in your workplace?
What organizational factors are facilitating WPB?
How severe is WPB?
How is WPB affecting the target?

Sensemaking

Is WPB visible to other workgroup members?
Is WPB negatively affecting the workgroup?
Do other workgroup members confirm WPB?
How willing are coworkers to confront WPB?

Maintaining

Should the target exit the organization?
Can self-narratives be revised to account for WPB?
Have norms to prevent future WPB developed?
How can organizational structures be revamped to prevent continued or future WPB?

Transforming

What effective resistance strategies are available?
Should the bully be avoided, confronted, or exposed?
Will mutual advocacy be effective?
Will contagious voice commence?

response may be necessary to relieve mounting psychological and physical strain. Abusive or hostile reactions in the workplace that occur infrequently will not warrant the same reaction. Thus, attending to risk involves gauging the extent and severity of workplace bullying as well as one's vulnerability to continued attacks.

Sensemaking

Once an employee has determined he or she (or a coworker) is at risk of being victimized by workplace bullying, he or she needs to engage his or her office cohort to test these assumptions. Engaging fellow coworkers will help make sense of the risk to the target and to the workgroup and perhaps the organization. At this point, it is imperative to uncover if abusive behaviors are visible to other employees. Have coworkers experienced similar forms of abuse? Can they verify that bullying is occurring? Can they confirm the accounts of targeted employees? Will coworkers testify to their own experiences with the workplace bully? Answers to these questions will help the victim make sense of the situation. In addition, targeted employees should speak with coworkers about the effect of workplace bullying on the workgroup. Are members intimidated? Less satisfied? Less likely to help one another when being bullied? Knowing the answers to these and other questions helps the targeted employee assess the risks presented to the workgroup.

Transforming

How can the risk presented by a workplace bully be reduced or eliminated? Employees can begin by choosing carefully from among potential resistance strategies. Targets can confront the bully, but this approach may fuel antagonism between the bully and members of the workgroup. Better yet, victims can begin a thoughtful trail of documentation of the frequency and variety of abuses perpetrated by the bully. Next, employees can seek the help of influential others, perhaps calling upon the human resources office, legal counsel, or a professional association's ombudsperson. This tactic puts the behavior of the bully under inspection and may expose the abuser. Mobilizing contagious voice and mutual advocacy will be helpful in this regard. If victims can get coworkers to share their experiences with influential others, resistance efforts will gain momentum and veracity. The risk may not abate if the target protests in isolation. After all, it will be the victim's word against the bully's, and that may not be enough to draw appropriate attention to the issue. If others are unwilling to share in resistance efforts, employees must turn to alternative risk management approaches. This may simply involve avoiding the bully. For example, the target can seek a transfer within the organization that moves him or her out of the reach of the workplace bully. Although these tactics vary considerably, they may contribute to a safer workplace. In some cases, the result may be closer to what we have called optimization. The organization may be prompted to change the conditions that enabled bullying to occur in the first place.

Maintaining

Once the risk of dealing with a workplace bully is reduced, targets can focus on long-term strategies to maintain risk at tolerable levels. This will involve determining if a workplace bully should be removed from the organization and implementing practices that discourage bullying behavior. Employees can, for example, provide feedback about establishing nonretaliatory reporting processes. They can ask for monitoring practices that expose workplace bullying. And employees can demonstrate the need to increase the perceived costs and sanctions for abusive behavior. Participation in training for workplace bullies, targets, witnesses, and managers also can contribute to the stabilization and maintenance of risk. Through training programs, workers can learn to identify bullying, how to report it properly, and how to deal effectively with a bullying employee. The benefits of training will help maintain risk at acceptable levels.

These types of organizational changes are more likely when employees act collectively. However, individual employees can also take action to maintain risk at acceptable levels. One option is to exit the organization. Exiting quickly reduces the risk of being bullied and gives the employee greater control over risk exposure. Of course, exit can introduce professional risk. Has the employee found a position somewhere else, or will she or he be unemployed and looking for work? Does the target intend to stay in the same profession, or will she or he need to seek training and qualifications necessary to work in another field? One final consideration regarding efforts to maintain risk concerns self-narrative. Regardless of whether a victim leaves an organization or a bully does, targets will need to "restory" their self-narrative to include a realistic assessment of the bullying episode. Doing so can help victims restore self-esteem and build their resolve as they contemplate future encounters with abusive coworkers. In this way, revising one's self-narrative functions to manage future levels of risk.

❖ CONCLUSION

To conclude this chapter, we share a poignant account provided by Roberta, a female letter carrier working for the United States Postal Service. Her story reflects many of the themes touched on in this chapter.

> At the time I was one of only two female letter carriers on the job, and this fact did not sit well with the male superior who, by law, could not deny us employment, but went about the business of making it nearly impossible for you to work there by creating a hostile work environment that only the strong could survive. Some of the policies and practices that he would employ to compel you to quit included overloading your route, following you while you were on the road, pulling your time card and punching back in while you were still on the road, robbing you of overtime because he had overloaded your route, and denying you access to overtime at time and a half. The female employees endured verbal abuse, sexual harassment, and the threat of physical abuse. I ran into trouble with my supervisor when he discovered that I was a college graduate. For some reason, that really ticked him off, and he made it his business to force me to quit via daily harassment of one form or another.
>
> Roberta, age 46

Attend to the risk that accompanies workplace bullying in this scenario. What features of workplace bullying are present? Is the bullying condoned by other organizational members? The victim recounts this episode with a narrative voice that sounds comparatively "thick-skinned," but what effects might have been experienced by employees at the time this event occurred? Would it be difficult to endure the kinds of abuses described on a daily basis?

Once it is determined that workplace bullying is occurring, we need to assess and make sense of the risk it presents. How could the victim's coworkers help her make sense of the situation? For example, can other letter carriers confirm that workplace bullying is occurring? What we cannot directly gather from the account is the effect that bullying is having on other coworkers. Can we assume that all letter carriers are condoning this behavior? Or is it a case of other workers remaining reticent because they fear the retribution?

What, then, can intimidated employees do to transform the risk affiliated with workplace bullying? Should they band together to bring attention to the bully's behavior? Should they file grievances, speak out as a coalition, or impugn the bully? How could concepts such as mutual advocacy and contagious voice help to transform risk in Roberta's workplace?

How can risk be stabilized and maintained in cases of workplace bullying? Can members of this workgroup recommend, with the obvious involvement of management, some form of formal reprimand for the bully? What might those recommendations be? What kinds of supportive actions can be taken to bolster victims? Or fellow coworkers who witnessed bullying? We also would need to consider how the organizational structures that monitor and address workplace bullying could be improved. For example, management could monitor employee feedback for signs of problematic supervision. What other actions could be taken? What other procedures implemented?

❖ REFERENCES

Chan, D. K.-S., Lam, C. B., Chow, S. Y., & Cheung, S. F. (2008). Examining the job-related, psychological, and physical outcomes of workplace sexual harassment: A meta-analytic review. *Psychology of Women Quarterly, 32,* 362–376.

Duffy, M., & Sperry, L. (2007). Workplace mobbing: Individual and family health consequences. *The Family Journal: Counseling and Therapy for Couples and Families, 15,* 398–404.

Harvey, M. G., Heames, J. T., Richey, R. G., & Leonard, N. (2006). Bullying: From the playground to the boardroom. *Journal of Leadership and Organizational Studies, 12,* 1–11.

Heames, J., & Harvey, M. (2004). Workplace bullying: A cross-level assessment. *Management Decision, 44,* 1214–1230.

Lewis, S. E. (2006). Recognition of workplace bullying: A qualitative study of women targets in the public section. *Journal of Community & Applied Social Psychology, 16,* 119–135.

Lewis, S. E., & Orford, J. (2005). Women's experiences of workplace bullying: Changes in social relationships. *Journal of Community and Applied Social Psychology, 15,* 29–47.

Lopez, S. H., Hodson, R., & Roscigno, V. J. (2009). Power, status, and abuse at work: General and sexual harassment compared. *The Sociological Quarterly, 50,* 3–27.

Lutgen-Sandvik, P. (2006). Take this job and . . . : Quitting and other forms of resistance to workplace bullying. *Communication Monographs, 73*, 406–433.

Lutgen-Sandvik, P. (2008). Intensive remedial identity work: Responses to workplace bullying trauma and stigmatization. *Organization, 15*, 97–119.

Lutgen-Sandvik, P., Tracy, S. J., & Alberts, J. K. (2007). Burned by bullying in the American workplace: Prevalence, perception, degree and impact. *Journal of Management Studies, 44*, 837–862.

Moayed, F. A., Daraiseh, N., Shell, R., & Salem, S. (2006). Workplace bullying: A systematic review of risk factors and outcomes. *Theoretical Issues in Ergonomics Science, 7*, 311–327.

Salin, D. (2003). Ways of explaining workplace bullying: A review of enabling, motivating and precipitating structures and processes in the work environment. *Human Relations, 56*, 1213–1232.

5

Negotiating Workplace Relationships

I was friends with my supervisor and had a pretty good relationship with this other employee and his family. We had all worked together for several years, through some challenging times, helping each other out, kind of like a team. When he (the other employee) got a bad review and protested it, I was in the middle and didn't know what to do. Who should I stick up for? What would the other employees think if I defended him but not them? I had to be careful because the supervisor was my friend, but she was my boss too! The other employee ended up not talking with me anymore. He ended up leaving and partly blaming me for a lack of loyalty to him. I lost my friendship with him and his wife. They never even invited me to their house after that. It took a long time for things to become "normal" around the office.

Kirsten, age 46 (Waldron, 2003, p. 163)

As the opening narrative suggests, employees function within a complicated web of relationships, one that spreads throughout the organization and across its boundaries to include friends and family members. Damage to any one of these relationships has consequences for our larger network of personal and professional ties. In the scenario presented above, Kirsten found that her relationship with Jake was harmed when she failed to defend him after he received a poor evaluation. Kirsten worked closely with Jake on team projects, and he expected her to support his appeal to their supervisor. Kirsten secretly agreed with the low rating. She was reluctant to question the supervisor's judgment. Unfortunately, the relational ramifications extended beyond their friendship. Kirsten's close ties with Jake's wife, Rosa, became strained. For her part, Rosa noticed that Jake was now more stressed about work, and this caused tension in their household. The relational fallout spread as coworkers shared informal assessments of the situation and realigned their allegiances to Kirsten and Jake. At the informal employee gatherings often hosted at Jake's home, Rosa swayed opinions by offering her own assessment of the situation. Kirsten's exclusion from these events ensured that her own version of the story went largely unheard. Given the anger directed at her by Jake and Rosa, the supervisor reevaluated relationships with other employees. Was she too close to her team members, leaving them to feel hurt and surprised when she called attention to performance lapses? Did they think she was a pushover when it came to performance evaluations? Should she create more distance in relationships with the staff, by curtailing her participation in their social events, like the Friday happy hour gatherings?

All experienced workers know that some relationship damage is inevitable in the course of a career. This is particularly true for leaders, as their decisions inevitably affect the financial rewards, career advancements, and egos of the members who report to them. Indeed, relational competence is a key to success in nearly every job. Employees who ignore relational communication are subject to any number of risks. They may be resented, mistrusted, and isolated by coworkers. In team situations, they fail to cultivate the support and goodwill required for collective success. Employees of relationally challenged supervisors are more likely to be unmotivated and disloyal. In extreme cases, they sabotage their manager's plans with the hope of forcing a change in leadership. For all of these reasons, this chapter is concerned with the role of communication in damaging, repairing, and maintaining work relationships. As the next chapter focuses on the special challenges of romantic work relationships, the current chapter will examine less intimate peer and supervisory relationships.

❖ WHY IS NEGOTIATING WORKPLACE RELATIONSHIPS IMPORTANT?

Damage to any significant relationship can be costly, but work relationships are worth maintaining for several reasons. First and most obvious, work relationships are often nonvoluntary. We have limited choice when it comes to teammates and supervisors, so it is in an employee's interest to maintain these ties and repair them when they are damaged. Second, relationship failure has career implications. Promotable employees are often those with good people skills. They are respected and often liked by peers and those with promotion authority. They maintain a relationship network as a source of mentoring, task advice, and social support. They tend not to burn bridges because, over the long term, poisoned relationships can be toxic to career success. Third, workplace relationships can be a source of positive morale. Good relationships help employees maintain a positive outlook. Ties to coworkers are a source of resilience when the job becomes highly demanding or economic downturns cause anxiety. Coworker relationships can be sources of calm when personal relationships are turbulent. Of course, strained work relationships can also be sources of distress. A fourth reason for minimizing relationship damage is task interdependence. Many jobs require employees to work in close cooperation, as they share information, divide the workload, and focus labor resources where they are most needed. Relationally incompetent employees may find themselves to be vulnerable when their tasks require the help of coworkers.

Relational competence is the ability to recognize and manage the varying types of social bonds that develop in work settings. One key distinguishing factor is status. Workers experience *status-equal* relationships with peers. In the United States, a key dimension of peer relationships is equality, but other important considerations are liking, belonging, loyalty, collaboration, and mutual respect. Understandably focused on the task demands of their jobs, peers often pay limited attention to the relational implications of their work interactions. But as Kirsten came to realize, relational messages are important. Jake interpreted her behavior as a sign of disloyalty.

Status-unequal relationships involve differences in power, as is the case in most supervisory relationships. Employees acquire status from their position in the formal hierarchy, but expertise, seniority, connections to powerful people, cultural prejudices, and a host of other factors also contribute. In addition to obvious differences in power, these relationships are defined along several other dimensions, including the degree of trust shared by the parties. Formality, the autonomy allowed lower status members, openness, and respect are other important relational dimensions. Natalia shared this unpleasant experience, which reveals the importance of mutual respect and trust in peer relationships.

> I worked with this other employee on an advertising campaign. It was a short deadline and we worked long hours for a week to design the campaign and sketch out some ideas for slogans and ad copy. This other employee seemed nervous that I would screw things up (I was pretty new to the agency but she has been there for 2 years). I felt she was constantly looking over my shoulder. Rather than talking about my ideas, she would just dismiss them. I was a "rookie" in her mind. But when it came time to present our different plans to our manager, she ended up liking mine best. To my amazement, my coworker quickly took the credit! I learned a hard lesson about trusting her. I realized that from now on, I needed to respect my own talent and speak up for myself. I definitely learned not to trust that person ever again.

Employees experience many variations within these two broad relationship types. For example, status-equal coworkers might work closely together on a work team as Natalia and her coworker described above did. Or they may merely share the same physical space. Some peers become confidants and even close friends by working so closely together. But others maintain a healthy dose of skepticism. As Natalia recounts, we cannot necessarily trust the motives or guarantee the behavior of colleagues with whom we work closely.

Researchers use the term *blended relationships* to describe coworker/friend attachments (Bridge & Baxter, 1992). Blended relationships are frequent and highly valued, but they can be complicated. In the scenario that opened this chapter, Kirsten was conflicted in her relationship with Jake. He expected her to be a loyal friend, but Kirsten knew that the success of their workplace collaborations depended on Jake's improved performance. It can be difficult to be both friend and coworker.

In the case of status-unequal relationships, researchers have long recognized substantive variations. One of those is the difference between supervisory and leadership bonds (Graen & Cashman, 1975). In *supervisory* relationships, communication is generally concerned with the task requirements of the job. It tends to be formal and downward directed. Members communicate with leaders in highly proscribed ways, and their influence is limited. The roles of the parties are well defined and inflexible. In contrast, communication in *leadership* relationships can be more informal, multidirectional, and free-flowing. Members are granted more autonomy and are encouraged to share ideas and to question their bosses. Of course, most relationships between members and leaders involve a mix of these qualities. It is more useful to think of a leadership-supervision continuum rather than two discrete relational categories. For some employees and managers, a leadership relationship develops over time, as the member's competence, commitment, and trustworthiness are established. In such cases, the leader may offer mentoring, inside information, and opportunities for professional growth. In short, a marker of relational competence may be the member's capacity to develop leadership-type bonds within status-unequal relationships.

❖ KEY RESEARCH STUDIES

Managing Relationship Threats

One way to minimize relational damage is to prevent it from happening in the first place. A study recently reported by Waldron and Sanderson (in press) illustrates the point. Their research examined how leaders and members behave in challenging workplace situations, such as those discussed in the chapters of this book. In particular, they examined how members persuaded reluctant leaders to accept new work procedures or changes in workplace rules. Situations such as these are potentially threatening to the member, the leader, and the status of their relationship (Waldron, 2003). For example, a technology-savvy sales employee might insist that a Web-based ordering system would improve on the current telephone procedure. However, the proposal may be interpreted by the supervisor as a threat to his or her authority or technical competence. In pressing the matter, the member risks being perceived as pushy, overly eager, a know-it-all. Waldron and Sanderson argued that these threat perceptions are managed not just by the behaviors deployed in the present. Relational history may be more important.

Central to that history are the patterns of relationship maintenance behavior that have developed over time (see Textbox 5.1). Through these routine patterns of interaction, coworkers find the answers to a number of relational questions. How well do I know you? Are you reliable, committed, and loyal? What kinds of information can we share? Are you open to change? Do I have to be careful around you? In the case of the sales ordering system, the answers to these relational questions will help both leader and member gauge the degree to which the proposal is considered a threat or merely the constructive suggestion of a loyal and confident employee. If leader and member have established a stable pattern of friendly communication (personal pattern) and shared commitment to task improvement (contractual pattern), the suggestion likely will be welcomed. If the pattern has been regulative, defined by defensiveness and control, proposals for change may be unacceptably threatening to both parties.

Textbox 5.1   Relationship Maintenance Patterns

Personal

A friendship pattern defined by sharing humor, using small talk, discussing personal plans and problems

Contractual

Showing compliance with rules and expectations; emphasizing tasks and accomplishments; conveying agreement with organizational objectives and values

Regulative

Careful self-presentation; editing negative content; controlling emotions; avoiding conflict; use of distancing language

Direct

Explicit talk about relational expectations; meta-communication; questioning perceived relational injustices

Extra-contractual

Expressing a willingness to exceed normal expectations; prioritizing work commitments over personal commitments; communicating an unusual degree of availability and loyalty

Source: Tepper (1995) and Waldron (1991).

To test this way of thinking, the researchers surveyed 319 full-time workers from a variety of professions (Waldron & Sanderson, in press). Each respondent rated the degree of threat they perceived in two scenarios (see Textbox 5.2). Each involved an employee attempting to persuade a supervisor. One was similar to the new-idea scenario mentioned above; the other involved a request for an unscheduled day off from work. The participants also reported on relationship maintenance patterns. Results confirmed that patterns of relational communication make these persuasive situations more or less threatening. In particular, members who reported more frequent use of regulative behavior felt more threatened by the prospect of lobbying their supervisor to accept new ideas. Those who used more direct and personal maintenance behaviors were less threatened but only when pressing their request for an unscheduled day off. The reduction in threat appeared to be modest. The largest consideration in both situations was leader-member exchange quality, which we discussed earlier. Those members who maintained leadership-type relationships were less likely to perceive persuasive attempts as potentially damaging to themselves, the supervisor, and the relationship. This effect was most pronounced when employees expressed innovative ideas.

Textbox 5.2   Which Scenario Is Riskiest? Why?

The "Day-Off" Scenario: To deal with a personal matter, it has become very important that you take an unscheduled day off from work one day next week. You have no vacation time remaining, and you must find another way to obtain the needed time off with pay. Consider what you would say or do to obtain the time off while still being paid your normal salary or compensation.

The "New Idea" Scenario: You have recently noticed that some aspect of your work could be performed more efficiently if an existing work procedure could be changed. However, you are not allowed to make this change without your supervisor's approval. Your supervisor has indicated that he or she is hesitant to allow the change for reasons that are unclear to you. Consider what you would do or say in this situation.

Source: Waldron and Sanderson (in press).

This study yields several practical implications. First, regular communicative investments in the supervisory relationship in the present may prove helpful when leader and member face a challenging situation in the future. Second, the *type* of maintenance communication matters. Leaders and members who routinely employ regulative (defensive, cautious) communication report that their relationship is threatened by nonroutine communicative encounters. Finally, relationship considerations are more important when the member is seeking a legitimate organizational goal, not just a personal favor. Exploiting a high-quality relationship to seek a favor was, at best, modestly successful.

Managing Deteriorating Workplace Friendships

Communication researcher Patricia Sias (2006) conducts research on the nature of workplace friendships. Her work confirms that these relationships are important sources of information, task assistance, camaraderie, and social support. However, as our opening scenario suggested, when work relationships deteriorate, they also can be sources of emotional stress. Failed relationships can lead to lowered morale, impaired task performance, and, sometimes, the loss of valued employees. Why do workplace friendships go bad? Sias and her associates (Sias, Heath, Perry, Silva, & Fix, 2004) asked workers to share stories of relationships that had gone sour. They carefully examined the narratives to identify the reasons for relationship decline (see Textbox 5.3). Some declines were attributed to changes in events external to the friendship, such as a promotion or personal problems. Others were attributed to the qualities of the friend, such as an annoying personality trait or an intentional act of betrayal. Regardless of cause, the deterioration of an important relationship puts one or both employees at risk. How? Consider these descriptions of the behaviors of workplace colleagues who were former friends, synthesized from our own surveys:

- Refuses to cooperate on shared tasks

- Takes credit for the work we accomplished together

- (Is now the boss) and goes out of his or her way to show that I am not favored

- Spreads rumors about me and encourages my coworkers to shun me

- Refuses to invite me to after work social gatherings

- Gives me the "silent treatment" whenever possible

Given these negative perceptions, employees should be mindful of the communication strategies they use when ending a friendship with a coworker.

Textbox 5.3 Why Workplace Friendships Sour

Problem personalities: An annoying personality trait, such as overbearingness, self-pity, or oversensitivity, makes the friendship untenable.

Conflicting expectations: The friends anticipate different outcomes or express different hopes. For example, team members might disagree on peer performance ratings or the amount of time they will devote to helping each other complete tasks.

Promotion: One of the friends is promoted to a position of authority. The friendship is changed by increased power differences, the need for more objective communication, or even envy.

Betrayal: Trust is damaged by a breach of confidentiality or failure to keep promises.

Distracting life events: A coworker's personal problems, such as marital strain, distract from work performance and strain the friendship.

Source: Adapted from Sias et al. (2004).

In her research, Sias located three primary approaches to ending a workplace friendship (Sias & Perry, 2004). The first, *cost escalation*, involves the use of negative communication to make the friendship undesirable. These include condescension, criticism, interruptions, insults, rumor mongering, and failing to cooperate. *Depersonalization*, the second approach, imposes restrictions on the relationship to make it less personal. Ceasing to share personal information, limiting conversations to the immediate concerns of the task, refusing to engage in social activities—each of these actions increases the social distance between the parties and makes clear that the parties are merely coworkers, not friends. A third approach is the *state-of-the-relationship talk*, which involves explicit discussion of the terms of the relationship and the desire to terminate the friendship.

Employees report a preference for the depersonalization strategy when disengaging from work friendships (Sias & Perry, 2004). The cost escalation approach is least preferred. Of course, employee reports may or may not accurately reflect the behaviors they actually use. Nonetheless, cost escalation strategies are risky, as they are likely to permanently damage the relationship. Before using them, an employee should consider the traditional advice: "Don't burn your bridges." You may find someday that the friend you spurned is now your boss. We would argue that cost escalation tactics are also unethical in many cases, in that they cause unnecessary harm to other human beings. Another consideration is effectiveness. Depersonalization is an indirect method, one that assumes that the spurned coworker will eventually get the message. In fact, the reasons for disengagement may never become clear to the offending coworkers, even if they come to understand that friendship is no longer desired. More explicit conversations about relationship status may help both parties understand why and how the relationship needs to change in the future. State-of-the-relationship talks may provide opportunities to clarify misunderstandings, ameliorate hurt feelings, and reinforce shared task commitments.

None of this should be construed as advice to tolerate unethical, abusive, or personally damaging work relationships. Severing or downgrading ties with coworkers is necessary when a relationship exposes you to unethical conduct, exploits your generosity, threatens your mental well-being, or impairs your job performance. Similarly, we are cautious in suggesting that workers respond strategically rather than emotionally in their work relationships. Experiences of indignation, fear, and joy are important relational signals. They tell us something important about the presence or absence of mutual regard, justice, and morality in our interactions with others. For example, feelings of indignation may arise in response to a prolonged pattern of relational unfairness.

A sharp, emotionally charged response may be the most honest and effective way to communicate the seriousness of the matter. For that reason, we suggest relational disengagement should be an emotion-guided, goal-sensitive form of communication. This approach gives voice to relational feelings while considering how emotional communication will affect relationships, identities, and tasks of the former friends. We provide an example of how this might be achieved in Textbox 5.4.

Textbox 5.4   **Emotion-Guided, Goal-Sensitive Communication**

Vielka, a mechanical engineer with a large auto manufacturer, chose this approach when her coworker, Hamdi, insisted on answering his cell phone during their product specification meetings. "I was really irked," she admitted, "because it seemed so rude and disrespectful. It completely interrupted the flow of our work." Vielka wanted to "read him the riot act" but decided not to embarrass Hamdi in front of their peers. Instead, she took him aside after a meeting and "told him his behavior was frustrating the rest of us. It was damaging his relationship with the team." Hamdi seemed surprised, but with a sheepish smile, he turned off his phone at the beginning of the next meeting. In this way, Vielka heeded her emotions while preserving her relationship with Hamdi. She helped him protect his work identity and helped the team get its work done more effectively.

Responding to Relational Wrongdoing

Work relationships are gratifying sources of camaraderie, emotional support, and task assistance. But they can be hurtful as well. Employees report that the bad behavior of peers and supervisors is a frequent source of emotional stress (Waldron & Krone, 1991). Some organizations are rife with stories of backstabbing competitors, disloyal team members, and callous supervisors. Add the inevitable strain generated by daunting deadlines and problematic personalities, and it is not surprising that responding to relational misconduct is a crucial communicative competency at work.

In a recent study of 109 working adults (average age = 36), communication scholar Sandra Metts and her colleagues (Metts, Cupach, & Lippert, 2006) explored possible responses to workplace transgressions. They began by defining three general categories of misconduct. *Incivility* refers to behavior that is demeaning, rude, selfish, impatient, condescending, disconfirming, or arrogant, among other descriptors (for discussion of *civility*, see Arnett, 2006). Incivility is often chronic, an ongoing pattern of bad relational behavior, although the intent of the actor is sometimes ambiguous. Nonetheless, incivility breeches the relational rules that call for mutual respect among peers and can harm an employee's identity and dignity.

A more intense form of conduct is *bullying,* a kind of mistreatment characterized by threatening, humiliating, and abusing behavior (Lutgen-Sandvik, Namie, & Namie, 2009). Sabotaging the performance of a coworker is another form of bullying (see Chapter 4). In many cases, bullies are supervisors who abuse formal power, but sometimes it is individual coworkers or groups of peers that inflict harm. Lutgen-Sandvik and colleagues (2009) report that workplace bullying is "shockingly common and enormously destructive" (p. 27). Indeed, victims often report deep emotional distress and long-term consequences. Metts and colleagues (2006) consider *abuse* to be a distinct subset of bullying behavior in that it occurs within status-unequal relationships. Leaders abuse their power through such practices as intimidation, taking unfair advantage of employees, manipulating information to create false impressions, or stealing the credit for employee accomplishments.

It is first and foremost the responsibility of the organization to correct employees who engage in incivility, bullying, and abuse. These behaviors often prevail because they are accepted, even encouraged, by an organization's culture. Nonetheless, when faced with misconduct, employees must craft a communicative response. They can remain (a) silent, (b) leave, (c) voice their objections, (d) enlist assistance, (e) seek revenge or retaliation, or, in some cases, (f) initiate a process that may lead to forgiveness and possible reconciliation. *Silence* is a common response when employees fear the consequences of speaking up about relational misconduct. It may provide protection in the short run, but in the long run, abused employees often find themselves ruminating constantly, growing increasingly angry and bitter, and experiencing stress-related physical symptoms. In the cases of serious bullying or abuse, some employees choose to *leave the organization.* As with an abusive marriage, leave-taking can be an empowering and freeing response, and it may be the most realistic one if the abuser is powerful and supported by management.

Voicing objection can involve face-to-face discussion, informal reporting to authorities, or formal reporting. These options are considered in more detail in Chapter 8. For now, we note that face-to-face interaction requires a certain confidence in one's communicative abilities and the skill to express concerns in a manner that is assertive but not aggressive. Reporting misconduct to higher authorities can be advantageous, particularly if the misconduct clearly violates organizational guidelines. In such cases, the organization may feel compelled to intervene, and the reporting employee may be protected from retaliation. Some employees share concerns informally (with a senior employee or HR representative) rather than (or before) using a formal grievance-filing procedure. In *enlisting assistance,* employees seek out an experienced mentor or credible innovation champion. They ask for a realistic assessment of options and consequences and a better understanding of how the misconduct is likely to be interpreted within the organization's culture. The champion may be asked to help promote the change. Before using *formal* reporting systems, employees should understand confidentiality practices, the potential for retaliation by the offender, and the degree of support he or she will receive from coworkers and management.

Employees who feel they have been victimized by coworkers sometimes seek *revenge.* They typically seek to even the score by inflicting harm on the transgressing coworker. While revenge brings a certain sense of satisfaction (and sometimes seems richly deserved), this response has several unfortunate consequences. First, the vengeful act can itself be a kind of misconduct, which may be negatively sanctioned by the organization. Second, the practice of revenge halts the communication process, making it unlikely that the transgressing employee will ever acknowledge wrongdoing, understand the harm that he or she caused, apologize, or offer to make amends. Third, revenge can lead to a spiral of harmful behavior as employees and their allies engage in reciprocating negative acts. Together, these responses to relational misconduct can result in a hostile work environment, one characterized by widespread relational damage, energy-draining grudges, and a paucity of constructive relational communication.

Forgiveness is a constructive alternative to revenge. This concept is more often invoked in discussions of personal relationships, but Waldron and Kelley (2008) argue that forgiveness can be a competent, hopeful, and potentially productive response to a damaged work relationship. They offer a communicative definition of forgiveness:

> Forgiveness is a relational process whereby harmful conduct is acknowledged by one or both partners; the harmed partner extends undeserved mercy to the perceived transgressor; one or both partners experience a transformation from negative to positive states, and the meaning of the relationship is renegotiated, with the possibility of reconciliation. (p. 5)

As noted in Textbox 5.5, forgiveness is not a way to excuse injustice or ignore bad behavior. It is instead a way for aggrieved parties to confront relational misconduct and renegotiate their relationship. From this point of view, the victim of misconduct has every right to hold a grudge or seek revenge, but through a process of negotiation, he or she agrees to let go of this right. The parties may or may not reconcile, but if they do so, the relationship should be more just, safer, and mutually respectful. At work, forgiveness is a process that can help employees put negative incidents firmly in the past, recover self-esteem, renew their faith in the system of organizational justice, and recommit to the rules and values of the workplace.

Textbox 5.5   What Forgiveness Is Not

- Avoiding responsibility for harm
- Excusing bad behavior
- Pardoning injustice
- Escaping consequences
- Overlooking wrongdoing

How does the forgiveness process work? Waldron and Kelley (2008) proposed a seven-part Communicative Tasks of Forgiveness (CTF) model (see Textbox 5.6). It starts with parties confronting the transgression, which requires the offender(s) to both acknowledge the harm that has been caused and to offer an apology. The emotional effects on the parties must be vented and managed. After exploring the causes of the incident (sensemaking), the parties seek and grant forgiveness, negotiate new relational terms, and monitor compliance with them. Metts and colleagues (2006) confirmed that aggrieved coworkers are more forgiving when sincere apologies are offered and anger has dissipated. It is not uncommon for one or more parties to a forgiveness negotiation to seek assistance of a third party such as a human resource professional, mentor, counselor, or spiritual adviser.

Textbox 5.6   Communicative Tasks of Forgiveness

1. Confront the transgression
2. Manage emotion
3. Make sense
4. Seek/invite forgiveness
5. Grant/accept forgiveness
6. Renegotiate rules and values
7. Monitor relational transition

As a communicative process, forgiveness can be taxing for both offender and victim. It requires the participation of multiple parties. Nonetheless, it provides a constructive alternative to revenge, bitterness, or alienation, all of which undermine the effectiveness of an organization's workforce. We summarize these and other key communication options related to negotiating workplace relationships in Textbox 5.7.

Textbox 5.7   Communication Options

Relationship Maintenance Tactics (Waldron, 1991, 2003)

Personal/informal
Regulative
Contractual
Extra-contractual
Direct

Disengaging From Workplace Friendships (Sias & Perry, 2004)

Cost escalation
Depersonalization
State-of-the-relationship talk

Responding to Relational Misconduct (Metts et al., 2006; Waldron & Kelley, 2008)
Silence
Leaving
Face-to-face confronting
Informal reporting
Formal reporting
Enlisting assistance
Revenge
Forgiveness

   Confront the transgression
   Manage emotion
   Make sense
   Seek/invite forgiveness
   Grant/accept forgiveness
   Renegotiate rules and values
   Monitor relational transition

❖ MANAGING WORKPLACE RELATIONSHIPS AND THE RISK NEGOTIATION CYCLE

Our relationships at work provide a sense of belonging. The longer they last, the more secure we feel in them. Indeed, with the passing of time, the terms *friend* and *coworker* blend together. But as we have noted throughout this chapter, workplace relationships are sites for the negotiation of risk. Poor maintenance practices place our relationships at risk of deterioration. In contrast, more productive forms of relationship maintenance make problematic situations less risky for workers and their supervisors. The scenario that started this chapter demonstrated that the deterioration of a workplace friendship can have wide-sweeping effects. Employees can manage that risk by using relationship disengagement tactics that are emotion guided and goal sensitive. As in our private relationships, we put ourselves at risk of getting hurt when we form close bonds with coworkers. The benefits are worth the risks. Yet, employees must decide how to respond when they are the victims of relational misconduct. So far, we have considered a variety of possible responses, ranging from silence to revenge to forgiveness. In helping the reader negotiate these complexities of work relationships, we reconsider the risk negotiation cycle as it applies to managing workplace relationships (see Figure 5.1).

Attending

The first step in managing risk is to take an inventory of one's work relationships. For example, employees should consider how they are on the workplace for friendships. Do they have other sources of friends? Because people spend so much time at work, it is likely that many friendships will be formed there. But a failure to cultivate friends outside of work leads to vulnerability. What happens when the workforce is "downsized" or peers are transferred to new locations? In addition, employees need to disengage from coworkers who put them at risk because of unethical or sloppy work practices. A balanced social network, with friends from inside and outside of work, is generally more resilient.

Another consideration is the quality of the relationship with one's supervisor. Is a leadership relationship desired, or is mere supervision acceptable? Employees enjoy the former if their boss shares inside information, seeks their opinions, grants some flexibility in defining their approach to work, and creates opportunities to develop skills. Those who have yet to experience these benefits should attend to the maintenance behaviors that define this important relationship. In particular, notice if one's approach is regulative, with a tendency to be defensive or avoidant in supervisory interactions.

Attend to the emotions that accompany interactions with peers and supervisors. Feelings such as indignation, dread, or guilt may be signals that something is amiss. They may help us avoid risky situations. Emotions can spur changes in work alliances. They may prompt

Figure 5.1 Negotiating Workplace Relationships and the Risk Negotiation Cycle

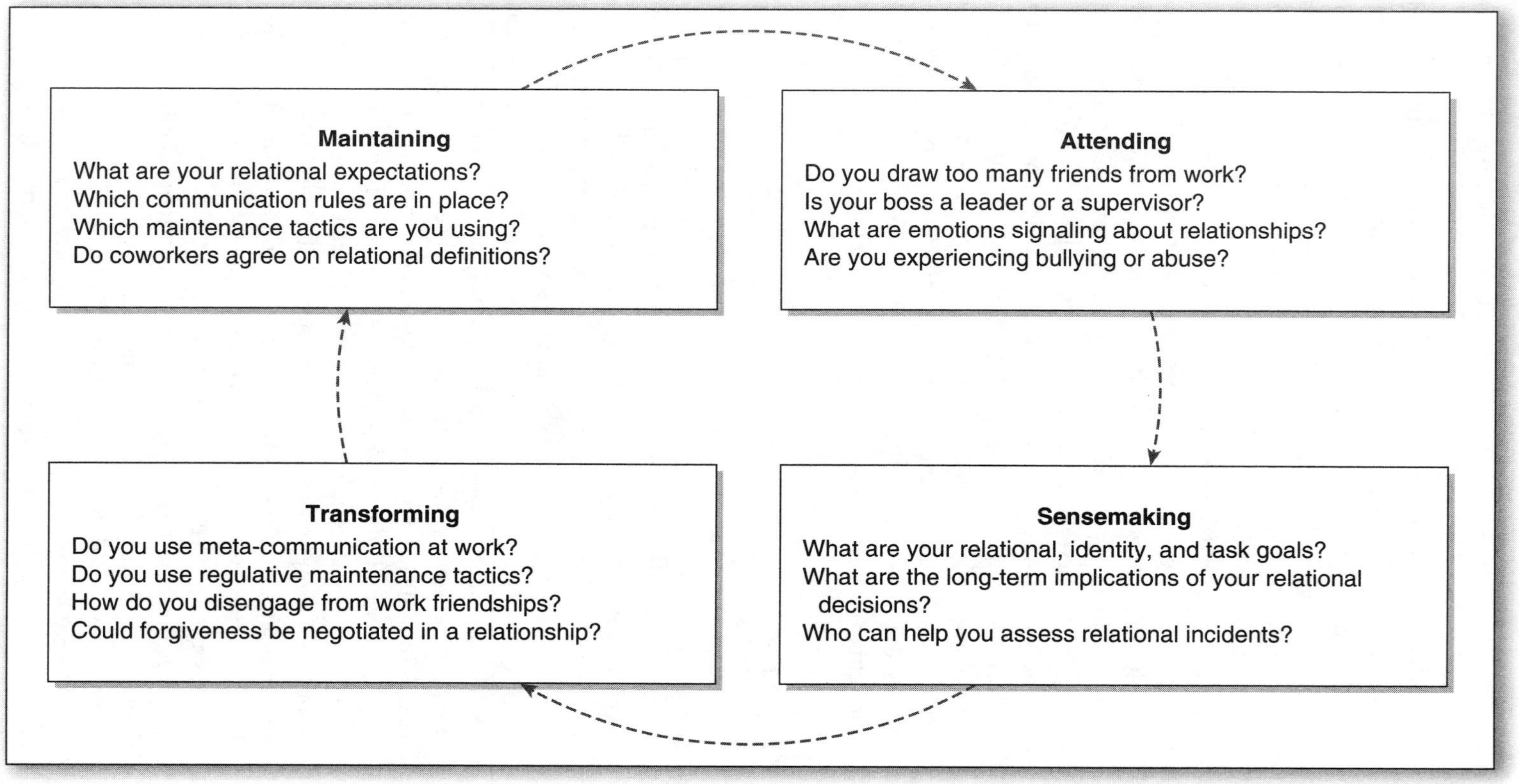

Attending

Do you draw too many friends from work?
Is your boss a leader or a supervisor?
What are emotions signaling about relationships?
Are you experiencing bullying or abuse?

Sensemaking

What are your relational, identity, and task goals?
What are the long-term implications of your relational decisions?
Who can help you assess relational incidents?

Maintaining

What are your relational expectations?
Which communication rules are in place?
Which maintenance tactics are you using?
Do coworkers agree on relational definitions?

Transforming

Do you use meta-communication at work?
Do you use regulative maintenance tactics?
How do you disengage from work friendships?
Could forgiveness be negotiated in a relationship?

questions about practices that make us uncomfortable. In addition, positive emotions shared with coworkers help us endure conditions that are temporarily unpleasant and stressful. Many workers need assistance as they listen to their emotions. Some will need the guidance of a counselor or experienced friend.

Sensemaking

The workplace is a web of relationships. The relational threads are many and varied, and they can be confusing. Before taking relationally risky action, consider both short-term and long-term communication goals. Communication behaviors have long-term implications for identity and task completion, as well as relationship management. If you decide to question your supervisor's decision, will she or he feel threatened? What evidence will help make the case while still respecting the supervisor's identity as the designated decision maker? If a relationship with a troublesome coworker is terminated, how will that affect the cohesion of the work team? Finally, the single-minded pursuit of task objectives can jeopardize relationships with peers. Failure to share the credit or offer assistance to peers may place these relationships at risk.

The advice of experienced coworkers or outside mentors can be valuable in the sensemaking process. As an example, consider that workers who have been bullied often experience disorienting confusion and self-doubt. They may even feel that their own behavior is to blame. An objective third party can provide a valuable reality check. They might confirm that the coworker is in fact out of line, know that the behavior has occurred in the past, and suggest possible responses. Or they might help to see relational situations from an alternative perspective. Maybe what appeared to be a condescending comment was really just an unintentional gaffe by a chronically absent-minded coworker. By consulting with a mentor, an employee could learn that a "friendly" relationship with the boss is causing coworkers to worry about favoritism. A general principle here is to consult with others before making rash judgments about workplace relationships.

Transforming

It is no exaggeration to say that communication is a primary means by which relationships are transformed, for better or for worse. In this chapter, we have identified a number of transformative practices. Some, such as the practice of forgiveness at work, may be unfamiliar. Others, including the state-of-the-relationship talk, may make you uncomfortable. But these practices have the potential to salvage relationships that are at risk of failure or at least preserve a functioning task relationship for those who can no longer be friends.

We have suggested that relationship maintenance behavior, the routine patterns of communication with a supervisor, has the potential to transform risky communication situations. Employees and supervisors who maintain their relationships through avoidance, editing bad news, and defensiveness are ill-prepared for truly challenging situations, such as disagreements over proposed innovations or negotiations over work rules. They simply find these situations more threatening than other employees. Among the implications: These employees rarely question the status quo; their innovative ideas go unrecognized; while other members gain influence and visibility, these folks go unnoticed.

Communication about the rules, expectations, and interactions that define a relationship featured prominently in this chapter. We suggested this meta-communication as a key to successful relationship disengagement. A state-of-the-relationship talk could (a) help former friends understand how expectations were violated ("Your inappropriate jokes make me uncomfortable, particularly when coworkers are present"), (b) indicate which new communication rules must be implemented ("From now on, please do not send me your humorous e-mails"), and (c) suggest which kinds of interaction boundaries will be imposed ("Let's focus our discussions on the work as much as possible").

We proposed that forgiveness could be a transformational process in the workplace. Serious relational transgressions threaten the moral codes that govern relationships, communities, and workgroups. Revenge is one way of reasserting that order, but it may destroy what remains of a damaged relationship, and it creates the conditions for a cycle of retribution and spreading feelings of hostility. Forgiveness is a process that calls attention to wrongdoing, holds the offender accountable, and creates possibilities for reconciliation. Offenders who explicitly recognize having broken the rules that govern organizational relationships may have a better chance of reconciling with coworkers. They may be less likely to repeat the offense. Ideally, the victimized employee is respected and may find justice in the process. The guiding principle is that parties consider an explicit process of relational negotiation rather than indulging their aggression or taking refuge in silence.

Maintaining

Once relational risks are transformed, communication practices are essential in maintaining safer relational terms. For example, the relationship maintenance behavior we labeled contractual helps a supervisor see that an employee is completing tasks, meeting expectations, and following rules. These behaviors may be particularly important for employees who are seeking to earn the trust of a supervisor after a damaging incident. Informal maintenance behavior, the routine small talk and light banter commonly shared among friends, is a means of monitoring the health of work relationships. It might reveal that the boss is cranky today or a coworker is distracted by family problems. In either case, this knowledge would allow an employee to adjust behavior to minimize relational stresses. Accordingly, this might not be the best time to ask the boss for that day off or the appropriate moment to tease a sensitive team member. In other words, relational information allows us to minimize behavior that might put work relationships (even temporarily) at risk.

Relationships are also maintained though definitions, expectations, and rules, some of which should be revisited. Periodically, leaders must scrutinize the communication rules that govern their interactions. Are all members expected to follow similar procedures when communicating with the supervisor, or do some get special access, more personalized attention, or more frequent opportunities? Why? What are the effects of these practices on member perceptions of favoritism and organizational justice? Members too should review their expectations for relationships with coworkers and leaders. Are any of these relationships putting them at risk? How important is personal loyalty to the relationship? What about trustworthiness, openness, and task competence? Do peers agree on the relative importance of these factors? Should communication be altered in light of these assessments to make relationships more trustworthy, open, or task oriented?

❖ CONCLUSION

In conclusion, we offer this slightly fictionalized account, based on a story shared by one of our students. At the time of this event, Emma was 23 years old. As you read it, consider what you have learned from this chapter.

> I used to be a server at a busy restaurant. It was my first job, and I was happy to become good friends with the hostess. Unfortunately, some days she would not show up for work, and I would have to cover for her. Sometimes she would call and ask me to take her shift on very

short notice. After a while, the manager just started to expect that I would always come in when they needed me. They would just tell me to come in, not even ask! Eventually, I had to tell the managers that I didn't want to do it all of the time. They got kind of mad, and I thought they were disrespectful of me. Later when my section was basically empty for hours, I would be afraid to ask them for more tables or to just send me home. Then they acted like I was losing interest in the job, and they would say, "We will look into it" or "Just wait, things will get better." I did care about the job, but I wanted the opportunity to make some tips. Fortunately, the bar manager was nice, and she respected all of the staff. She had been working there for a long time, and she gave me some advice about dealing with the other managers and getting respect for myself. Things got better after that.

Attend to the qualities of the relationships Emma experiences at work. Consider the status-equal and status-unequal relationships in which she participates. Which of these proved problematic? Why? Is there any relational misconduct occurring? What are Emma's emotional reactions signaling in this situation? What type of relationship does she appear to have with her boss? How does this exacerbate her dilemma?

With regard to sensemaking, Emma needs to understand how this workplace friendship is affecting her task and identity goals. Earlier, we described the workplace as a web of relationships. How is she affected by her hostess friend's behavior? How has the spillover from her workplace friendship shaped her supervisors' perceptions? And, in turn, how has the tension resulting from her workplace friendship led to changes in her work performance? What does Emma do to try and make sense of this chain of events? Which employee helped Emma understand her situation?

How could Emma transform the risk she faces? Should she disengage from her relationship with the hostess? If so, which disengagement approach would be best? Should she consider depersonalization or a state-of-the-relationship talk? Consider the responses to relational misconduct. Should she confront the hostess? Make a formal complaint? Or seek revenge? Could forgiveness be an option in this situation? Under what conditions? Would it help to engage in meta-communication? What might she say, then, to manage the relational risk in this situation? To the hostess? To the boss? To other coworkers?

Once Emma has established improved workplace relationships, what can she do to maintain them? What expectations should she have for her workplace friendships? What should others expect from her? Consider the forms of relationship maintenance communication discussed earlier in this chapter. Which of these would be most helpful in Emma's relationship with her supervisor? Her workplace friends? Could this organization benefit from more explicit workplace rules? For example, should there be more formalized procedures for switching shifts and the assignment of tables to serve?

❖ REFERENCES

Arnett, R. C. (2006). Professional civility: Reclaiming organizational limits. In J. M. Harden-Fritz & B. L. Ohmdahl (Eds.), *Problematic relationships in the workplace* (pp. 233–248). New York: Peter Lang.

Bridge, K., & Baxter, L. A. (1992). Blended relationships: Friends as work associates. *Western Journal of Communication, 56,* 200–225.

Graen, G. B., & Cashman, J. F. (1975). A role making model of leadership in formal organizations: A developmental approach. In J. G. Hunt & L. L. Larson (Eds.), *Leadership frontiers* (pp. 143–165). Kent, OH: Kent State University Press.

Lutgen-Sandvik, P., Namie, G., & Namie, R. (2009). Workplace bullying: Causes, consequences, and corrections. In P. Lutgen-Sandvik & B. Sypher (Eds.), *Destructive organizational communication* (pp. 27–52). New York: Routledge.

Metts, S., Cupach, W. R., & Lippert, L. (2006). Forgiveness in the workplace. In J. M. Harden-Fritz & B. L. Ohmdahl (Eds.), *Problematic relationships in the workplace* (pp. 249–278). New York: Peter Lang.

Sias, P. M. (2006). Workplace friendship deterioration. In. J. M. Harden-Fritz & B. L. Ohmdahl (Eds.), *Problematic relationships in the workplace* (pp. 69–88). New York: Peter Lang.

Sias, P. M., Heath, R. G., Perry, T., Silva, D., & Fix, B. (2004). Narratives of workplace friendship deterioration. *Journal of Social and Personal Relationships, 21,* 321–340.

Sias, P. M., & Perry, T. (2004). Disengaging from work relationships: A research note. *Human Communication Research, 30,* 589–602.

Tepper, B. (1995). Upward maintenance tactics in supervisory mentoring and nonmentoring relationships. *Academy of Management Journal, 38,* 1191–1205.

Waldron, V. (1991). Achieving communication goals in superior-subordinate relationships: The multi-functionality of upward maintenance tactics. *Communication Monographs, 58,* 289–306.

Waldron, V. (2003). Relationship maintenance in organizational settings. In D. J. Canary & M. Dainton (Eds.), *Maintaining relationships through communication: Relational, contextual, and cultural variations* (pp. 163–184). Mahwah, NJ: Lawrence Erlbaum.

Waldron, V., & Kelley, D. (2008). *Communicating forgiveness.* Thousand Oaks, CA: Sage.

Waldron, V., & Krone, K. J. (1991). The experience and expression of emotion in the workplace: A study of a corrections organization. *Management Communication Quarterly, 4,* 287–309.

Waldron, V., & Sanderson, J. (in press). The role of subjective threat in upward influence situations. *Communication Quarterly.*

6

Monitoring
Organizational Romance

Over a year ago, I was promoted, much to the dismay of my store manager, Dave. Dave and I never truly saw eye to eye. Ever since the man came to our store, he's never liked me. He doesn't smile, laugh, or even appreciate me. I'm a damn good employee, and he never recognizes me. Basically, I was promoted, and my manager Dave wasn't happy. He constantly spent time with a coworker named Anna. I began watching their friendship develop. They went from laughing to flirting to escapades in the backroom. Everyone began to notice their behaviors, but I was the gossiper in the store. I spread the news of the relationship so fast. I felt like the National Enquirer. Everyone knows you don't ever have a relationship with a coworker. It's against policy. I felt like Paul Revere telling the colonists that the British were coming. I made a phone call and talked to my district manager. I only saw them kiss, but being the over-dramatic queen that I am, I completely blew the situation out of proportion. It went from a simple peck on the cheek to total soft core porn. I'm devious. The district manager approached Dave with the issue. Dave didn't deny the budding relationship. Two days later, he was transferred!

Nicky, age 21

We spend a great deal of time at work, where we often meet people with similar skills, talents, and interests. It is not surprising, then, when coworkers develop romantic relationships. Some do so with full awareness of the risks that accompany workplace romance. Others are blinded by the strength of their attraction. They overlook the risks and fail to take the necessary precautions. The scenario above illustrates some of the unintended consequences. Dave was transferred not because he and Anna were romantically involved but due to their indiscretion, their flirtatious conduct that "everyone began to notice." The experience of this couple reminds us that workplace romance can be risky. But employees can manage these relationships in ways that reduce or manage the risk to themselves and their coworkers.

As a context for developing and maintaining romantic ties, the workplace is unique. How? Consider the role of Nicky, the employee who obviously had her differences with Dave. She seems to feel quite justified in reporting Dave's behavior to the district manager and takes some pleasure in embellishing the story. Dave works within a web of relationships, and his behavior with Anna reverberates across these connections, some of which are strong and others that make him vulnerable. Nicky and Dave share a negative relational history, and this provides a motive for her "outing" of the romantic relationship. We can speculate that Dave and Anna could have been more discriminating in their displays of affection at work—that they should have kept the relationship "under the radar." But Nicky's report reminds us that workplace romances must be conducted in a manner that is compliant with organizational policies and sensitive to the social dynamics of the workgroup.

The purpose of this chapter, then, is to look more closely at those communication practices that help employees manage the relational and organizational risks that accompany workplace romance.

❖ WHY IS MONITORING ORGANIZATIONAL ROMANCE IMPORTANT?

The Prevalence of Organizational Romance

Intimate workplace relationships are on the rise for several reasons. First, the gender composition of the workplace has changed dramatically over the past few decades, making it much more viable to develop opposite- or same-sex romantic relationships at work (Powell & Foley, 1998). Pair this with the average amount of time working adults spend at the workplace, which has increased steadily over the past few decades (Pierce, Aguinis, & Adams, 2000), and we can see why workplace romances readily occur. In addition, people are working in more team/group settings where they are brought together for periods of time, often without supervision, to work intensely on specific projects (Pierce, Byrne, & Aguinis, 1996; Powell & Foley, 1998; Quinn, 1977). These factors coalesce to form an environment in which people discover mutual interests and come to know one another well, an environment ideal (aside from the fact that it occurs at work) for the development of a potential romantic relationship. According to some of the many polls conducted on workplace romance (see Textbox 6.1), essentially three out of four employees have dated someone at work, and a similar percentage of managers approve of dating coworkers. The prevalence of workplace romance is counterbalanced, however, by the potential risks or outcomes associated with these relationships.

Textbox 6.1	**What the Statistics Tell Us About Organizational Romance**

Regarding managers...

    30% reported having at least one workplace liaison[1]
    74% reported approving of dating coworkers[1]
    21% approved of dating subordinates[1]
    50% reported dating subordinates[2]

Regarding employees in general...

    71% of employees reported that they had dated someone at work[2]
    71% reported avoiding workplace romances[4]
    76% believe that workplace romance can lead to conflict in the organization[4]
    52% reported that workplace romance was discouraged by management[4]

Regarding workplace dating policies...

    70%–72% of HR professionals reported that their companies had no policies[3,5]
    7%–14% reported that they have an unwritten understanding[3,5]
    13%–18% have written policies[3,5]
    48%–55% with (un)written policies permit consensual dating but discourage it[3,5]

Regarding the consequences for workplace romance policy infractions...

    42% transfer within the company[3]
    27% termination[3]
    26% counseling[3]
    25% formal reprimand[3]
    7% demotion[3]

(Continued)

Regarding the reasoning for having workplace dating policies . . .

88% potential for sexual harassment[3]

75% potential for retaliation if the romance ends[3]

60% concerns about morale of coworkers[3]

46% concerns about lowered productivity of those involved in the romance[3]

38% view that workplace romances are unprofessional[3]

Sources:
[1] 1994 survey conducted by the American Management Association
[2] 1998 America Online Survey
[3] 1998 Society for Human Resources Management Member Survey
[4] 2002 *USA Today* poll
[5] 2006 Society for Human Resources Management Member Survey

Concerns Associated With Organizational Romance

Interestingly, similar proportions of employees report avoiding romantic relationships at work, often because these relationships lead to conflict among coworkers. Yet, despite these worries, employees often find themselves in workplace romances. Clearly, love, attraction, and desire are powerful forces, even at work. The literature suggests many reasons for a cautious approach. Powell and Foley (1998) argued that romantic connections at work face greater scrutiny than other relationship types, such as those among coworkers or team members. Coworkers seem particularly concerned about the capacity of romantic ties to create distractions or inhibit the productivity of the intimate partners.

The Possible Outcomes of Organizational Romance

Our narrative at the beginning of the chapter highlighted an inescapable truth: Workplace romances prompt speculation and gossip. Powell and Foley (1998) argued that this is so because "workplace romances may invoke, among others, issues of love, sex, family, power, justice, ethics, and norms regarding acceptable behavior in the workplace" (p. 421), all of which are provocative topics for discussion. Employees can expect that workplace romances will result in gossip from coworkers. Beyond gossip, though, there are other serious repercussions potentially tied to workplace romances (Mainiero, 1986). When physical and sexual attraction is not reciprocated between employees, unwelcome flirtation and advances can quickly shift to sexual harassment (Pierce & Aguinis, 2001). When a romance ends but one party continues to pursue the relationship, charges of sexual harassment are quite possible (Pierce et al., 2000). Also, claims of retaliation or actual retaliation may occur between previous partners when a workplace relationship ends badly (Pierce & Aguinis, 2001).

What all of this makes clear is that mismanaged or failed relationships can have negative effects on morale, performance, and productivity. One common problem: Coworkers may perceive that romantic partners received favored treatment, even when that is not the case. Others find that their interactions with the romantic partners become awkward (Riach & Wilson, 2007). In the worst cases, romantic ties create conflicts of interest and biased decision making. Fellow employees may complain of unnecessary distractions from group tasks (Powell & Foley, 1998; Quinn, 1977).

Despite these concerns, organizational romance is viewed positively in some organizations. In some, they are a welcome part of the corporate culture. At Half Price Books, many employees have forged romantic ties, so many that the chief executive believes them to be a contributing factor to company success and the "feeling of family" that pervades its culture (see Textbox 6.2). Quinn (1977) found several positive outcomes associated with organizational romances, including increased coordination, lower tensions, improved teamwork, improved productivity, and improved work flow. In a related study, Anderson and Hunsaker's (1985) findings revealed that nearly a quarter of the people they surveyed believed that workplace romances had a positive impact on the organization. Similarly, Riach and Wilson (2007) reported that managers in some organizations believed that romances enhanced cohesion, improved productivity, and fostered employee satisfaction. We would argue that these benefits are more likely when the romantic partners engage in risk-managing communication practices.

Textbox 6.2 Romance at Half Price Books

Sharon Anderson Wright is the chief executive of Half Price Books, a chain that sells used books and magazines generating $120 million in business annually. The chain was founded by her mother, Pat Anderson, and the man she was dating for 21 years. Sharon met her husband, now the vice president for merchandising, during a renovation at the Dallas store she managed over a decade ago.

According to a piece titled, "St. Valentine, He's in Human Resources" (Belkin, 2004) that appeared in the *New York Times*, "There are now nearly 20 couples in senior management at Half Price Books, and 7 of the 17 district managers met their spouses at work." Sharon Anderson Wright quipped, "I won't even begin to guess how many couples are working for us total. Books can be darn romantic."

(Continued)

Textbox 6.2 *(Continued)*

The chief executive reports that the idea of instituting a workplace dating policy comes up occasionally but never really gains traction because she says, "That would be so hypocritical for us." Furthermore, she is somewhat realistic about managing amorous workplace relationships, concluding that management probably could not control these relationships if they tried. She does, however, report that complications do arise, noting that certain workers are not eligible for promotions because they would end up directly supervising their spouses, whereas other couples break up, still have to work together, and bring their issues to the office. But she claims those issues are a reasonable trade-off for the "feeling of family" that emerges from the romantic workplace relationships.

Organizational Policies on Workplace Romance

To protect against claims of sexual harassment, nepotism, or favoritism, a limited number of organizations have adopted workplace dating policies (Karl & Sutton, 2000; Wilson, Filosa, & Fennel, 2003). These usually stipulate the types of intimate relationships that are unacceptable (e.g., supervisor-subordinate romantic relationships vs. coworker relationships), and specify sanctions for offenders of the policy (e.g., transfers, written warnings). Some provide clear guidelines for relational conduct at work (Wilson et al., 2003). Guidelines pertain to the public display of affection or the inappropriate use of sexual innuendo, as well as disclosure of the relationship to management. According to the Society for Human Resource Management, the number of companies with workplace dating policies has not changed significantly in recent years, and the numbers remain modest, increasing from 13% in 1998 to 18% in 2006 (see Textbox 6.1). The number of companies purporting to have unwritten policies dropped from 14% in 1998 to 7% in 2006. The drop is likely due to the tension between management's desire to avoid litigation while respecting employee privacy (Wilson et al., 2003).

The repercussions for violating a workplace dating policy can be quite serious. Organizational responses range from relatively lenient interventions such as informal counseling to more serious and formal interventions, including verbal reprimands, written warnings, transfers, and termination (Karl & Sutton, 2000). Karl and Sutton (2000) found that, in general, employees deemed counseling to be the fairest response to workplace romances. However, employees favored stricter sanctions when the performance of the couple had suffered or the romance was highly visible.

Conversely, employees preferred that management should take no action when the performance of romantically involved employees had improved.

When formal policies are absent, managers must determine when to intervene. Brown and Allgeier (1995) found that managers were more likely to do so when the relationship involved members of unequal status or there was evidence that the relationship was hampering the larger workgroup. Because dating policies vary across organizations, wise employees familiarize themselves with both written and informal policies as well as workgroup norms. Failure to do so increases the risks of workplace romance.

Textbox 6.3   Love Contracts

The Web site HR.BLR.com aims to provide advice and answers related to human resources. A column on the Web site devoted to organizational romance detailed what should be included in organizational policies governing workplace dating.

According to labor and employment practice attorney Marilyn Sneirson, employees signing "love contracts" need to agree to certain prescribed expectations about behavior and to confirm that the romantic relationship is consensual ("'Love Contracts' Lessen Liability," 2006).

In addition, love contracts need to clarify that

- employees sharing the same reporting level will not take a position that results in one partner directly supervising the other;

- in instances where the romantic partners are already in a hierarchical relationship, the supervising partner will remove himself or herself from any decision making that affects the subordinate employee;

- disputes arising from the relationship will be resolved through arbitration;

- either party will be able to terminate the relationship without the fear of retaliation;

- employees will agree to waive their rights to pursue claims of sexual harassment linked to events that occurred before signing the contract.

❖ KEY RESEARCH STUDIES

Models of Workplace Romance

In the seminal piece of work in this area, Quinn (1977) administered survey questionnaires and conducted interviews to learn about employees' perceptions of workplace romance. People in the study were asked to report about a time when they had been "closely associated, as a third-party observer, with a romantic relationship between two members of the same organization" (p. 32). Quinn found that proximity was the major determinant of organizational romance. In particular, three types of proximity accounted for the development of romantic relationships: ongoing geographical proximity, proximity due to ongoing work requirements, and occasional contact. The first involves simply sharing workspace, which accounted for 63% of all reported romances. The second results from spending time performing shared work tasks such as training, consulting, and business travel, which accounted for 77% of all romances. There is considerable overlap between these two. Occasional contact, in contrast, occurred when people met at work but did not see one another regularly due to shared work space or tasks. Quinn's work also revealed that people attributed romances to three motives: job (e.g., financial rewards, advancement), ego (e.g., adventure, excitement), and love (e.g., companionship, meaningful long-term relationship).

The visibility of romantic relationships contributes to their impact. Relationships became more visible when participants spent noticeable amounts of work time chatting, took long lunches together, had long discussions behind closed doors, and physically displayed affection at work. Another impact factor was coworker observations of changes in three aspects of work behavior: competence, power relations, and positivity. Changes in competence involved relationship members becoming preoccupied, doing less work, missing commitments and meetings, producing lower quality work, and making costly errors. Changes in power entailed showing favoritism for one another, providing one another with more power, isolating one another from other coworkers, and flaunting newfound power. Interestingly, there were positive behavioral changes when coworkers observed that romantic partners became easier to deal with interpersonally and when romantic partners became more productive workgroup members.

Textbox 6.4   Behavioral Changes Due to Workplace Dating

Riach and Wilson (2007) examined employee dating in English pubs. The excerpts below, drawn directly from their work, reveal all three types of behavioral changes.

Changes in Competence

Another worker spoke of a relationship between a team leader and a bar worker who became "really lazy and tired all the time." "Like when she had been working late shifts he would always be late in for work in the morning and he'd spend a lot of the time phoning her, or if she came in talking to her, and not doing his work" (p. 87).

Changes in Power

For example, one female manager told the story of a girl who was disliked by other staff for being "conniving" and was given favourable shifts and treatment after beginning a relationship with one of the managers (p. 86).

Changes in Positivity

Another worker said that the effect could be positive if the couple is happy and those around them feel happy (p. 87).

Organizational members react to workplace romance in different ways, depending on the impact of the relationship on the workgroup. They may tolerate the relationship by choosing to ignore it or counseling participants about the potential risks. They may react negatively by ostracizing participants, undermining their work, and sabotaging their efforts. They may complain to supervisors. Discussions among coworkers sometimes spread unfounded speculation and amplified perceptions of favoritism. Quinn (1977) reported that the informal employee network was sometimes the source of distortion and negative evaluations of the couple. Management's responses to organizational romance included punitive action (e.g., warnings/reprimands, terminations, and transfers), positive action (openly discussing, counseling), or no action (ignoring, avoiding, waiting for the situation to resolve itself). Although this work is now dated, it provided the foundation for our understanding of how coworkers respond to organizational romance.

Research on workplace romance languished for two decades, only to resurface in the late 1990s (Brown & Allgeier, 1995; Pierce, 1998; Pierce et al., 1996; Powell & Foley, 1998). Pierce et al. (1996) conducted a comprehensive literature review on the topic. They produced an elaborate model of the antecedents, moderating factors, and consequences of workplace romance. According to these scholars, workplace romance begins when propinquity (spatial proximity) and repeated exposure allows coworkers to discover similarities in attitudes. Similarity leads to interpersonal attraction. But how does similarity lead to romantic interest? Pierce et al. argue that workplace pressures such as time deadlines, competitive demands, and other anxiety-provoking situations give rise to physiological arousal, which coworkers mislabel as sexual attraction or romantic interest. People with similar attitudes may develop feelings of sexual and romantic attraction when confronted with the arousing situations inherent in a competitive work environment. Obviously, many coworkers neither experience nor act upon such feelings. Why do certain employees pursue organizational romances when others do not? According to the researchers, pursuit is more likely when coworkers hold favorable attitudes about organizational romance, work in more accepting organizational cultures, and enjoy more job autonomy.

The work of Pierce et al. (1996) also considers consequences for employees, members of the workgroup, and the organization. The authors concluded that job productivity, worker motivation, and job involvement decreased in early stages of organizational romance and increased in later stages. They contended that job productivity and job involvement increased when love motives were present but changed little when ego motives were in play. In addition, they suggested that hierarchical romances (i.e., relationships between supervisors and subordinates) produced greater decreases in participant and coworker job productivity than lateral relationships between equally ranking coworkers. They argued that hierarchical romances, particularly highly visible ones, had a negative effect on coworker morale, whereas lateral romances had a positive affect on coworker morale. Workplace romances appear to bolster the satisfaction of organizational members who already feel satisfied with particular aspects of their job. Apparently, and perhaps not surprisingly, employees who enter into workplace romances for job motives can expect to generate more gossip, particularly negative gossip, than those who enter into such relationships because of love motives. Finally, Pierce et al. asserted that low-status employees were more likely than high-status employees to be terminated or relocated due to an office romance. Overall, this work reveals that perceived motives of the partners and the nature of those relationships (hierarchical or lateral) shape the reactions of coworkers. They clearly consider how the relationship alters the power dynamics of the workgroup.

The Web site jobschmob.com provides an outlet for employees to vent about frustrating workplace issues. Employee postings appear in categories such as Bosses from Hell, Interview Stories, and Office Romance. The fact that power dynamics surface as a result of organizational romance is patently clear in the following fictionalized anecdote, which is typical of the postings under the Office Romance category.

> I work for a company that will remain anonymous. A senior officer at the company had a longtime relationship with one of her direct reports. Everyone knows that it is a bad idea to date your boss or, for that matter, your subordinate. This can only result in a messy conflict of interest. Now, even though everyone knows about their affair, we all have to tiptoe around them.

Apparently, employees know about this relationship, but they choose not to comment, since one of the parties is a senior officer. What remains unclear from this employee's commentary is the degree to which the hierarchical romance inhibits productivity. However, the fact that employees feel the need to post anonymous comments to Web sites would suggest that the relationship affects the larger workgroup. So why is it that organizational romance proves so challenging and disruptive for fellow coworkers? How do you feel about organizational romance (see Textbox 6.5)?

Power Dynamics in Organizational Romance

Organizational romances are clearly risky in some organizational environments and become more challenging and problematic when hierarchical in nature (Mainiero, 1986). In lateral relationships, neither party can influence the organizational status or standing of the other member. However, in hierarchical relationships, influence is bidirectional. The higher status partner can alter performance expectations of the lower status partner, and the lower status partner can leverage the relationship to achieve favorable assignments and schedules. Whether real or merely perceived, these practices can be highly disruptive.

Textbox 6.5 **Where Do You Stand on Organizational Romance and Workplace Dating?**

Below are statements that Powell (1986) used to assess students' attitudes about organizational romance. In his study, more than 350 undergraduate and graduate management students completed a survey questionnaire comprising 18 items. Study participants used a 7-point scale that ranged from *strongly disagree* (1) to *strongly agree* (7) to indicate the degree to which they concurred with each statement.

Ten of the original items appear below. How would you respond?

1. Sexual relations foster better communication between the workers involved.

2. Some sexual intimacy among coworkers can create a more harmonious work environment.

3. Management should take strong steps to discourage sexual propositions toward coworkers.

4. Supervisors who direct sexual attention toward their subordinates should be reprimanded.

(Continued)

Textbox 6.5 *(Continued)*

    5. Any worker who directs sexual attention toward another should be reprimanded.

    6. It is all right for someone to look for a marriage partner at work.

    7. It is all right for someone to dress attractively to draw the attention of coworkers.

    8. I would be offended by a coworker flirting with the supervisor.

    9. I would never get intimately involved with a coworker.

    10. I would never get intimately involved with my supervisor.

Coworkers become concerned when romantic partners act as a power coalition (Mainiero, 1986). This is evidenced by such practices as inequitable task allocation or resource distribution. One effect is that employees begin to carefully edit messages out of fear that they will be shared with the more powerful romantic partner. Hierarchical romances are problematic when coworkers perceive that one of the partners is exploiting relational access and unjustly acquiring rewards. Reactions, which can "range from social disapproval to outright hostility and acts of sabotage" (Mainiero, 1986, p. 758), create dysfunction within the workgroup, which moves employees to seek management intervention.

Workplace Romance and Sexual Harassment

Not all intimate workplace relationships last. In fact, one report indicated that almost half dissolve (Henry, 1995). When workplace romances end, the possibility for sexual harassment between partners increases (Pierce & Aguinis, 2001; Pierce, Broberg, McClure, & Aguinis, 2004). According to Pierce and Aguinis (2001), the likelihood of sexual harassment emerging from dissolved workplace romances can be tracked directly back to the original motives for entering into such relationships. They proposed a typology of workplace romances, which included (a) companionate love (both parties have love motives), (b) passionate (both parties have love and ego motives), (c) fling (both parties have ego motives), (d) mutual user (both parties have job motives), and (e) utilitarian (one partner has job motives, whereas the other has ego motives).

Pierce and Aguinis (2001) argued that passionate and companionate relationship types lead to indirect forms of sexual harassment such as unwanted sexual attention, gender-based sexual joking, and innuendoes. These can be contrasted with more overt forms such as sexual coercion or assault. Apparently, relationships underpinned by love motives allow the former partners to see one another as complex and multidimensional individuals rather than sexual objects. However, continued displays of romantic interest can be perceived as harassment.

By comparison, utilitarian and user relationships are motivated by professional advancement. The relationship may dissolve, but the motives remain, creating the potential that sexual coercion could be used for career advantage. Finally, Pierce and Aguinis (2001) contended that employees who enter into workplace romances for ego reasons (e.g., the fling) will be less likely to engage in sexually harassing behavior once the relationship dissolves because they recognize that flings are short-lived. The partners are less invested in these relationships in the first place, and are ready to move to a new relationship to meet their ego needs (see Table 6.1).

Several other factors can contribute to the emergence of sexual harassment when workplace romances dissolve (Pierce & Aguinis, 2001). For example, position power can play a major role. Will one of the former partners abuse their power? Clearly, this is more likely with hierarchical workplace romances than with lateral ones. In addition, we need to consider how the relationship ends. Is it terminated by mutual agreement or is it the preference of one partner? Does one partner harbor bitterness about the breakup? When relationships end bilaterally with positive affect, the risk of sexual harassment is negligible.

When workplace romances end unilaterally, the individual who wants the relationship to continue may persist in displaying and seeking affection. In these instances, desire to rekindle a romance or the

Table 6.1	Factors Contributing to Sexual Harassment Stemming From Organizational Romance		
Motives for Entering the Relationship	**Type of Relationship**	**Relationship Dissolution**	**An Organization's Sexual Harassment Guidelines**
Job/Ego/Love	Lateral/ Hierarchical	Bilateral/ Unilateral	Explicit and enforced/ Lax

Source: Adapted from Pierce and Aguinis (2001).

drive to continue satisfying ego needs can manifest in sexual harassment (Pierce & Aguinis, 2001). Cases such as these are frequently submitted to simplyfired.com, a Web site designed to provide people with an outlet for discussing and seeking feedback on their firing. We have constructed the following fictionalized account based on a synthesis of various stories appearing on the Web site.

> Paul was totally smitten with his coworker Sheila. The pair arranged a weekend getaway in Atlantic City. During the trip, Paul sensed that something was amiss. He questioned her commitment to the relationship, and his doubts seemed well founded when he discovered upon their return that Sheila was also dating another coworker from the office. Paul was distraught. When he confronted her, Sheila got defensive and asked him to back off. Paul was confused—he thought they were in love. He demanded an explanation. Sheila replied to his continued attempts to contact her by filing a harassment complaint with human resources. In the end, Paul lost his job, while Sheila kept hers. Paul is bitter to this day.

This account reveals the potentially serious repercussions (i.e., termination) that result when former romantic partners in the workplace fail to agree on the future of the relationship and the nature of appropriate behavior at work. Paul lost not only his love interest at the time but also his job, as Sheila construed his continued interest as sexual harassment. Was she acting hastily in this situation when she reported him for sexual harassment? Perhaps, but perceptions of sexual harassment are more likely when a former partner expresses anger, resentment, or jealousy. Scorned partners may not go quietly, and their relationship repair efforts can easily cross the line of sexual harassment.

A final consideration in Pierce and Aguinis's (2001) model is an organization's tolerance for sexual harassment. Dissolved romantic relationships are less likely to lead to sexual harassment when organizations have clear and strict guidelines about sexual harassment. Consider the rejected lover who continues to use inappropriate sexual innuendo with a former partner. In a company with well-developed guidelines, there is no ambiguity about the inappropriateness of such communication behavior. For that reason, employees typically will be more confident in labeling it as such and reporting it to management.

Organizational Romance

Riach and Wilson (2007) set out to determine what people perceived to be the "rules of engagement for romance" (p. 85). They interviewed employees from a chain of pubs in the United Kingdom. Don't let it interfere with your work, don't "screw the crew" (i.e., managers should not date subordinates), and don't date the customers were rules that surfaced in their study. Their work produced some unique findings as well. For example, when employees perceived workplace romances unfavorably, they were more likely to make negative attributions about those involved in these relationships, leading to the commonly held notion "that bad people have bad organizational relationships" (p. 86). In addition, they found that a certain tension underscored employees' feelings about workplace romances. That is, employees reported that workplace romances had a positive effect on the workgroup yet caused some uncertainty. For instance, an employee reported that having a couple in the workplace made interacting more friendly and casual in some instances but also more awkward in other situations.

Managing the risks of organizational romance can be a challenge for the partners and their coworkers, but as we have made clear in this chapter, communication practices largely determine the success of workplace romances. We summarize the communication options in Textbox 6.6.

Textbox 6.6   Communication Options

Communicative Displays of Workplace Romance (Quinn, 1977)

   Spending noticeable amounts of work time chatting
   Taking long lunches together
   Having long discussions behind closed doors
   Displaying physical affection at work

Communicative Responses to Workplace Romance (Quinn, 1977)

   Ignore
   Gossip
   Counsel
   Ostracize
   Undermine/sabotage
   Complain to management

Communicative Responses to Hierarchical Workplace Romance (Mainiero, 1986)

   Communication distortion
   Social disapproval
   Displays of hostility
   Demonstrations of sabotage

(Continued)

Textbox 6.6   *(Continued)*

Communicative Acts That Denote a Power Coalition and Exploitation (Mainiero, 1986)

Ostracizing workgroup members
Reassigning tasks
Promoting the subordinate partner
Flaunting newfound power

Communicative Acts That Signal Sexual Harassment After Relational Dissolution (Pierce & Aguinis, 2001)

Continued expressions of interest
Continued sexual advances (due to unchecked ego motives)
Displays of negative affect (e.g., anger, resentment, jealousy)

❖ MONITORING ORGANIZATIONAL ROMANCE AND THE RISK NEGOTIATION CYCLE

Employees must attend to the factors that make romantic relationships more or less risky in their workplace. They can use communication to assess their relational assumptions and make sense of their options. The risk of these relationships can be transformed when employees are prudent and discerning in their communication. Indeed, many romantic relationships have been initiated and nurtured by people who work together. However, to maintain a safe environment for partners and their peers, organizational policy and relational behavior must be responsive to the potential risk of mismanaged organizational romances. The risk negotiation cycle (Figure 6.1) provides the framework for our analysis of these possibilities.

Attending

When attending to or detecting risk, we believe employees should consider at least four key issues. First, what is the apparent motive of a coworker for engaging in a workplace romance? A workplace romance initiated for ego or career advancement motives is far riskier than one based on love motives. The first way to manage risk is to avoid relationships based on more questionable motives. Rest assured that your coworkers will assess your motives as they attend to the risks it creates for them. Another consideration is the tolerance of the organization for workplace romance. Is there a formal dating policy in place? And, if so,

Figure 6.1 Monitoring Organizational Romance and the Risk Negotiation Cycle

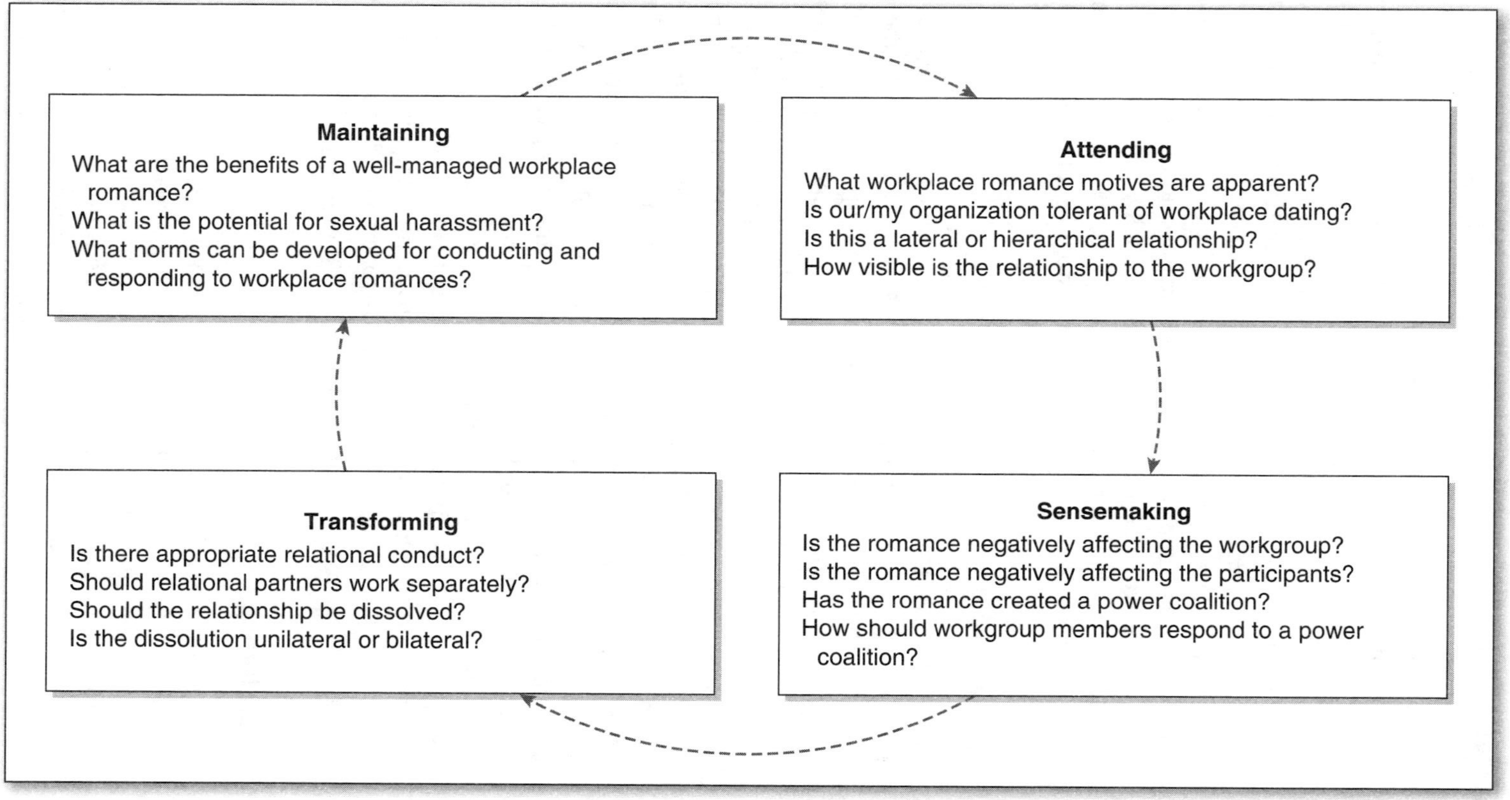

Attending

What workplace romance motives are apparent?
Is our/my organization tolerant of workplace dating?
Is this a lateral or hierarchical relationship?
How visible is the relationship to the workgroup?

Sensemaking

Is the romance negatively affecting the workgroup?
Is the romance negatively affecting the participants?
Has the romance created a power coalition?
How should workgroup members respond to a power coalition?

Maintaining

What are the benefits of a well-managed workplace romance?
What is the potential for sexual harassment?
What norms can be developed for conducting and responding to workplace romances?

Transforming

Is there appropriate relational conduct?
Should relational partners work separately?
Should the relationship be dissolved?
Is the dissolution unilateral or bilateral?

is it enforced? What are the informal norms governing workplace dating? By attending to these questions, employees can anticipate the consequences of organizational romance. When formal policies are present, the risk of formal sanctions, such as transfers or reprimands for workplace dating, is greater. A third major consideration is the nature of the relationship. Is it a lateral relationship between coworkers, or is it a hierarchical relationship that involves a supervisor and subordinate? The former will introduce less risk for participants and the workgroup; the latter comes with considerably more risk. Finally, when assessing risk, employees need to consider the visibility of the relationship. As participants, employees can reduce the risk by adopting a low profile.

Sensemaking

Before initiating or accelerating an intimate relationship, employees can seek the assessment of trusted coworkers. How would the relationship affect them or others? If the relationship has begun, employees should monitor the perceptions of peers and look for signs of distress or disruption. Do they see evidence that productivity, job involvement, or motivation of the romantic partners has slipped? Are they concerned about favoritism or exploitation? These discussions may reveal negative impacts, but positive assessments may also be forthcoming. Mentors or dispassionate observers can help employees make sense of their options, giving consideration to the organization's history, culture, policies, and norms. For example, on the advice of a mentor, the partners could decide to report the existence of their relationship to a manager or human resources officer.

Coworkers can make the partners aware of gossip or misperceptions that might be spreading across the organization's networks. The couple may learn that peers are carefully monitoring interactions with the couple or feeling awkward. This discovery could prompt them to make constructive changes in their behavior at work.

Transforming

We see three possible ways to transform the risk created by workplace romances: appropriate relational conduct, removal of one relational partner from the workgroup, and dissolution of the relationship. Employees involved in a workplace relationship can adjust their relational conduct. In a hierarchical relationship, perceived abuses of power can be avoided by such actions as recusing oneself from evaluation and promotion decisions and scrupulously declining opportunities to gain career advantage from romantic ties to a powerful employee. In lateral relationships, ensure that displays of affection and time spent together are minimized, that personal productivity remains high, and that awkwardness with coworkers is addressed in a nonthreatening manner. When disruption to the workgroup is an issue, the possibility of reassignment should be explored. The reality is that some personal relationships become a distraction to employees, and at least one partner should be relocated to reduce risk to the larger workgroup. Similarly, physical relocation may be the best alternative when relationships dissolve but one partner continues to pursue it. Relocation may reduce the likelihood of sexual harassment.

Indeed, partners may find that a highly disruptive relationship should be dissolved. This is more likely with utilitarian or mutual user relationships than compassionate and passionate relationships. Coworkers can help reduce the risk in these instances by counseling romantic partners to consider the importance of the relationship juxtaposed against the disruption it may be causing. Less important relationships can be dissolved bilaterally and without further disruption to the group. Relationships that dissolve unilaterally may prompt former partners and workgroup members to reengage the sensemaking process as they explore ways to reestablish relationship norms.

Maintaining

Maintenance of a safe relational environment involves clear understandings of the relational behaviors that are permissible in the workplace. Development of communication norms is important because organizational romance is not an isolated event. In fact, workplace romances will continue to form as long as members work long hours together in emotionally intense environments. Like the pub employees who developed rules of engagement for dating in the workplace, organizational members can develop informal norms when formal guidance is lacking. In so doing, workgroups engage in optimization. They increase the possibility that the benefits of organizational romance will outweigh its risks. The degree to which a relatively risk-free environment is maintained will depend on the motives of those who enter romantic relationships. For example, passionate relationships will be more enduring but potentially more disruptive if and when they dissolve. Relationships based on a desire for special access or career advancement are risky for the partners and their peers. Restrictions on hierarchical relationships may be helpful in maintaining a safe environment.

❖ CONCLUSION

To conclude this chapter, we share an additional account about workplace romance. This account is taken from an article in *Nation's Business* that chronicled workplace romances gone awry. It reads as follows:

> The controller of a small company in the Southeast and a warehouseman made no bones about their adulterous relationship, kissing and pawing each other ostentatiously. The two eventually left their spouses and married. But the warehouseman soon took advantage of his new wife's high standing in the company, overstepping his authority and, unbeknown to her, sexually harassing female workers. Fed up, the owner told the controller that her husband was being fired for those abuses, whereupon both spouses angrily quit and threatened to capsize the firm. (Meyer, 1998, p. 57)

Attend to the motives of the couple described in this account. Which of the motives described in this chapter are evident? Have the partners assessed the organization's tolerance for workplace dating? The controller and warehouseman appear to be in a hierarchical relationship. How is power affecting the risks created by this workplace romance? Finally, are these romantic partners mindful of how their relationship is affecting coworkers?

How would other employees make sense of this situation? What consequences will a relationship such as this have on workgroup dynamics? Productivity? Clearly, the warehouseman feels somewhat emboldened by the status acquired from the romantic involvement. Has a power coalition emerged? And, if so, how might coworkers change how they respond to their peer? Finally, what is the connection between this particular organizational romance and the occurrences of sexual harassment reported in this case?

To transform some of the risk introduced in this case, coworkers would need to look at the conduct of the relational partners and perhaps confront it. Should they urge the couple to "cool it" with the public displays of affection, to "think twice" about misusing power, or to "wake up" to the damage the relationship might be inflicting on the workgroup and the company? A discussion with these particular romantic partners may not be feasible due to power dynamics. Would approaching management be a reasonable alternative? Should management ask the partners to dissolve the relationship? Transfer one of the employees? Dismiss them if they continue to allow the romance to interfere with the workplace?

Finally, how could this company maintain a safer environment for its employees? Should they create clearer guidelines for the conduct of relationships? What should they be? Could the workgroup develop informal norms for handling problematic workplace romances in the future? What would these entail? For example, members could define rules for public displays of affection or caution budding couples about the potentially disruptive effects of romance on team performance. What kinds of guidelines would minimize the chances of romantic relationships leading to sexual harassment?

❖ REFERENCES

Anderson, C. I., & Hunsaker, P. L. (1985). Why there's romancing at the office and why it's everyone's problem. *Personnel, 62,* 57–63.

Belkin, L. (2004, February 15). St. Valentine, he's in human resources. *New York Times,* p. 10/1.

Brown, T. J., & Allgeier, E. R. (1995). Managers' perceptions of workplace romances: An interview study. *Journal of Business & Psychology, 10,* 169–176.

Henry, D. (1995). Wanna date? The office may not be the place. *HR Focus, 72,* 14.

Karl, K. A., & Sutton, C. L. (2000). An examination of the perceived fairness of workplace romance policies. *Journal of Business and Psychology, 3,* 429–442.

'Love contracts' lessen liability from consensual workplace dating. (2006, February 6). Retrieved June 23, 2009, from http://hr.blr.com/whitepapers.aspx?id=17668

Mainiero, L. A. (1986). A review and analysis of power dynamics in organizational romances. *Academy of Management Review, 11,* 750–762.

Meyer, H. R. (1998). When cupid aims at the workplace. *Nation's Business, 86,* 57–59.

Pierce, C. A. (1998). Factors associated with participating in a romantic relationship in a work environment. *Journal of Applied Social Psychology, 28,* 1712–1730.

Pierce, C. A., & Aguinis, H. (2001). A framework for investigating the link between workplace romance and sexual harassment. *Group & Organization Management, 26,* 206–229.

Pierce, C. A., Aguinis, H., & Adams, S. K. R. (2000). Effects of a dissolved workplace romance and rater characteristics on responses to sexual harassment accusation. *Academy of Management Journal, 43,* 869–880.

Pierce, C. A., Broberg, B., McClure, J. R., & Aguinis, H. (2004). Responding to sexual harassment complaints: Effects of a dissolved workplace romance on decision-making standards. *Organizational Behavior and Human Decision Processes, 95,* 66–82.

Pierce, C. A., Byrne, D., & Aguinis, H. (1996). Attraction in organizations: A model of workplace romance. *Journal of Organizational Behavior, 17,* 5–32.

Powell, G. N. (1986). What do tomorrow's managers think about sexual intimacy in the workplace? *Business Horizons, 29,* 30–35.

Powell, G. N., & Foley, S. (1998). Something to talk about: Romantic relationships in organizational settings. *Journal of Management, 24,* 421–448.

Quinn, R. (1977). Coping with cupid: The formation, impact, and management of romantic relationships in organizations. *Administrative Science Quarterly, 22,* 30–45.

Riach, K., & Wilson, F. (2007). Don't screw with the crew: Exploring the rules of engagement in organizational romance. *British Journal of Management, 18,* 79–92.

Wilson, R. J., Filosa, C., & Fennel, A. (2003). Romantic relationships at work: Does privacy trump the dating policy? *Defense Council Journal, 70,* 78–88.

7

Dealing With Difference

❖ ❖ ❖

In my position as director of graduate programs in a multicultural university college of business, I have the ultimate responsibility for selecting students for admissions to our graduate programs. Before accepting this position, I had dealt with fairly homogeneous groups and little cultural diversity. However, in my current position, I deal on a daily basis with international applicants whose cultural norms and educational backgrounds present challenges. For example, I often meet with prospective international female applicants from different cultures whose husbands accompany them to our meeting. It is not uncommon in those situations for the husbands to "take over" the conversation and do the talking for their wives. Being accustomed to dealing with intelligent women who speak for themselves, I find myself becoming tense in these situations. I will then begin to direct all of my questions directly to the woman and respond to the husband's questions looking directly at the woman. I will not discuss her with him or refer to her as she. I will face her and use "you" when speaking.

Martha, age 60

Martha is struggling with a kind of communication challenge that is encountered in multicultural work environments. The situation is complicated by her limited experience in these situations. Martha adapts her communication in a way that seems reasonable within her cultural frame of reference. Is she correct in addressing the women in these situations? Or should she speak to the men? Or both? What do your own cultural norms suggest? In some cultures, men are expected to speak for women; in others, this practice is considered chauvinistic. How should cultural difference be managed in the workplace? There are no easy answers to these questions. Employees should not expect to respond optimally to all of the multicultural challenges faced in an increasingly diverse workplace. However, cultural sensitivity and effective communication practices can be useful in managing intercultural interactions.

In this chapter, we use the term *difference* to characterize diversity in gender, ethnicity, race, age, disability, language, cultural background, or sexual orientation. As the workplace continues to diversify, employees are required to interact with people who differ in values, norms, preferences, and interaction patterns. Employees may interact on a regular basis with people they would not readily encounter outside of work. For example, straight employees will work alongside openly gay coworkers. American employees are likely to interact with Chinese, Russian, Indian, and South African coworkers. Healthy employees might work closely with chronically ill coworkers, such as those suffering from muscular dystrophy, AIDS, or Parkinson's disease. All of these scenarios are more likely now than they were in the past.

Of course, employees don't check their cultural baggage at the office door. Rather, organizations and individual employees must develop the communication competencies that help them thrive in a workplace that is rich in diversity. Dealing with difference appeared to be stressful for Martha, but anxiety can be reduced by increasing cultural sensitivity and learning to be interculturally effective in interactions (Ulrey & Amason, 2001). How is dealing with difference a risky communication activity? For starters, the mismanagement of intercultural encounters puts workgroups at risk of reduced performance, employee dissatisfaction, and turnover. Claims of discrimination and harassment present additional risk. Cultural incompetence can undermine an employee's professional standing and place his or her organization's reputation at risk. To explore the risk and opportunities associated with difference, we begin with an examination of its importance in the changing workplace.

❖ WHY IS DEALING WITH DIFFERENCE IMPORTANT?

The Diversifying Workplace

The workplace is becoming increasingly diverse for a host of reasons, including the integration of the world market through globalization, the rise of multinational corporations, and the increase in employees working in foreign countries (Konrad, 2003; Seyman, 2006). All of this is occurring while the population of available workers continues to diversify (Fine, 1991). The mixing of cultures influences the identities of individual employees as well as workgroup norms, management practices, conflict patterns, and communication styles (Christian, Porter, & Moffitt, 2006; Konrad, 2003; Seyman, 2006).

In response to these trends, organizational leaders have embraced different approaches for "managing" workplace diversity and have offered several arguments for encouraging it (Horwitz, 2005; Konrad, 2003). First, to stay competitive, organizations need to recruit from a broad spectrum of demographic constituents. Second, a diverse population coupled with globalization creates a more diverse customer base. And third, culturally diverse workforces possess a greater variety of information and experience and may outperform homogeneous workgroups on creative and problem-solving tasks. While these arguments make good business sense, Konrad (2003) warned that they are also flawed in important ways. For example, simply positioning diversity as something to be managed ignores the ingrained interaction patterns within organizations that tolerate levels of stereotyping and discrimination. Hiring diverse employees primarily to interface with customers of their own cultural group limits cultural group members to only these organizational roles, acting as a form of segregation. So workforce diversity can have a positive impact, but we cannot assume that it will.

The Benefits of Workplace Diversity

Workplace diversity appears to lead to organizational improvement in several areas (Hermon, 1996; Kirby & Richard, 2000). It can improve the balance of power and access to decision making within organizations while bolstering employee competence, job satisfaction, job involvement, and organizational commitment (Kirby & Richard, 2000). In addition, workplace diversity initiatives have been shown to raise the sensitivity of senior managers to diversity issues and concerns, increase career opportunities for women and minorities, and improve interpersonal relationships among employees (Hermon, 1996). Thus, there appear to be some clear benefits derived from workplace diversity. Not surprisingly, corporations actively recruit culturally diverse employees. See Textbox 7.1, which features HERSHEY'S efforts to promote workforce diversity.

Textbox 7.1   Workforce Diversity at HERSHEY'S

Many organizations now use their corporate Web sites to speak directly to current and prospective employees about their workforce diversity policies and initiatives. The text below appears on the HERSHEY'S Web site.

"The story of Hershey's diversity is told through its Great People. Hershey's strength comes from bringing together people of diverse backgrounds, ideas and interests. We provide a number of opportunities for all employees to learn, grow and incorporate their best into the work environment and the community:

An annual companywide Inclusion Day celebration emphasizing the diversity of local communities

Lunch & Learn speakers who discuss topics from new immigrant experiences to personal empowerment for minorities and women

An in-depth website employees can use to find information about a vast array of diversity subjects

Diversity email newsletters designed to educate employees on specific aspects of diversity as well as to inform them about why those differences are important to our business."

Source: www.thehersheycompany.com/careers/diversity.asp

Even though there are obvious advantages to cultivating workforce diversity, positive outcomes are not ensured. A review of studies examining workplace diversity concluded "that the most typical relationship between demographic diversity and organizational performance is no relationship" (Svyantek & Bott, 2004, p. 307). Similarly, Christian et al. (2006) concluded from their literature review that diversity "can improve group performance by providing groups with a wider range of perspectives and a broader skills base" (p. 460) but noted that cultural diversity "can be detrimental to group cohesion and performance because the diversity in personal backgrounds has the potential to exert a negative influence" (p. 460).

Thus far, scholarship has shown that diversity can prove beneficial or detrimental to group cohesion. This was illustrated in one employee's report about a London branch of an American financial services company's receipt of a major diversity award:

So a big e-mail was sent out to say that we had won this *gender* equality award. The senior investment bankers who sent out the note talked about this gender equality award and women in the workplace etc. and didn't specifically mention the lesbian and gay network at all; and yet, we won it because of our lesbian and gay network! My manager read that e-mail, noticed that we weren't mentioned, and sent a note copying me and all his managers and senior managers to say "and, of course, we wouldn't have won this award had it not been for the good work that the lesbian and gay network has done." (Ward & Winstanley, 2004, p. 227)

This account reveals how management's celebration of a major honor overlooked the contributions of the organization's gay and lesbian network. Management's communication about the award resulted in friction rather than cohesion. The e-mail that management sent risked alienating an active and productive portion of the workforce in the company. Fortunately, a supervisor mitigates this risk by responding to the e-mail with one that fully recognizes the contribution of gay and lesbian employees. Ward and Winstanley (2004) characterize this story as a cautionary tale, revealing how risky communication about diversity can be in an organization, even one committed to recognizing and celebrating it.

The Challenges of Workplace Diversity

Perceptions of fairness are entangled with cultural diversity (Kirby & Richard, 2000; Richard, Kochan, & McMillan-Capehart, 2002). Even when workplace diversity programs are in place, they may fail to alleviate employee concerns related to fairness. Consider the member of the dominant cultural group who raises questions when being passed over for a position. Alternatively, consider the highly qualified diverse candidate who raises questions about whether a position was offered primarily as part of a diversity initiative. Both employees may feel that hiring practices designed to increase workforce diversity are unfair. Confirming this, Kirby and Richard (2000) assessed corporate workplace diversity efforts and discovered that sizable proportions of employees reported concerns with opportunity, inclusion, and the balance of power in their respective organizations. Similarly, Hermon (1996) found that participation in workplace diversity initiatives, while perceived favorably by some, led to feelings of resentment for others.

The *social categorization* perspective suggests that workforce diversity can be detrimental to employee satisfaction and performance (Christian et al., 2006; Horwitz, 2005). In organizations, group members categorize others into "in" (inclusive) and "out" (outcast) groups based on relevant features of diversity—race, gender, sexual identification, and so on. Such categorizations, in turn, lead to poor group relations because of in-group biases, and tendencies to denigrate the out-group. Intragroup conflict, miscommunication, and lack of trust can impede the performance of diverse workgroups (Horwitz, 2005). So, too, can conflicts characterized by anger, frustration, and distrust (Richard et al., 2002). These mixed research findings led Richard et al. (2002) to speculate that the relationship between workplace diversity and group effectiveness/performance was curvilinear, with groups being more effective with low and moderate levels of diversity and less effective when dealing with higher levels of diversity.

Workforce diversity is a necessary and important component of the contemporary workplace. Employees need to develop skills to manage complex relationships with diverse coworkers and customers. Otherwise, employees risk ostracizing others, alienating themselves, damaging workgroup relationships, and jeopardizing workgroup performance.

❖ KEY RESEARCH STUDIES

Communication Forms

Scholars have adapted the work of Barnett Pearce (1989) to advance ideas about which communication practices are more or less effective in multicultural workplaces (Grimes & Richard, 2003). According to this conceptualization, employees treat others as natives or nonnatives. We communicate with natives as members of the in-group and judge them by in-group standards. In contrast, we communicate with nonnatives as a distinct group with their own criteria for making judgments and expect them to adapt their communication to in-group standards. The other dimension is the degree to which people are open to change. Those who are closed to change do not adopt other perspectives and assumptions; in contrast, those who are open to change learn new sensemaking processes and understandings.

When these two dimensions are considered together, four possible forms of communication emerge (see Table 7.1). In the *monocultural* form of communication, there is no openness to change, and everyone is treated as a native. Essentially, this form of communication occurs only in highly insular communities that have little contact with other cultural groups. *Ethnocentric* communication embraces clear distinctions between in-groups and out-groups and remains closed to change. Communicators using the ethnocentric form recognize other groups but tend to judge them as inferior. They rely heavily on scripts in certain settings (e.g., business meetings, formal events like weddings, and so on), which serve to keep interactions predictable.

Table 7.1   Forms of Communication

Form of Communication	Challenges and Shortcomings	Benefits
Monocultural		
Everyone is native	Highly insular	
Closed to change	Little contact with out-groups	
Ethnocentric		
Clear in-groups/ out-groups	Judge out-groups as inferior	
Closed to change	Rely heavily on scripts	
	Use stereotypes readily	
	Alienation of coworkers	
Modernistic		
Everyone is nonnative	Disconnected from groups	
Open to change	Absence of overarching values	
	Social isolation	
	Tolerance of misunderstanding	
Cosmopolitan		
Everyone is native/ nonnative		Value difference
Open to change		Cultural learning
		Multiple perspective taking
		Understanding

Source: Adapted from Grimes and Richard (2003).

In contrast, in the *modernistic* form of communication, everyone is viewed as nonnative, and ways of understanding remain open to change. Communicators using the modernistic form do not place a great emphasis on tradition but rather value novelty and innovation. They are less interdependent and are not connected to one particular group. Thus, modernist communicators are less focused on group identity and may have difficulty relating to people who value group membership. However, modernistic members can become disillusioned because there is no overarching set of values to which they can subscribe.

Finally, *cosmopolitan* communication weaves "together useful elements from each of the other forms" (Grimes & Richard, 2003, p. 15). In this form, everyone is treated as both nonnative and native, and ways of understanding are both open to and exempt from change. Others are considered "simultaneously native and non-native" (p. 15), appreciation for genuine differences between people is expressed, the shared human experience of learning a given culture without judging one way of learning and understanding as superior or inferior to another is recognized, and individual knowledge and sensemaking practices are retained with the acknowledgment that they are merely one way of understanding.

Grimes and Richard (2003) suggested that adopting an ethnocentric form of communication was problematic for diverse workgroups because of the reliance on simple scripts and stereotypes that limit, ignore, and devalue the real or potential contributions of nonnative group members. They concluded that ethnocentric communicators lose significant input and alienate valuable coworkers. Similarly, the modernistic form brings complications to the workplace. Employees who do not subscribe to a modernistic form of communication may find themselves socially isolated when they cling to organizational traditions deemed obsolete and dated. For example, employees who appreciate moving cautiously through decision-making processes by sharing oppositional viewpoints and collectively discussing issues may end up being characterized as "old timers" unable to adjust to the pace and demands of the modern workplace. This is not to say that modernistic communicators would be against this type of discussion but rather that they may let certain traditions trail away in the wake of what is new and novel in contemporary organizational expectations and practices. In addition, because they are change and future focused, modernistic communicators tolerate misunderstanding.

The cosmopolitan form of communication represents the optimal choice for interacting in a culturally diverse workplace (Grimes & Richard, 2003). Cosmopolitan communicators can be expected to work well in everyday interactions because they value and embrace differences and remain open to change. They also do not assume everyone else is like them, and they are open to new ways of understanding. Cosmopolitan communicators support a range of discussion and appreciate multiple perspectives, making them effective agents for facilitating multicultural group processes.

Privileged Discourse and Muted Voices

Scholars have recognized that organizations privilege certain discourses while muting others (Fine, 1991, 1996; Meares, Oetzel, Torres, Derkacs, & Ginossar, 2004; Orbe, 1998). Fine (1991) argued for a framework of organizational communication that recognized the assumption of difference rather than the assumption of homogeneity as the norm. She maintained that resisting privileged discourse and creating harmonic discourse are necessary for understanding multicultural communication in organizations. Resisting involves recognizing privileged discourses, calling them into question, and creating space for alternative discourses to be heard. Multicultural discourse becomes harmonic when "all voices retain their individual integrity yet combine to form a whole discourse that is orderly and congruous, in much the same way that musicians create harmony" (p. 266).

We can look again to the work of Ward and Winstanley (2004) for evidence of how certain discourses are privileged and others muted in diverse workplaces. In the following anecdote, a gay employee describes how the investment company solicited participation for diversity focus groups:

> They sent out this big e-mail with voting buttons to click on if you wanted to attend a forum. There were 11 buttons in total, representing the different diversity groups; the first button was for 'American Expatriates in Europe,' followed by one for gender issues and one for race issues. However, they didn't give gay employees a button, like they gave everyone else. Instead, they had this narrative at the bottom where they said if you are interested in sexual orientation issues please contact this separate phone number. Now what they were trying to do was give someone with sexual orientation issues a confidential route, but they didn't realise the implications. There were a lot of apologies, and "we didn't realise," blah, blah, blah. Gay colleagues who saw it thought it was for people who aren't out. It was actually straight friends of mine who came to me and said, "I don't think it's very fair for you guys, why don't you get a button? Are they trying to lock you away by giving you this secret phone number?" (p. 226)

While management's effort to protect the confidentiality of gay employees seemed well intentioned, it backfired because it served to mute the voice of gay and lesbian employees in the diversity discussion. Management claims to have misunderstood the implications of its actions, which further fuels the perception that powerful organizational discourses, both knowingly and unknowingly, mute diverse employees.

Orbe (1998) explored the concept of muted voices in a co-cultural model of organizational communication that considers two key factors: the communication approach of the employee and the preferred outcome of the employee. Co-cultural employees, or members of an out-group, can adopt an aggressive approach, an assertive approach, or a nonassertive approach. Nonassertive communication is characterized by inhibition and nonconfrontation. Orbe characterizes aggressive communication practices as "hurtfully expressive, self-promoting, and assuming control over the choices of others" (p. 247) and noted that co-cultural members moved to this communication approach when nonasservtive and assertive attempts were ineffective. Finally, people can strike a balance between nonassertive and aggressive communication approaches by adopting an assertive style. The assertive style necessitates promoting one's own rights, needs, and desires while being mindful of violating the rights of others. In this way, it is self-enhancing and expressive without being overbearing and aggressive. Orbe noted that often members of the dominant culture construe assertive communication approaches as aggressive. Some co-cultural group members reported relying on one particular communication approach as innate to their character (e.g., being a nonassertive person). Others, though, claimed to strategically select from and move between the approaches as was necessary for a given situation.

In terms of preferred outcomes, co-cultural group members may pursue assimilation, accommodation, or separation from the dominant group. "Assimilation involves attempts to eliminate cultural differences, including the loss of any distinctive characteristics, to fit in with dominant society" (Orbe, 1998, p. 243). In contrast, accommodation seeks association with a dominant culture, but not at the expense of sacrificing distinctive cultural features. Accommodation requires resistance when alternative voices are muted and the promotion of a multicultural workplace that appreciates diversity. Separation involves a rejection of a coherent dominant culture in favor of separate group identities and social structures. Separation stems from the belief that it is unrealistic to assume intergroup relationships will change in any meaningful way.

Overlaying the preferred outcomes and the communication approaches reveals nine possible communicator orientations that co-cultural group members may adopt (see Table 7.2). If assimilation is the preferred outcome, employees can adopt nonassertive, assertive, or aggressive orientation. Minimizing cultural differences, exercising politeness and attentiveness to members of the dominant culture, and censoring oneself in response to inappropriate and offensive comments characterize a *nonassertive assimilation* orientation. This approach may facilitate assimilation into the dominant group, conflict-free interactions, and improved social standing, but members using this approach risk loss of identity and self-worth. They may feel guilty for accepting the power of dominant groups.

With an *assertive assimilation* orientation, cultural differences are downplayed but not at the expense of marking oneself invisible. Rather, people overcompensate in their work and interactions to draw attention to their efforts, manipulate commonly held stereotypes to

Table 7.2   Co-Cultural Communication Orientations

Co-Cultural Communication Orientation	Example Behavior
Nonassertive assimilation	A Hispanic employee letting a joke about illegal aliens slide
Assertive assimilation	An Asian employee positioning himself as the "go to" guy for computer problems
Aggressive assimilation	A female saleswoman derogating fellow female saleswomen for lacking the ability to "close the deal"
Nonassertive accommodation	A gay coworker attending out-of-office workgroup social gatherings with his partner
Assertive accommodation	A young and enthusiastic newcomer seeking out a well-tenured and older coworker as a mentor
Aggressive accommodation	An African refugee challenging coworkers in a marketing brainstorming session to account for people who have not grown up in safe suburban environments
Nonassertive separation	An English-as-second language speaker remaining quiet in group deliberations
Assertive separation	A lesbian employee consistently reminding her peers about the accomplishments of notable gays
Aggressive separation	Muslim employees disrupting an annual employee appreciation luncheon that falls during Ramadan

Source: Adapted from Orbe (1998).

their advantage, and strike stated or unstated agreements with members of the dominant culture to ignore co-cultural differences. These practices may be advantageous to securing social status in the dominant group but again present considerable risk to the employee. It takes great psychological effort to adhere to problematic stereotypes and overcompensate on a continuing basis.

Co-cultural members practice *aggressive assimilation* by dissociating themselves with any behaviors typically associated with one's cultural group, engaging in ridicule of themselves or other cultural group members, and strategically distancing themselves from any association with cultural group members. Here, too, the benefits of assimilation are apparent (e.g., social standing), as well as the previously mentioned disadvantages (e.g., identity and psychological risk). In addition, the practices associated with this orientation achieve assimilation outcomes at the risk of alienating co-cultural group members and fraying potentially important social relationships with them. Those using an aggressive assimilation orientation may be labeled "sellouts" by their fellow co-cultural group members.

A *nonassertive accommodation* orientation occurs when employees hope to "delicately challenge the status quo of the organizations in which they participate" (Orbe, 1998, p. 254). This orientation allows employees to dispel stereotypes and to increase their visibility. When executed effectively, co-cultural group members can influence decision-making processes without drawing negative reactions from members of the dominant culture. The shortcomings with this approach are the risk of appearing too passive to other co-cultural group members and the inability to promote any major organizational changes.

An *assertive accommodation* approach involves interacting with dominant group members authentically and networking with like-minded employees to change onerous organizational processes. Those using this approach may cultivate the support of the dominant group as they educate others about cultural differences. People who choose this orientation walk a tightrope of sorts, balancing the challenges of appearing not aggressive enough to co-cultural group members and perhaps too aggressive to dominant cultural members. Clearly, the stress of balancing these constraints makes this strategy potentially risky.

Aggressive accommodation involves open confrontation with the dominant cultural group. "The focus for an aggressive accommodation is to become a committed part of the organization and then work from within to promote significant change regardless of personal cost" (Orbe, 1998, p. 256). These tactics can be tempered with the use of the assertive practices to moderate the perception of being too separatist. Employees using this approach seek radical change at the risk of becoming isolated from both the dominant group and their co-cultural peers. They also risk being labeled as radical, oversensitive organizational members who too often play the race, ethnicity, or difference "card."

The final set of orientations revolves around the desire to seek separation. The *nonassertive separation* orientation primarily concerns avoiding and psychological distancing (e.g., not facing or sitting away from others). Nonassertive separation also may involve engaging in behaviors that reinforce marginalized standing (e.g., not speaking up in meetings). Clearly, these strategies reduce the stress and tension of dealing regularly with difference, but they undoubtedly limit the ability of co-cultural employees to bring about organizational change.

Promoting the accomplishments and contributions of co-cultural groups and embracing the positive aspects of common stereotypes are indictors of an *assertive separation* orientation. This orientation works to bolster co-cultural unity and self-determination and to promote group members as role models. The segregation that affords these benefits, however, also hampers the group by isolating members, limiting their interactions with and influence on the dominant cultural group.

The final orientation, *aggressive separation,* promotes the urgency of separation, which "is sought through whatever means necessary" (Orbe, 1998, p. 259). People who adopt this orientation will chronically criticize those who choose to assimilate and will engage in acts of organizational sabotage to confront the dominant cultural group. These practices empower and give voice to the co-cultural group but endanger work identity (e.g., being labeled as an extreme radical) and professional viability (e.g., experiencing legal, political, or institutional retaliation in response to acts of aggression).

Cultural Diversity and Identification

In the first chapter of this book, we discussed risk to identity. This risk is pronounced when dealing with differences between coworkers. Brickson (2000) developed a model of the important connections between identification and diversity (see Table 7.3). In culturally diverse organizational settings, people alternate between three fundamental yet distinct means of identification. They can draw upon any or all three in a given interaction. However, employees typically prefer one of the three.

Personal identification stems from desires to enhance personal well-being, references individual traits and behaviors for self-knowledge, and relies on comparisons to others for gauging self-worth. A *relational identification* entails enhancing relational partners' well-being, referencing

Table 7.3   Means of Identification

Type of Identification	Attendant Identity Questions
Personal identification	Have I achieved my personal goals?
	Have I mastered my job responsibilities?
	Have I performed well compared to other employees?
Relational identification	Have I attended to the needs of my workplace peers?
	Have I played the role of a supportive coworker well?
	Have I lived up to my coworkers' relational expectations?
Collective identification	Have I contributed to my workgroup's well-being?
	Have I upheld the standards of my workgroup?
	Have I embraced my workgroup as superior to others?

Source: Adapted from Brickson (2000).

roles in specific contexts and relationships for self-knowledge, and anchoring self-worth in role performance assessed against one's own or a partner's standards. *Collective identification* involves ensuring the group's well-being, garnering self-knowledge through comparisons against a prototypical group standard, and measuring self-worth by making comparisons to an out-group. Consider the example from the beginning of the chapter. As Martha interacts with her prospective students, she needs to recognize their identities as unique individuals but also take into account their roles in particular kinds of marriages and their membership in cultures that might be very different from her own.

Dimensions of Interaction in Culturally Diverse Workgroups

Larkey (1996) recognized five dimensions that characterized interactions between and among members of diverse workgroups. The first, *inclusion/exclusion,* speaks to the practices we use to either marginalize or include people "in the network of information, contacts, and opportunities" (p. 300). Communicatively, this typically occurs only in the presence of selected coworkers. Members may regulate participation in conversations through linguistic and nonverbal cues. They may alter the content of the conversation in the presence of "unwelcome" others. Employees also signal *convergence/divergence,* or the degree to which they are willing to adapt their interaction patterns to others (e.g., dialect, slang, use of the speaker's primary or secondary language). Convergence is the practice of adjusting communication, whereas divergence is resistance to change.

The *varied ideation/conforming ideation* dimension of interaction helps to explain why decisions in culturally diverse workgroups aren't always enhanced by the differing perspectives. Groups must adopt a varied ideation to realize the benefits of including diverse ideas. In contrast, those with a conforming ideation value normative views and are uncomfortable when diverse opinions are expressed. *Understanding/ misunderstanding* is another dimension of interaction that affects group processes. Misunderstanding occurs when there is a mismatch of meanings and expectations due to discrepancies in language use, communication patterns, and values. *Positive/negative evaluations* are grounded in biases and stereotypes. Negative evaluations are revealed when members use labels or tell stories that affirm harmful stereotypes. Positive evaluations are revealed in messages that affirm member diversity.

Several dimensions of interaction become apparent in the following story provided by a Native American woman and social worker:

> Last week . . . I was coming into the building and my supervisor was outside smoking a cigarette. My supervisor is a White male dressed in his suit and his tie. DSS [Department of Social Services] has security guards now that are present in our building. So I start toward the elevator. Now I'm walking with my supervisor. He's White and my face is brown. The security guard says to me, "Hey where are you going?" I said, "Are you talking to me?" He says, "Yeah, you going to welfare?" So I said, "Excuse me?" My supervisor says to me, "You don't have to answer that question, he has no right to ask you that." I said, "But you don't understand what the bigger picture is, that he thinks that People of Color are all going to welfare." My supervisor said, "No, that's not what it is about . . . He's just doing his job. He has to ask everybody." I said, "That's exactly what it's about." (Bell, 2003, p. 13)

We see elements of inclusion/exclusion when the questions of the security guard strike the Native American woman as exclusionary. To her, these questions stem from an underlying discourse that stereotypes people of color as welfare recipients. The supervisor tries to diffuse the situation by encouraging the employee to disregard the security guard's questions. But the questions have brought a negative evaluation (people of color need and seek welfare) to the surface, which is in fact recognized by both the social worker and her supervisor. The supervisor hopes to dismiss this as a misunderstanding. The social worker, though, concludes that the supervisor doesn't "get it." The story reveals how several dimension of interaction complicate and charge communication between diverse people.

Thus far, we have introduced concepts that can help employees develop a more nuanced understanding of the factors that make workplace differences both beneficial and potentially risky. By communicating mindfully, employees reap the benefits of diversity and negotiate its challenges. In Textbox 7.2, we summarize the communication options presented in this chapter.

Textbox 7.2   Communication Options

Communication Forms (Grimes & Richard, 2003; Pearce, 1989)

  Monocultural
  Ethnocentric
  Modernistic
  Cosmopolitan

Co-Cultural Communication Orientations (Orbe, 1998)

  Nonassertive assimilation
  Assertive assimilation
  Aggressive assimilation
  Nonassertive accommodation
  Assertive accommodation
  Aggressive accommodation
  Nonassertive separation
  Assertive separation
  Aggressive separation

Dimensions of Interaction in Culturally Diverse Workgroups (Larkey, 1996)

  Inclusion/exclusion
  Convergence/divergence
  Varied ideation/conforming ideation
  Understanding/misunderstanding
  Positive/negative evaluations

❖ DEALING WITH DIFFERENCE AND THE RISK NEGOTIATION CYCLE

Dealing with difference is a challenge for all parties involved. Members of the dominant culture risk offending minority group members and vice versa. When offenses occur, group productivity, workplace relationships, and employee satisfaction and commitment likely suffer. To more fully understand the potential risks and how to deal effectively with them, we apply the risk negotiation cycle (see Figure 7.1).

Attending

When attending to difference, employees can assess the communication forms and orientations used by coworkers. Are interactions characterized by a monocultural, modernistic, cosmopolitan, or ethnocentric form? If an ethnocentric form of communication is apparent, can all employees be expected to adopt the dominant cultural group's way of thinking? This will depend to some degree on the communication orientation of the participants. If a co-cultural interactant prefers one of the assimilation orientations, an ethnocentric form of communication might be less detrimental than under other circumstances. Indeed, if someone is working to assimilate, he or she may find ethnocentric modes of interaction predictable and manageable. However, ethnocentric communication is rarely the right choice. If diverse employees seek to accommodate or to separate, then ethnocentric communication exacerbates individual, relational, and organizational risk.

A second consideration is identification. Are participants relying on personal, relational, or collective bases of identification? Are they stimulated by self, relational, or collective motives? Self-motives may lead to stronger ethnocentric or assimilation tendencies. That is, the comfort of belonging unquestionably to a dominant culture or the desire to avoid the struggles associated with being an out-group member could move employees to use ethnocentric forms of interaction. Operating from collective motives could prove difficult as an employee may be motivated to support the larger collective, the dominant cultural group, or any number of co-cultural groups. Those steeped heavily in collective identification with dominant or co-cultural groups will find interaction with nongroup members to be challenging and risky. However, those who hold a strong identification with the organization are more likely to support one another and less

Figure 7.1 Dealing With Difference and the Risk Negotiation Cycle

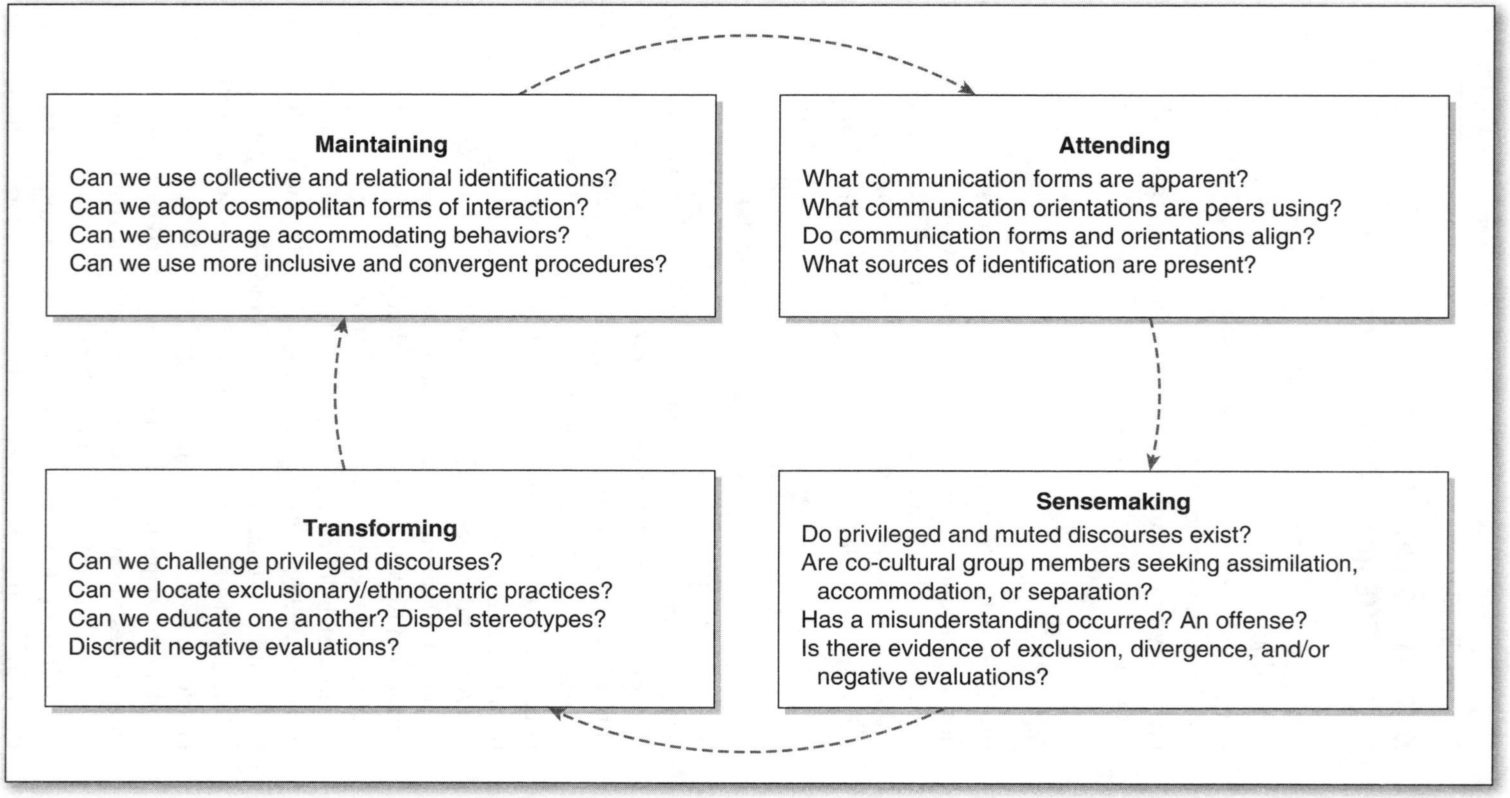

Attending

What communication forms are apparent?
What communication orientations are peers using?
Do communication forms and orientations align?
What sources of identification are present?

Sensemaking

Do privileged and muted discourses exist?
Are co-cultural group members seeking assimilation, accommodation, or separation?
Has a misunderstanding occurred? An offense?
Is there evidence of exclusion, divergence, and/or negative evaluations?

Maintaining

Can we use collective and relational identifications?
Can we adopt cosmopolitan forms of interaction?
Can we encourage accommodating behaviors?
Can we use more inclusive and convergent procedures?

Transforming

Can we challenge privileged discourses?
Can we locate exclusionary/ethnocentric practices?
Can we educate one another? Dispel stereotypes?
Discredit negative evaluations?

likely to alienate others. In these ways, risk can be assessed by considering the communication forms and orientations of participants and how they align or diverge.

Sensemaking

Employees can seek the counsel of coworkers to make sense of interaction patterns. This consultation process can help them gauge the risk presented in their interactions with diverse coworkers. The assessment will be more accurate if consultations include members of dominant and co-cultural groups. Doing so may reveal that the dominant culture is clearly intolerant of differences—that a privileged discourse is in place to which members have contributed, even if unknowingly. Failure to adjust interactions as a dominant cultural group member (e.g., being less ethnocentric and more sensitive to co-cultural group concerns) in this instance risks further alienation of valued coworkers. Through the sensemaking process, employees may discover high levels of resignation and desires for separation among co-cultural members. Efforts to assimilate or accommodate to the dominant culture could be construed as "selling out."

Sensemaking, then, alerts the employee to potential risks and suggests means for managing them. Consider our discussion of the dimensions of intercultural interaction. Was there understanding or misunderstanding between interactants? Checking the perceptions and understandings of members from both dominant and co-cultural groups may reveal the source of misunderstanding. Similarly, feedback from participants may indicate why one or more interactants were offended. Offenses may be attributed to practices of exclusion (e.g., the regular use of negative stereotypes in conversations). They may surface when conversational partners practice divergence (e.g., co-cultural members' communication signals separation and resignation). Or they may manifest when an undercurrent of negative evaluations provides the interpretive subtext for conversations (e.g., the perpetuation of lower expectations on certain tasks due to ingrained stereotypes of particular co-cultural groups). The occurrence of any of these offenses, knowingly or unknowingly, would produce and enhance risk, particularly if the offense went unnoticed and unaddressed. In contrast, interactions characterized by inclusion, convergence, and positive evaluations more readily reduce risk. Through sensemaking, we can determine the levels of misunderstanding, the magnitude of potential offenses, and the risk that accompanies these concerns.

Transforming

Once the apparent risk and its sources are identified (e.g., offenses, misunderstandings), employees can work toward transforming risk. This may involve questioning organizational values that previously remained uncontested and privileged. Managing the risks stemming from cultural difference requires persistence and nuanced communication. For example, a simple apology for cultural insensitivity may alleviate tension in the short term, but it fails to address the organizational practices that disadvantage diverse members and make them targets of disrespectful behavior. Despite the apology, the perception that dominant cultural group members "just don't get it" may persist. The risk is not so much transformed as merely postponed until the next time a similar offense or misunderstanding arises.

How, then, can employees truly transform risk when dealing with difference? We believe that the answer comes from questioning privileged discourses and listening for muted voices. Risk may be transformed by recognizing and challenging the communication practices that exclude and marginalize organizational members, as well as confronting the communication patterns, such as conforming ideation, that prove ethnocentric. Fostering an open and questioning climate for dealing with difference requires organizational members to interact in an authentic manner to educate one another, dispel stereotypes, and discredit negative evaluations. In other words, risk is transformed when deep-seated cultural differences in the workplace are acknowledged and addressed through mindful communication.

Maintaining

A safe environment for all employees is maintained by the communication practices of individuals and the policies of the organization. Interactions among diverse employees are made safer when participants use their communication to learn about the perspective of others before making judgments. Focusing on the best interests of the organization, as opposed to one's own interests, is a way of finding common ground. A cosmopolitan form of communication, one that recognizes the important and unique contributions of others without sacrificing one's own, fosters mutual respect. This approach requires a certain humility as one seeks the input of others even as the likelihood of misunderstanding is accepted and welcomed. Communication orientations that facilitate accommodation may reduce the risk perceived by diverse members of the organization. Employees can be inclusive and convergent in interactions while practicing varied ideation in group decision making. When workgroups sustain these risk management efforts, they stand to reap the benefits of cultural diversity. The optimal outcome is a more innovative workforce that finds difference energizing rather than intimidating.

❖ CONCLUSION

The following scenario concerns gender differences in the workplace. It chronicles a saleswoman's experience with gender inequity that puts her and her organization at risk.

> A few years ago, I was running a team of consultants in software applications when I was asked by the director of sales to apply for a position in sales. He was impressed with the amount of revenue I had been able to generate for the company on the consulting side and thought I should give sales a try. So I interviewed for it and was awarded the position. As part of the initial contract, I was offered a package that stipulated I would retain my same salary that I earned as a consultant for the first 3 months as a sort of trial period. The thinking was I could decide whether or not I liked sales, if it was for me, and if not I could return to my consulting position without taking a cut in pay. It seemed completely reasonable at the time, but I was aware that the salary I was brought in at was easily 25k less than the men holding the same sales positions with the same sales targets. In that first quarter, I blasted my sales targets, exceeding them all. It was clear that I could do as well as the men in sales and that I should be compensated with a similar salary and incentives. So I went to see HR about having my salary adjusted after the initial trial period. The director of HR said, "Give me a week and I'll get back to you." A week later, I was told that there was "no budget" to give me the equivalent salary and that I would continue to receive less pay because I had less sales experience. I reminded the director of HR that I'd interviewed and won the position, that I was recruited because the director of sales knew I had generated considerable revenue as a consultant for the company, and that I had exceeded all of my sales targets. And I'll never forget her response. She told me, "You're a victim of your own success." I was ready to leave the company, but I was sort of trapped because I would need more sales experience, at least a year, before I would be seriously considered for another sales position elsewhere.

> Miranda, age 36

Attend to the risks Miranda faces in this situation. Who constitutes the dominant cultural group? In what ways is Miranda a nonnative? What mode of communication does Miranda encounter in this case? Is she faced with monocultural, ethnocentric, modernistic, or cosmopolitan modes of communication? Consider the different forms of identification. What appears to be the locus of identification for Miranda? Is it individual, relational, collective, or some combination of these? What communication orientation is she using? How effective does it appear to be?

Miranda must make sense of the risk she has encountered. Is she confronting a privileged discourse? What kinds of values are privileged in this organization? What can Miranda learn from fellow coworkers, particularly other saleswomen? She may be able to determine which communication orientations they are using. Do her female coworkers appear to be adopting separation, assimilation, or accommodation orientations? Refer to the dimensions of interaction discussed earlier. What evidence do you see of exclusion? Of misunderstanding? Of conforming ideation?

What, then, can Miranda do to transform risk in this situation? Given her status, should she adopt a nonassertive, assertive, or aggressive communication orientation toward the dominant group? What would be the risks associated with each approach? Clearly, Miranda feels she will have to stay in this organization for the time being. Going forward, should she assimilate? Accommodate? If she were to accommodate, what communication behaviors should she use? Should she challenge the prevailing or privileged discourse? How might she do that in a way that minimizes risk?

Ideally, Miranda can maintain the risk of being a successful saleswoman in a male-dominated sales force at manageable levels. She can draw attention to the privileged discourse while accommodating to the dominant cultural group and espousing a more inclusive collective identity. However, to create an environment of relative safety requires changes in the organization itself. What should these changes be? Consider how dominant cultural group members might adjust their communication. How might they adjust their communication forms? Their interaction patterns? Should they reconsider their collective values and organizational policies? For example, is it right that seniority trumps sales performance? Which group of employees benefits from the current system? How would the organization benefit from reassessing equity in its compensation standards?

❖ REFERENCES

Bell, L. A. (2003). Telling tales: What stories can teach us about racism. *Race Ethnicity and Education, 6,* 3–28.

Brickson, S. (2000). The impact of identity orientation on individual and organizational outcomes in demographically diverse settings. *Academy of Management Review, 25,* 82–101.

Christian, J., Porter, L. W., & Moffitt, G. (2006). Workplace diversity and group relations: An overview. *Group Processes & Intergroup Relations, 9,* 459–466.

Fine, M. G. (1991). New voices in the workplace: Research directions in multicultural communication. *Journal of Business Communication, 23,* 259–275.

Fine, M. G. (1996). Cultural diversity in the workplace: The state of the field. *Journal of Business Communication, 33,* 485–502.

Grimes, D. S., & Richard, O. C. (2003). Could communication form impact organizations' experience with diversity? *Journal of Business Communication, 40,* 7–27.

Hermon, M. V. (1996). Building a shared understanding and commitment to managing diversity. *Journal of Business Communication, 33,* 427–442.

Horwitz, S. K. (2005). The compositional impact of team diversity on performance: Theoretical considerations. *Human Resource Development Review, 4,* 219–245.

Kirby, S. A., & Richard, O. C. (2000). Impact of marketing work-place diversity on employee job involvement and organizational commitment. *Journal of Social Psychology, 140,* 367–377.

Konrad, A. M. (2003). Special issue introduction: Defining the domain of workplace diversity scholarship. *Group & Organization Management, 28,* 4–17.

Larkey, L. K. (1996). The development and validation of the Workforce Diversity Questionnaire: An instrument to assess interactions in diverse workgroups. *Management Communication Quarterly, 9,* 296–337.

Meares, M. M., Oetzel, J. G., Torres, A., Derkacs, D., & Ginossar, T. (2004). Employee mistreatment and muted voices in the culturally diverse workplace. *Journal of Applied Communication Research, 32,* 4–27.

Orbe, M. P. (1998). An outsider within perspective to organizational communication: Explicating the communicative practices of co-cultural group members. *Management Communication Quarterly, 12,* 230–279.

Pearce, W. B. (1989). *Communication and the human condition.* Carbondale: Southern Illinois University Press.

Richard, O. C., Kochan, T. A., & McMillan-Capehart, A. (2002). The impact of visible diversity on organizational effectiveness: Disclosing the contents in Pandora's black box. *Journal of Business and Management, 8,* 265–291.

Seyman, O. A. (2006). The cultural diversity phenomenon in organizations and different approaches for effective cultural diversity management: A literary review. *Cross Cultural Management: An International Journal, 13,* 296–315.

Svyantek, D., & Bott, J. (2004). Received wisdom and the relationship between diversity and organizational performance. *Organizational Analysis, 12,* 295–317.

Ulrey, L. U., & Amason, P. (2001). Intercultural communication between patients and health care providers: An exploration of intercultural communication effectiveness, cultural sensitivity, stress, and anxiety. *Health Communication, 13,* 449–463.

Ward, J., & Winstanley, D. (2004). Sexuality and the city: Exploring the experience of minority sexual identity through storytelling. *Culture and Organization, 10,* 219–236.

8

Expressing Dissent

I never seemed to catch her [my boss] doing wrong things until my coworker started bringing it to my attention. I started to notice her not showing up on time, yet clocking herself in as if she had been there all day. She would go run some personal errands on company time all of the time. I let it go, assuming it was none of my business, until the day she had a huge team meeting on the staff needing to be on time and how she was going to start writing us up if we were late. I could not believe my supervisor, who should be a role model, could be such a hypocrite.

Gina, age 23

In the scenario above, Gina finds herself troubled by both the behavior of her boss and the double standard her boss has established. What should she do in this situation? Should she speak to her boss directly? A coworker? Her boss's boss? Or should she continue say nothing? In this case, Gina opted to circumvent her boss. As a result, according to Gina, her supervisor "lost some of her freedoms as a supervisor and could not be trusted like before."

Typically, we don't set out to undermine our supervisors, but at times, as this example illustrates, we find ourselves in situations that necessitate the expression of dissent. Kassing (1997) defines dissent as the expression of disagreement or contradictory opinions about work-place policies and practices. In this instance, dissent occurred due to a workplace practice that involved some degree of organizational wrongdoing. In other cases, dissent may be expressed in response to organizational policies that employees find to be flawed. For example, consider the case of Aamir, a loan originator:

> Without notice, the pay structure had been changed for all loan originators. Previously, originators were paid on how many loans they closed. But the new change would mean that originators would be paid on tiers. Tier 1 was 50%, tier 2 was 70%, and tier 3 was 90% commission. This was great for originators that originated high loan amounts, but I originated only CRA loans, which were low-income loans, which would mean that I would never exceed the 50% tier unless I tripled in new clients. I worked twice as hard and still the loan amounts would never exceed that 50%.
>
> Aamir, age 28

Clearly, this policy puts Aamir at a disadvantage with regard to earning commission in his organization. It seems unfair that he should be penalized by a compensation system while others benefit. But what should he do about it? Aamir can express dissent to his supervisor about the policy, to his coworkers, or to friends and family outside of work. He chose to speak to someone in management about his concerns.

As we will see in this chapter, the expression of dissent within organizations creates several kinds of risk for employees. Will dissenting lead to retaliation or reward? Appreciation or disdain? Action or inaction on the part of management? Kassing's (2007) study suggests that dissenters sometimes experience retaliation. Unfortunately, Gina finds herself in the unenviable position of reporting on her boss. On the surface, this is an act of insubordination and disloyalty, yet the manager to whom she reported her concerns responded by monitoring Gina's boss more closely and by verifying the allegations. In the end, Gina's boss was "put on notice" and relieved of some of her duties. The work situation improved for employees. Gina experienced no retaliation. Taisha reported a less successful experience.

> When I was working as a RA in the dorms, my boss began to show disrespect for our staff by making up or changing information she was supposed to relay to us. She would also show up late to my individual meetings. I wrote a letter to the top guy at Residential Life with certain concerns about the job (not just about her, but about many concerns) and suggestions. I sent her a copy of the letter. We had a staff meeting a couple days later, and my boss was up in arms about following the

chain of command. Actually, the only reason I didn't follow procedure was because my boss never followed through, and I had a personal invitation from the top guy to contact him personally with any concerns that I had. My boss was pissed, and she took it out on me the rest of the year and made my life and working experience a nightmare.

Taisha, age 21

Was Taisha right in going to the "top guy"? Should her boss have been "pissed"? What we do know is that Taisha's communicative choice to dissent resulted in retaliation. What could she have done differently, if anything, to change this outcome? To answer these questions, we need to look to the literature and some key studies.

❖ WHY IS EXPRESSING DISSENT IMPORTANT?

Dealing With Organizational Constraints

Upon joining an organization, we encounter a variety of constraints—when to arrive and to leave, how to dress, what tasks to perform, and so on. Some degree of constraint is necessary for organizations to operate optimally; otherwise, our work lives would be confusing and chaotic. However, sometimes organizational constraints prove burdensome. What if employees were required to wear black uniforms while working outdoors in the height of summer? This policy would create potential health risks associated with heatstroke and heat exhaustion. In this case, employee dissent might move management to rethink a harmful policy and create a dress code that would be more seasonally appropriate. Expressing dissent, then, is a kind of communication that questions and, when necessary, challenges organizational constraints.

Drawing Attention to Overlooked Issues

As it turns out, organizations often focus constraints on the communication of employees. Workers face restrictions when speaking about organizational matters. American citizens speak freely about politics, the economy, or the local sports team. You can share your opinions about presidential candidates, the economy, or the performance of the football coach. But at work, employees tend to censor themselves when it comes to critiquing their coworkers, managers, and companies. Failing to do so could put at risk your employment or standing among workplace peers. At times, though, dissent is essential as it brings attention to problems that would otherwise go unnoticed.

Lupé found that expressing dissent was necessary because working conditions were both unfair and unrealistic.

> I work for a retail store that does at least $200,000 a week. They expect us to greet and assist every guest that comes in the store even though we are always short staffed. We are also expected to do several jobs and get paid for one. My argument was that they should not implement a "greet-and-assist" plan if understaffed.
>
> Lupé, age 42

Lupé deals daily with the challenge of being short staffed and the expectation to meet and assist every customer. Her dissent about this situation calls attention to the inherent difficulty she experiences in trying to follow the "greet-and-assist" plan. Management may not recognize the difficulty this situation presents, failing to see that an effective and courteous greet-and-assist plan will be difficult to execute without adequate staffing. Lupé's decision to share her concerns brought the issue to management's attention. Of course, the skill with which Lupé communicated her concerns will influence her manager's response.

Exposing Unethical Behavior and Organizational Wrongdoing

Organizations and the people who manage them do not always operate ethically. Unethical behavior continues to occur in contemporary organizations, and oftentimes it is the expression of dissent from employees that exposes organizational wrongdoing. Textbox 8.1 reveals how dissent occurred in response to unethical practices in the subprime lending industry. In this instance, the organization asked employees to forge federally mandated lending documents to close high-interest loans. This unethical practice yielded profits for the company. However, behavior of this kind created a lending crisis that in turn contributed to a national and global economic recession. The case highlights the power and importance of dissent in contemporary organizations.

Textbox 8.1   Employee Dissent and the Subprime Mortgage Crisis

Founded in 1922, the Ethics Resource Center (ERC) is a nonprofit devoted to the advancement of organizational ethics. The ERC seeks to advance high ethical standards and practices in organizations and to serve as a resource for both public and private institutions. In October 2008, Jason Zuckerman, a principal at the Employment Law Group in Washington, D.C., detailed his experience with employee dissent and subprime lending in a guest column that appeared on the ERC's Web site (www.ethics.org).

Zuckerman recounted the story of an employee from the mortgage industry who retained his firm for legal council. This particular employee felt he had experienced retaliation when he questioned his sales manager's directive to increase the company's subprime lending, which involved forging federally mandated disclosure forms. These were the very forms that let borrowers know about the disadvantages of subprime loans. Mortgage companies benefited from pushing such sales because these loan products came with much higher interest rates, which meant they were more lucrative for the lender. In response to employee dissent, the sales manager withheld sales leads—a clear act of retaliation for an employee whose compensation was largely based on commissions. The company, in turn, took the dissenting employee's retaliation case as an affront to its mission of making housing more affordable for the low-income borrowers.

Zuckerman reports that 3 short years later, the company had lost more than $1 billion from subprime mortgages. Zuckerman concluded that much of the financial crisis triggered by the subprime mortgage industry could have been averted by attending more closely to those employees who expressed dissent about the questionable practices perpetuated in the industry.

Providing Corrective Feedback

The subprime lending example also highlights the capacity of dissent to serve as a form of *corrective feedback* (Hegstrom, 1995). By sharing dissent, employees draw attention to organizational trouble spots. In the subprime lending industry, these included fraudulent and unlawful practices; in other organizations, they may include health and safety practices, flawed sales and marketing strategies, or lack of clarity in job descriptions and role responsibilities. Such feedback provides management with the opportunity to correct problems. It also signals employees' concern about organizational well-being. When employees express dissent with the intention of providing corrective feedback, they display an investment in bettering their respective organizations. Ideally, management appreciates such feedback. In this way, employees, management, and the organization all benefit from the expression of dissent.

❖ KEY RESEARCH STUDIES

Employee Responses to Dissatisfaction

Dissent is a communicative response to workplace conditions, practices, and policies that we find dissatisfying. Hirschman (1970) posited that employees respond to dissatisfaction through voice, loyalty, or exit. He contended that when faced with dissatisfying conditions, employees would choose to exit the organization or to stay and give voice to their concerns. Loyalty, in turn, is thought to influence employees' decisions to use exit or voice. Employees with higher degrees of loyalty are more likely to voice and those with lower levels to exit. Farrell (1983) expanded on the model, suggesting that employee responses to dissatisfaction should include neglect, which is characterized by lateness, absenteeism, and increased errors.

A Model of Employee Dissent

Kassing (1997, 1998) developed a model for understanding the factors that would affect how employees choose to express dissent. He argued that the expression of dissent begins when an employee experiences a *dissent-triggering event.* Subsequent research reveals a wide range of dissent-triggering events (Hegstrom, 1999; Kassing & Armstrong, 2002; Redding, 1985; Sprague & Ruud, 1988). Table 8.1 provides a typology of possible dissent-triggering events and examples of each drawn from actual employee accounts. As you can see, multiple and varied issues can trigger employee dissent, some concerning ethics and fairness, some dealing with decision making and organizational change, and others relating to inefficiency and resources.

Table 8.1   Dissent-Triggering Event Examples

Employee treatment (fairness and employee rights)	"I was not receiving my paycheck in a timely manner."
Organizational change (changes and implementation of changes)	"In July we transitioned into a new software system. This caused problems with client billing over several months."
Decision making (decisions, decision-making processes)	"Management made a unilateral decision to change a software program without conducting a needs assessment."
Inefficiency (inefficient work practices and ineffective processes)	"At an old catalog job I worked, near the end of my time there they hired an extra photographer to speed things up, yet they did not hire an extra copywriter. So, the work bottlenecked because I could not write fast enough to supply two photographers."
Role/responsibility (unclear, unrealistic, or unmet roles and responsibilities for self and others)	"There was disagreement regarding reassignment of work duties."

Resources (use and availability of organizational resources)	"Members of my department were in desperate need of latex gloves. . . . However, because our department answers to both a building-level supervisor and a district-level supervisor, both were at odds with whose budget the funds would come from."
Ethics (unethical practices or expectations of employees)	"I disagreed with some of the lack of clarity and honesty the company was allowing/ encouraging employees to convey to customers."
Performance evaluation (employee evaluations or the evaluation process)	"A supervisor was unfairly writing up employees who she did not like."
Preventing harm (practices or policies that endanger self, coworkers, or customers)	"I addressed my safety and other members of staff's safety."

Source: Adapted from Kassing and Armstrong (2002).

According to Kassing (1997), the employee then sorts through individual, relational, and organizational factors to answer two critical questions: (a) What is the probability of being perceived as constructive or adversarial, and (b) what is the likelihood of experiencing retaliation for expressing dissent? Individual factors include personality and communication traits such as being apprehensive or argumentative. Research findings indicate, for example, that employees who are more argumentative express more dissent to management (Kassing & Avtgis, 1999). Relational factors concern the types and quality of relationships employees have with their coworkers and supervisors. Not surprisingly, employees who have higher quality relationships with their supervisors express dissent more readily to them (Kassing, 2000b). Organizational factors include the climate and culture. Studies illustrate that employees are more likely to express dissent when they perceive that their opinions are valued (Kassing, 2000a, 2006).

Employees try to determine if their dissent will be perceived by bosses and peers as constructive or adversarial. They assess the likelihood of retaliation. On the basis of these considerations, workers choose the appropriate audience for dissent messages. When employees view dissent as risky at work, they direct messages to family members and nonwork friends because the risk of retaliation is low. This practice is known as *displaced dissent.* In contrast, employees who feel comfortable and secure in sharing their dissent are more likely to engage in *upward dissent*, directing their concerns to management. At times, employees want others in the organization to hear their concerns but worry that management will be unreceptive. In these instances, dissent is sometimes shared only with coworkers, a practice known as *lateral dissent* (Kassing, 1997, 1998). Because expressing upward dissent to management and supervisors provokes the greatest degree of risk, it has received particular attention in subsequent studies.

Upward Dissent Expression

By asking employees to report about specific instances in which they dissented to management, Kassing (2002) determined that employees used five distinct strategies for expressing upward dissent. *Direct-factual appeal* involves supporting one's dissent claim with physical evidence, knowledge of organizational policies and practices, or personal work experience. *Solution presentation* is the practice of suggesting a way to resolve a troubling issue. Repeated efforts to draw attention to the problem are referred to as *repetition*. "Going around the boss" to a higher authority is known as *circumvention*. The final strategy, *threatening resignation*, expresses the intention to exit the organization if management is unresponsive to the need for change. This same study revealed that employees used direct-factual appeal and solution presentation regularly and frequently. In contrast, circumvention and threatening resignation were used sparingly.

In a follow-up study, Kassing (2005) asked employees to rate the competence of each strategy. Solution presentation was perceived as most competent, followed by direct-factual appeal. These approaches appear to focus attention on problems and evidence rather than people and their relationships. They minimize the relational damage that sometimes accompanies dissent. In contrast, the strategies of repetition, circumvention, and threatening resignation were perceived to be less competent. Yet Kassing's (2002) study established that employees sometimes use these less competent strategies. Why would people choose less competent strategies given that there are clearly superior alternatives? Kassing (2007, 2009) explored this in subsequent studies.

Practicing Circumvention

Going around the boss can be risky. What are the possible effects on supervisory relationships? What will be the outcomes for an organization? Kassing (2007) addressed these questions by asking employees to describe a time when they felt it was necessary to go around their boss to someone higher in the organizational chain of command. Responses indicated a range of relational and organizational outcomes. Although circumvention led to decline within the superior-subordinate relationship in about half of the cases, in the other cases, it produced neutral or positive relational effects, including improved understanding between the parties (see Table 8.2). With regard to organizational outcomes, the results were sometimes desirable (see Table 8.3). Kassing concluded that circumvention should be used judiciously: It can sometimes be effective in bringing about change, but it frequently undermines supervisory relationships.

Table 8.2	Typology of Relational Outcomes Resulting From Circumvention
Deterioration	Subordinates noted a decline in superior-subordinate relationship quality and/or work conditions.
Neutrality	Subordinates reported no notable change in the relationship because circumvention produced ineffectual outcomes or because circumvention exposed inadequacies regarding how supervisors initially handled issues.
Compromise	Supervisors and subordinates addressed the concern at issue, the circumvention, or both in a way that protected their status and their mutual identities.
Development	Subordinates reported being thanked and feeling appreciated when circumvention produced favorable outcomes for supervisors.
Understanding	Supervisors tacitly approved of and deemed legitimate the issues raised by employees that the supervisors did not or could not address effectively.

Source: Kassing (2007). Used by permission.

Notice in Table 8.3 that circumvention sometimes resulted in an absence of corrective action. Some dissenters actually experienced retaliation, including the imposition of intolerable working conditions, reprimands, and, in some cases, termination. So what tips the scales in favor of the dissenter? What makes him or her more likely to be seen as constructive? Less likely to experience retaliation? The answer lies in whether dissent is motivated by principle or personal gain.

An Issue of Principle or a Matter of Personal Advantage

The contrast between matters of principle and personal gain was first introduced by Graham (1986) and explored further by other dissent scholars (Hegstrom, 1999; Sprague & Ruud, 1988). *Principled dissent* is

Table 8.3	Typology of Organizational Outcomes Resulting From Circumvention
Favorable for the dissenter	Circumvention allowed employees to achieve goals and to compel supervisory action.
Triggering agent sanctions	Circumvention resulted in some form of reprimand or sanction for the dissent-triggering agent (i.e., supervisors, coworkers, customers).
Organizational improvement	Circumvention led to corrective action that addressed either workplace conditions or corporate policies and practices that were beneficial to other employees as well as or in addition to the dissenter.
Absence of corrective action	Circumvention failed to produce any or enough corrective action on the part of management.
Disadvantageous for dissenter	Circumvention created confrontational representations of dissenters and produced retaliation.

Source: Kassing (2007).Used by permission.

expressed in response to actions that violate a standard of justice, honesty, or economy, whereas *personal advantage dissent* is expressed in response to personal motives (e.g., wanting time off, seeking a raise, etc.). Although the definitions of these types of dissent appear distinct, in practice they can blend together. At times, issues of principle affect people directly, leading them to be motivated to speak out not simply because an issue is unethical or morally wrong but also because it affects them individually.

> When I chose to leave the Active Duty Army and join a National Guard Unit in an early release program, my immediate commander (company CO) signed my paperwork with an approval or positive endorsement. When his boss, the battalion commander, found out about it, he made my company commander change his endorsement to a "no." I felt that this was unjust or possibly even illegal influence on my commander's decision, and I brought it up.
>
> Jared, age 31

In this example, Jared deals with a mixture of motives for dissenting. He is personally motivated to see that his endorsement is accurate and favorable, but he also is concerned about the ethics and legality of the behavior exhibited by the battalion commander who overrode the decision of a subordinate officer. This case illustrates how principled dissent can be tinged by personal advantage motives. Sherron Watkins, an Enron employee who blew the whistle on the energy company's questionable accounting practices, found herself in a similar situation. She dissented not only because she believed the accounting practices were ethically questionable but also because she was concerned for her career and the possible professional damage she might suffer if Enron was exposed.

Textbox 8.2   Organizational Wrongdoing at Enron

Originally an energy company that owned power plants, water companies, and gas distributors, over time Enron evolved into a powerful energy trader. Before collapsing, Enron was America's seventh largest company, having been named "American's Most Innovative Company" by *Fortune* magazine 6 years in a row from 1996 to 2001.

To disguise corporate losses, a network of partnerships was established. These partnerships served to hide debts by buying up losing businesses from Enron. In turn, Enron appeared more profitable than it actually was, and stock prices remained high, being inflated and overvalued.

In 2001, Sherron Watkins, Enron's vice president for corporate development, wrote a seven-page letter to her boss, Enron Chairman Kenneth Lay, informing him of her concerns regarding the company's accounting practices. She wrote, "I am incredibly nervous that we will implode in a wave of accounting scandals," adding that "the business world will consider the past successes as nothing but an elaborate accounting hoax."

When the accounting scheme was exposed publicly and Enron buckled, the company left behind more than $30 billion in debt, corporate shares that were worthless, and 21,000 unemployed workers around the world.

Kassing (2009) looked more carefully at employees' reasons for going around the boss. Not surprisingly, the primary motive was some perceived flaw in their supervisor's behavior. This included supervisors' failure to act on employee concerns, poor performance with regard to general management principles, unfair use of power, poor treatment of employees, and unethical behaviors such as stealing from the company, sexually harassing employees, and abusing company policies. To avoid being construed as adversarial, employees generally attempted to emphasize the principled nature of their dissent claim *along with* personal motives for expressing dissent. Kassing concluded that people see circumvention as constructive when the motives for dissent appear principled in nature and the issues are comparatively serious (see Table 8.4).

Earlier in the chapter, we discussed the case of Aamir, the loan originator. Aamir found the new compensation system to be unfair for

Table 8.4	Considerations Regarding the Perception of Circumvention	

Issue Severity	Nature of Dissent	Dissent Construal
High	Principled	Constructive
Low	Personal advantage	Destructive

Source: Adapted from Kassing (2009).

officers who generated certain types of loans. By default, they could not qualify for the highest levels of compensation. In essence, Aamir's concern is one of personal advantage. His potential to earn income has been compromised by the new system. In response, Aamir expressed upward dissent by going to management. Let's assume that in doing so, he circumvented his immediate supervisor. How did he minimize the risk of going around his boss? Aamir frames his argument around fairness, a quality that most employees understand and value. In so doing, Aamir shifts the focus of his argument from purely personal gain to a matter of concern to all loan originators. For management, the issue is not simply "Aamir is upset that he won't make as much in commission," but rather "the new compensation scheme is flawed and inequitable." Viewed this way, the matter has broader and more severe implications. Aamir's dissent is more likely to be perceived as a legitimate and constructive criticism of organizational policy. For a summary of the communication options available to Aamir and other employees who choose to express dissent, see Textbox 8.3.

Textbox 8.3	Communication Options

Choice of Audience (Kassing, 1997, 1998)

Upward dissent
Lateral dissent
Displaced dissent

Upward Dissent Strategies (Kassing, 2002)

Direct-factual appeal
Solution presentation
Repetition
Circumvention
Threatening resignation

Nature of Dissent (Graham, 1986; Hegstrom, 1999)

Principled

Personal advantage

❖ EXPRESSING DISSENT
AND THE RISK NEGOTIATION CYCLE

Expressing dissent is inherently a risky proposition because it involves threatening the organizational status quo and management. It is not a practice to engage in lightly, certainly not without some consideration of the factors that reduce or heighten risk to the dissenter. We use the risk negotiation cycle to better understand how organizational participants manage risk when expressing dissent (see Figure 8.1).

Attending

We have suggested a variety of factors that exacerbate or alleviate the risk faced by dissenters. Employees should attend to individual factors, including how satisfied, loyal, and committed they feel. Relational considerations include the quality of bonds with supervisors and coworkers. Will expressions of dissent put these relationships at risk? Organizational factors require attention. How tolerant is management of employee dissent? How has it responded to employee dissenters? Has the organization created mechanisms (e.g., suggestion systems) that facilitate the process? Attending to these matters helps employees form a risk assessment. If the organizational culture values voice and feedback and you are a satisfied employee with strong working relationships, you may judge risk to be low. In contrast, organizations that treat dissenters punitively signal less tolerance for employee dissent. Poor-quality supervisory relationships limit the communication options. In these cases, dissent is risky and more likely to lead to retaliation. By attending to these risk factors, employees decide on the audiences for dissent messages and the communication strategies they will use.

Sensemaking

Sensemaking emerges at different points in the dissent expression process. Dissenting to coworkers and nonwork friends and family provides an audience that confirms not only concerns but also your risk assessment. The coworker who responds to your dissent claim with, "I agree with you completely, but I'd never say that to management," signals that expressing dissent to management is a risky proposition.

Figure 8.1   Expressing Dissent and the Risk Negotiation Cycle

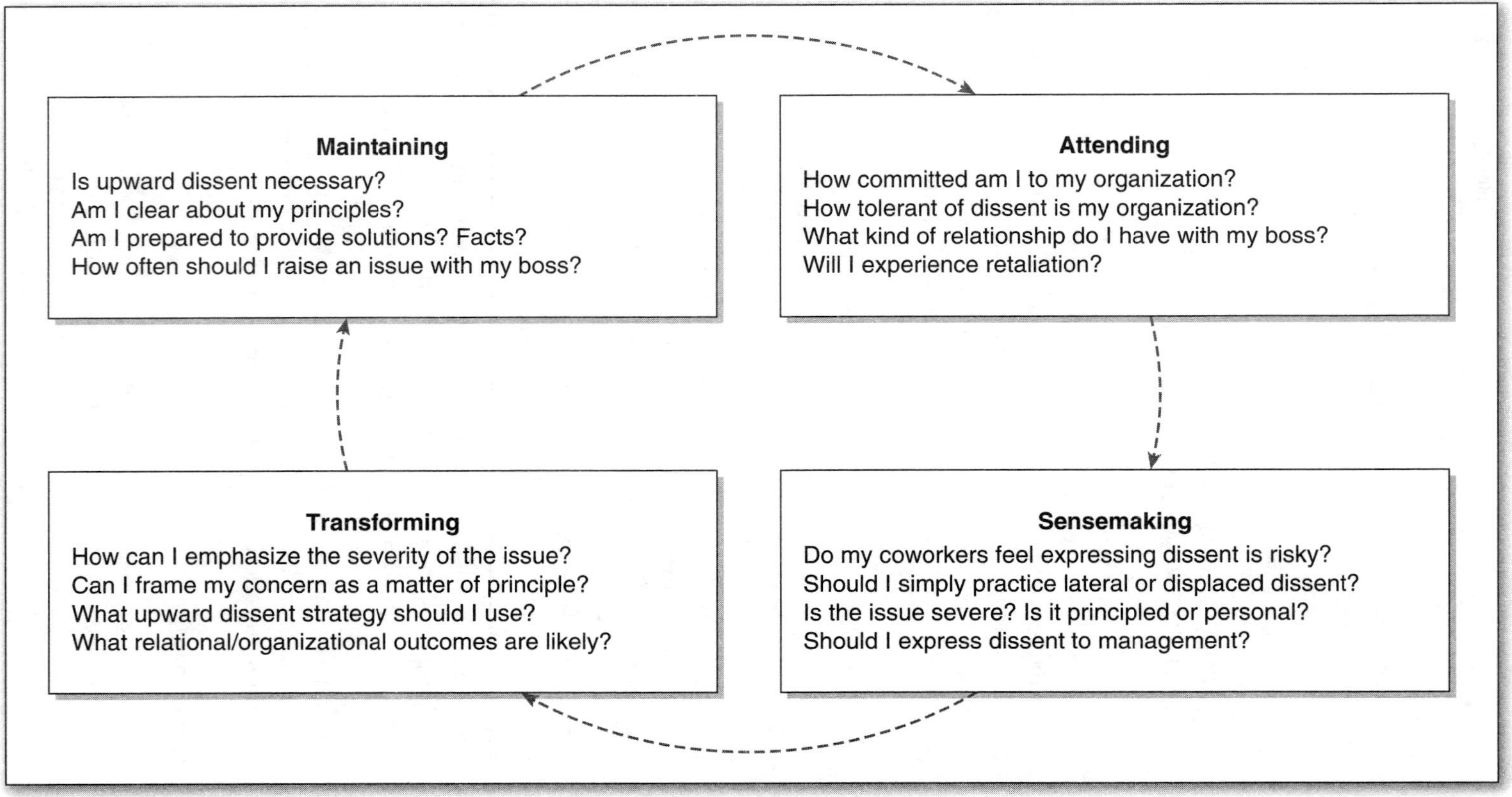

Attending

How committed am I to my organization?
How tolerant of dissent is my organization?
What kind of relationship do I have with my boss?
Will I experience retaliation?

Sensemaking

Do my coworkers feel expressing dissent is risky?
Should I simply practice lateral or displaced dissent?
Is the issue severe? Is it principled or personal?
Should I express dissent to management?

Maintaining

Is upward dissent necessary?
Am I clear about my principles?
Am I prepared to provide solutions? Facts?
How often should I raise an issue with my boss?

Transforming

How can I emphasize the severity of the issue?
Can I frame my concern as a matter of principle?
What upward dissent strategy should I use?
What relational/organizational outcomes are likely?

Thus, lateral and displaced dissent messages can be important elements of a risk management process.

Previewing your dissent strategy with coworkers or mentors is a valuable kind of sensemaking. It can help you determine if your message will be perceived as principled or personal. For example, one of the authors recently felt it was necessary to challenge an organizational decision to close the campus daycare center where his child was enrolled. He objected to the closure on personal grounds, but also for reasons of principle, as the closure would negatively affect students and other employees. After an unsuccessful attempt to express upward dissent to the vice president using a direct-factual appeal strategy, he considered circumvention—sending an e-mail to the president of the university. He sought the advice of two colleagues before doing so. Both cautioned him about the potential repercussions of circumventing a senior leader at the university. Their advice helped him choose a less risky approach.

Transforming

Lateral and displaced dissent are transforming in that they reduce the risk associated with expressing dissent directly to management. Expressing dissent to coworkers and to people outside of work provides relative safety. However, lateral and displaced dissent will not result in significant organizational change. Optimal outcomes can sometimes be achieved through the expression of upward dissent, but these gains come with a higher degree of risk. Dissent can lead to optimization when it involves corrective feedback, addressing some flawed organizational policy or practice that stands to be amended. What can be done to increase the effectiveness of dissent? First, emphasize the severity of the issue. Second, focus on principled rather than personal-advantage concerns, or at least use a combination of the two. And finally, choose the upward dissent strategies that have been identified as more competent and less relationship threatening (e.g., solution presentation). When the first two suggestions are implemented, it is certainly possible to obtain optimal outcomes, even when using less competent strategies, such as circumvention (Kassing, 2007). However, combining all three of these suggestions reduces risk and increases the likelihood of optimization.

Maintaining

Once we have attended to, made sense of, and transformed risk, we want to maintain it at acceptable and safe levels. This may involve appropriate use of displaced and lateral dissent. Dissent about less serious issues is best directed to coworkers and others outside of work. It is wise to avoid overburdening supervisors with repeated expressions of personal-advantage messages. Also, reserve your dissent messages for relatively serious matters. The safety of dissent is maintained when employees use routinely those strategies that focus on facts and solutions and less on personal relationships. Have a solution in mind when expressing dissent to supervisors so that the interaction is constructive rather than destructive. It is less productive to repeatedly raise the same concerns (i.e., repetition) or raise them without factual support or solutions. Employees can honor the supervisor's role and status in the organization by sharing dissent with him or her first and avoiding circumvention. Going around the boss should be reserved for situations when the supervisor has failed to be responsive to serious and well-documented concerns. Employees manage risk when they document a trail of constructive actions taken to raise a supervisor's awareness of the issue.

❖ CONCLUSION

In closing, we provide two additional accounts that represent two very different outcomes. In the first, Derek expresses dissent about a safety issue in an attempt to prevent harm.

> I was working for an airplane charter company. Fueling aircraft was one of our duties. Fuel spills weren't uncommon. One of the fuelers spilt what I thought to be approximately 25 gals of jet fuel. It's very hard to gauge exactly how much was spilled, but I thought it should be cleaned up no matter what. It was a very busy time for us. My supervisor didn't think it was important to clean up because of our busy schedule. I went to the director of operations because I had already confronted my supervisor. This type of behavior was common when we were busy (not cleaning up spills). The issue was partially resolved. We had a routine meeting where fuel spills and the importance of cleaning them was addressed.
>
> Derek, age 26

Below, Marcus recounts the unfairness he perceived upon taking a new job as coworkers shifted their work to him. His experience is not unusual. Workgroups often test the newcomer. As we see, Marcus decided to speak with his supervisor rather than dissenting directly to his coworkers. We cannot determine from the account whether he also engaged in displaced dissent. Would he have taken a different approach if his concerns had been shared with a mentor? Would Marcus have placed himself at less risk?

I was a new hire and my coworkers were pushing large amounts of their duties onto me. I went to my supervisor and gave him specific instances as examples and he questioned the other workers. They denied it and he said there was nothing else he could do. I went to his supervisor and we were all called in and the issue discussed. My supervisor acted different toward me after and avoided talking to me. Although the issue was resolved I felt left out of the group dynamic thereafter.

Marcus, age 26

When attending to risk, employees like Derek and Marcus must consider an organization's tolerance for dissent. Do the organizations featured in these stories appear more or less tolerant of dissent? What about the employees' apparent relationship with their respective organizations? One is a newcomer, the other a seasoned enough veteran to know that fuel spills of a certain magnitude ought to be a concern. What is the quality of the relationships Derek and Marcus have with their supervisors? Are these problematic in any way? How do these relationship qualities affect the expression of dissent? Finally, what is the risk of retaliation for these two employees?

When it comes to sensemaking, consider the role of coworkers in these scenarios. What could Derek and Marcus learn by observing their coworkers? Derek and Marcus also must make sense of issue severity. How serious is a jet fuel spill? How serious is the problem Marcus faces with his new coworkers? Are these matters of principle or personal advantage? What could Marcus do to emphasize the seriousness and principled nature of his concern? Are the issues grave enough to warrant the attention of management? Or would it be better to practice lateral or displaced dissent?

To transform risk, our dissenters need to choose an appropriate communication strategy. How does Derek do this? Both of our dissenters resorted to circumvention. What strategies did they employ before moving to circumvention? Do these appear to have been the most competent choices? What other alternatives could have been used? What were the apparent relational and organizational outcomes of circumvention?

Finally, what should Derek and Marcus do in the future to maintain risk at acceptable levels? Should they express lateral and displaced dissent instead of or in combination with upward dissent? Do they have well-defined principles that will guide them in future interactions? Have they jeopardized relationships with coworkers? Supervisors? How will this affect their future decisions about expressing dissent? The problems experienced by these employees may continue into the future. Should they continue to raise their concerns with their supervisors? How often? Would it be risky to do so? What are the alternatives?

❖ REFERENCES

Farrell, D. (1983). Exit, voice, loyalty, and neglect as responses to job dissatisfaction: A multidimensional scaling study. *Academy of Management Journal, 26*, 596–607.

Graham, J. W. (1986). Principled organizational dissent: A theoretical essay. In B. M. Staw & L. L. Cummings (Eds.), *Research in organizational behavior* (Vol. 8, pp. 1–52). Greenwich, CT: JAI.

Hegstrom, T. G. (1995). Focus on organizational dissent: A functionalist response to criticism. In J. Lehtonen (Ed.), *Critical perspectives on communication research and pedagogy* (pp. 83–94). St. Ingbert, Germany: Rohrig University Press.

Hegstrom, T. G. (1999). Reasons for rocking the boat: Principles and personal problems. In H. K. Geissner, A. F. Herbig, & E. Wessela (Eds.), *Business communication in Europe* (pp. 179–194). Tostedt, Germany: Attikon Verlag.

Hirschman, A. O. (1970). *Exit, voice, and loyalty.* Cambridge, MA: Harvard University Press.

Kassing, J. W. (1997). Articulating, antagonizing, and displacing: A model of employee dissent. *Communication Studies, 48*, 311–332.

Kassing, J. W. (1998). Development and validation of the Organizational Dissent Scale. *Management Communication Quarterly, 12*(2), 183–229.

Kassing, J. W. (2000a). Exploring the relationship between workplace freedom of speech, organizational identification, and employee dissent. *Communication Research Reports, 17*, 387–396.

Kassing, J. W. (2000b). Investigating the relationship between superior-subordinate relationship quality and employee dissent. *Communication Research Reports, 17*, 58–70.

Kassing, J. W. (2002). Speaking up: Identifying employees' upward dissent strategies. *Management Communication Quarterly, 16*, 187–209.

Kassing, J. W. (2005). Speaking up competently: A comparison of perceived competence in upward dissent strategies. *Communication Research Reports, 22*, 227–234.

Kassing, J. W. (2006). Employees' expressions of upward dissent as a function of current and past work experiences. *Communication Reports, 19*, 79–88.

Kassing, J. W. (2007). Going around the boss: Exploring the consequences of circumvention. *Management Communication Quarterly, 21*, 55–74.

Kassing, J. W. (2009). Breaking the chain of command: Making sense of employee circumvention. *Journal of Business Communication, 46*, 311–334.

Kassing, J. W., & Armstrong, T. A. (2002). Someone's going to hear about this: Examining the association between dissent-triggering events and employees' dissent expression. *Management Communication Quarterly, 16*, 39–65.

Kassing, J. W., & Avtgis, T. A. (1999). Examining the relationship between organizational dissent and aggressive communication. *Management Communication Quarterly, 13*(1), 76–91.

Redding, W. C. (1985). Rocking boats, blowing whistles, and teaching speech communication. *Communication Education, 34*, 245–258.

Sprague, J. A., & Ruud, G. L. (1988). Boat-rocking in the high technology culture. *American Behavioral Scientist, 32*, 169–193.

9

Proposing New Ideas

The head chef called a meeting to "brainstorm" new menu ideas. It didn't work out so well. As it turned out, she already knew what she wanted—just to "import" her last restaurant's menu ideas, with a few minor upgrades. Every idea we came up with, she found a reason to shoot it down. Obviously, we stopped suggesting things pretty quickly. No one wanted to be criticized for being, as she said, "out of date" or "unrealistic." After work that day, some of us went out together and brainstormed our own "ideal menu." It was fun, with everyone chiming in, coming up with some really creative dishes. Some were pretty wild and would never sell. But even after we got serious about pricing and customer tastes, we realized that some of these menu items would give us a real advantage over other restaurants in town. I shared some of the ideas on my Facebook, and even some of my super-critical "foodie" friends liked them right away. Some of us want to start our own place someday. Now we have some great ideas to get us going.

Abu, age 26

A bu works in the restaurant described above as an assistant chef. His experience sounds frustrating, but it is not unusual. It would be naive to think that all new ideas are worthwhile, but employees feel stymied when their creative ideas are resisted, criticized, or simply ignored. Pressing a reluctant supervisor to consider a potential innovation often seems risky. Abu's boss, the chief chef, seemed threatened by the loss of creative control, and her brainstorming sessions were mainly used to seek affirmation for her own creative impulses. To preserve a valued mentoring relationship, Abu kept the new menu ideas to himself until he took a more senior job in the kitchen of a competing establishment. In other words, he chose not to put his relationship at risk by pressing for innovation. Unfortunately, by squelching the creativity of her employees, Abu's boss may have placed her own organization at a competitive risk. Her resistance encouraged a creative employee to take his skills elsewhere, and she may find herself losing customers to the more innovative cuisine that Abu is dishing up at his new location.

❖ WHY IS PROPOSING NEW IDEAS IMPORTANT?

As in Abu's situation, the communication of innovative ideas can be risky for those who try it and for those who fail to cultivate it. Indeed, it would be no exaggeration to say that innovation is an essential ingredient to success in the contemporary marketplace, with its rapidly changing markets, fierce competition, and increasing globalization (Nanda & Singh, 2009). "Innovate or die," warned the management guru Tom Peters (1999) in his best-selling tome, *The Circle of Innovation*. In the decade since, events have made his words seem prophetic. Take the implosion of General Motors (GM) that unfolded over the past year. After receiving billions of dollars in bailout funding from the federal government, GM filed for bankruptcy. The sources of GM's difficulties are many, but one seems undeniable. As gas prices skyrocketed and consumers became more sensitive to environmental concerns, GM continued to produce expensive, gas-guzzling vehicles. Unable to design and quickly launch innovative and appealing smaller cars, GM and other American automakers clung too long to the brawny trucks and SUVs that once raked in huge profits (see Textbox 9.1).

Textbox 9.1   Innovate or Die (Again)

In the 1970s, gas prices surged as the Organization of Petroleum Exporting Countries (OPEC) constricted petroleum output. For the first time in history, Americans clamored for smaller, more fuel-efficient cars. It soon became apparent to consumers that the few available American models were unattractive, costly, or unreliable, particularly compared to imports manufactured in Japan. General Motors, Ford, and

Chrysler—the Big Three American car companies—built their reputations on large, heavy cars, and they were slow to recognize the change in consumer demand. As a result, their share of U.S. auto sales began a steep slide that continues today. The situation became so dire that Chrysler had to request an unprecedented government bailout to stay afloat. Led by its new plain-talking CEO Lee Iacocca, Chrysler promised to change its ways. And it did, launching an aggressive effort to create innovative and market-responsive models and paying back the money it borrowed.

Fast forward three decades. Chrysler is once again in deep financial trouble, Ford is struggling to keep its head above water, and the massive General Motors is in free fall. Fed up with continued requests for government bailouts and the slow pace of change, President Barack Obama essentially "fires" GM CEO President Jim Waggoner. A poster child for Detroit's obliviousness to changing market conditions, Waggoner's claim to fame at GM was the commercialization of the Hummer, a huge military vehicle that averages somewhere around 10 miles per gallon.

Like GM, many older companies are battered and bruised by the demands for constant innovation. They cling too long to once successful products. In the past, market leaders could develop new products at a relatively leisurely pace, but now research and development is a continual concern, and product development cycles are short. Globalization trends make it much more likely that foreign competitors will offer competing products at a cheaper cost or with improved quality. Where brand loyalty and local relationships were once primary motivators for consumers, these days, customers enjoy easy access to products created by a huge array of national and international producers. Increasingly savvy consumers are demanding new and creative products. The demand for innovation extends beyond the for-profit sector. Led by a new brand of social entrepreneurs, nonprofits and charitable organizations are rethinking traditional approaches to raising money, delivering services, and connecting with constituents. For example, in *Momentum*, her popular book on the topic, Allison Fine (2006) presses organizations to rethink their outreach efforts. In this spirit, she argues that intensive use of social media (rather than reliance on traditional mass mailings) is an innovative characteristic of next-generation activist organizations.

Of course, U.S. culture has long embraced the myth of the entrepreneur—those innately curious, unconventional, risk-taking, go-it-alone visionaries who grow revolutionary businesses from humble roots in a garage or basement. Microsoft founder Bill Gates may be the prototypical example. Increasingly, the illusive qualities of entrepreneurship are coming under the scrutiny of university educators and even large philanthropic organizations such as the Ewing Marion

Kauffman Foundation (http://www.kauffman.org/). Firm in their belief that entrepreneurism is the cure for all that ails American commerce and civic life, these organizations cultivate the innovative spirit in students, budding business owners, and social services leaders by providing instruction, encouragement, and seed money. These programs exist on many university campuses. Despite this enthusiasm and the undeniable importance of innovation, these efforts should be met with healthy skepticism (see Textbox 9.2).

Textbox 9.2   Entrepreneurial Brainwashing?

Can you require employees to be innovative? At our university (Arizona State), one of several funded by a large grant from the Kauffman Foundation, administrators' enthusiasm for entrepreneurialism is clear. Shortly after receiving the multimillion dollar gift, they elevated entrepreneurialism to the status of a core value of the university, akin to critical thinking and responsible citizenship. Administrators imposed a new set of innovation mandates. All first-year students would be required to learn that entrepreneurism is a core academic value, just like academic honesty. Moreover, entrepreneurialism would now be an essential element of every discipline. Faculty and students were surveyed to make sure they fully embraced the innovative spirit. Some of the more innovative faculty and students were troubled by this top-down approach.

Given that entrepreneurs are noted for "swimming against the tide," wasn't it odd to force all students to be one? Given that many entrepreneurs failed to appreciate the value of a college education (including Bill Gates, until after he was rich), was it wise to teach our students to emulate them uncritically? At a minimum, shouldn't we encourage them to think through the ethical implications of entrepreneurialism, to consider what is good for our society, as well as what is good for the individual entrepreneur? After all, wasn't it the entrepreneurs on Wall Street whose innovative trading practices yielded riches for themselves and disaster for the larger economy?

While we applaud our own employer's enthusiasm for innovation, the literature leaves us doubtful that innovations are produced through top-down processes and forced compliance with managerial mandates. Others share our skepticism. While some innovations require large organizational investments, the kind that only can be authorized by the highest levels of management, many organizations require a much less dramatic change in communication practices (Getz & Robinson, 2003). New and better ideas often emerge when organizations simply do a better job of listening to their customers and cultivating creativity through the communication practices of their own employees. And, as we emphasize in this chapter, an increasingly important communication competency of high-performing employees is their capacity to stimulate, promote, and implement innovation. Our intention in this chapter is to focus on the kinds of interactions and communication practices that will help you and your peers make innovative contributions at work. At the same time, we encourage you to think about innovation as a collective process, one that requires us to respect our peers and consider the larger interests of the organization.

❖ KEY RESEARCH STUDIES

Collections of Creatives

Thomas Edison, the famous creator of the light bulb, the phonograph, and so many other revolutionary inventions, is often portrayed as a fount of individual creativity—the "wizard of Menlo Park." But Francis Jehl, long-time assistant at his New Jersey laboratory, is often quoted as saying this: "Edison is in reality a collective noun and means the work of many men." Indeed, contemporary researchers of organizational innovation conceptualize creativity as a team process (Thompson & Hoon-Seok, 2006). A recent field study of creative problem solving in six innovate organizations included observations at Design Continuum, the company that helped Reebok create the Pump shoe, an innovative and wildly successful answer to the Nike Air line of athletic shoes (Hargadon & Bechky, 2006). The authors found that the complex problems of the modern workplace are rarely solved through the persistent efforts of an individual genius. Instead, they emerge from the brainstorming *interactions* of creative people ("collectives of creatives") with diverse expertise, who find ways to combine their efforts in momentary flashes of collective inspiration.

> Within the project team, a few people knew about the client's demands, another knew about inflatable splints, another about IV bags, and others about pumps. The social interactions within these brainstorms enabled connecting these ideas across members of the organization. Only during these momentary interactions did the design team come to recognize how their disparate knowledge . . . could be relevant to designing a better basketball shoe. (Hargadon & Bechky, 2006, p. 485)

Lauded as among the most creative shoes ever designed, the Pump generated $1 billion in revenues in just its first year. But what were the key communication practices that made these "momentary interactions" so conducive to the development of the Pump shoe? Hargadon and Bechky (2006) observed four distinctive kinds of communication.

- *Help seeking:* Help-seeking behavior ensured that more and different people participated in problem solving. It was initiated formally, for example, by inviting diverse specialists to brainstorming discussions. In successful companies, seeking help was engrained in the culture, as employees informally solicited wide-ranging opinions, often in hallway chats and after-work bull sessions. Seeking the help of those from different disciplines, occupations, and even cultures was encouraged and not stigmatized, as it is in companies that value only individual achievement.

• *Help giving:* Responding to help requests generously and quickly was a second communication practice that spawned innovative solutions. Innovative organizations eschewed the "it's not my job" mentality, and they encouraged collaborative as well as individual problem solving. Help-giving communication was considered a valued kind of organizational citizenship behavior. It sometimes involved asking questions as well as suggesting answers. Referring back to our opening vignette, Abu and his colleagues started with the question about new menu items, but in the course of their brainstorming, a new question emerged: "If we started our own restaurant, how could we make it truly different from the competition?"

• *Reflective reframing:* Reframing occurred in those creative moments when teams made new sense of the problems they faced. The Reebok Pump team used members' diverse experiences with IV bags and water pumps to reimagine the inner workings of a tennis shoe. In this way, the creative team generated different points of view, or "frames." This reframing process required a mindful effort to welcome unfamiliar ideas, delay criticism, and explore how familiar ideas might be adapted to new problems. Collectively, the members pursued multiple creative paths simultaneously, and they often found ways to combine and integrate divergent perspectives.

• *Reinforcing:* Reinforcing behaviors made collective creativity rewarding rather than burdensome. It involved giving credit to those who were willing to share ideas and let go of ownership. Members of creative firms found participation in brainstorming sessions to be motivating and intrinsically rewarding—an important aspect of the organizational culture. Many believed that their supervisors valued collective creativity. Verbal recognition and eventual promotion were linked to the processes of help seeking, help giving, and reframing. Those who were uncomfortable with these behaviors were negatively sanctioned and sometimes left the organization.

A Lesson From the Arts

The arts are hubs of creativity. With that in mind, organizational researchers have examined the creative processes used by artists. The work of successful theater directors received particular attention in a recent research paper (Ibbotson & Darso, 2008). The researchers observed and interviewed successful directors, noting that (like managers everywhere) directors must inspire and respect creative activity within boundaries imposed by timelines, budgets, and the need to coordinate the diverse talents of writers, costume designers, stage managers, and actors. Creativity must be maximized in the early stages of play development as roles and scripts are created and costumes conceived. But as the production of a play proceeds, the need for innovation is replaced by the necessity of careful coordination and conformity with the script. Costumes can't be redesigned after opening night, and the actors can't rewrite the script. This creative narrowing process parallels the one used in business as organizations create and then standardize a new product or service.

Ibbotson and Darso (2008) argue that successful directors are masters at introducing what they call "creative constraints." For directors, creativity is a boundary phenomenon. It emerges when boundaries are suggested, questioned, crashed up against, and then reimagined. Constraints are not instructions or targets or pathways. Instead, they are boundaries or challenges, within which the actors are encouraged to fully explore roles, take personal ownership of them, and produce their best creative interpretations. For example, the actors might be told that a character must convey a convincing sense of emotional desperation or that a scene should make the audience quake in their boots. But the actors are not told *how* to make the emotion convincing or the audience afraid. Good actors are motivated by these challenges, and they frequently create performances that are so unique that even the director could not have imagined them. From the theater, we learn that innovation can't be micromanaged, but it does require nurturing from an inspired and inspiring creative person. The authors articulate several specific communication practices of successful directors (see Textbox 9.3).

Textbox 9.3   **Communication Practices of Successful Theater Directors**

- Introducing challenging constraints rather than easily obtainable ones
- Trusting "the talent" as they define their roles
- Carefully observing, listening, and reframing as the creative process unfolds
- Accepting that false starts are inevitable and helpful
- Adding new constraints when creativity ebbs
- Developing synergy from the interactions of the actors
- Incorporating emerging ideas into an evolving artistic vision

---

Source: Adapted from Ibbotson and Darso (2008).

The notion of creative constraints can be easily applied outside the theater. For example, a new loan product offered by a regional bank should be competitively priced, easy to understand, convenient for customers, and relatively low risk. But the means of meeting these constraints could be left to the members of a product development team, who might question the traditional means of pricing (Could interest rates be adjusted based on customer payment performance?), delivering (Could sales be made by a third party rather than in-house staff?), and explaining the product (Would a 24-hour podcast offer better information than the standard brochure?). In the workplace, creativity can be killed by rigid goals, distrustful communication, and micromanaging team leaders. In contrast, theater directors select promising talent and use poetic language to construct an inspiring vision of how the play might move an audience. In other words, they use an approach that challenges rather than suppresses the creative spirit of employees.

Innovation Champions

In an often-cited study completed two decades ago, Jane Howell and Christopher Higgins (1990) reported the results of their in-depth interviews of what have come to be called "innovation champions." As they noted,

> There is no shortage of creative ideas in corporate America. However, for innovation to occur, someone must take the creative idea, guide it through the trying period when resistance is at its peak, and persevere until it becomes an innovation. In short, every idea needs a champion. (p. 40)

After an intensive screening process, the researchers selected 28 people who successfully promoted major technology changes in their organizations. As part of the study, each innovation champion was interviewed for several hours. The researchers identified some common personality characteristics: self-confident, persistent, energetic, and willing to take risks. Successful champions were generally credible people; they enjoyed long tenure in the organization, had accumulated considerable expertise, and had experience in many different locations and tasks.

This study and later work (Howell & Shea, 2006) also identified key communication practices of innovation champions. Successful champions articulated a compelling vision about the impact of the new technology, making the idea seem exciting and worthwhile. They also linked the new idea to the organization's larger values. Champions were adept at relational communication and team building. They developed innovation teams by encouraging risk taking, granting the team the freedom to experiment with new ideas, and inviting them to develop their potential through involvement in new projects. Innovation champions recognized the contributions of others by sharing credit for innovative ideas. They also served important boundary-spanning functions, such as scouting outside the organization for useful information and resources, protecting the innovation team from outside threats, and building communication links across departments and functions.

Howell and Higgins (1990) argued further that the process of championing was as important as the individual qualities of champions. In fact, the process appears to be quite different, depending on the larger organization's culture and its communication preferences. Three fundamental approaches were observed:

- *The rational process:* Provide a convincing, evidence-based persuasive presentation to key decision makers. After approval, build a coalition of innovation supporters.

- *The participative process:* Persuade a coalition of innovative supporters, make your presentation to decision makers, and argue that you have developed widespread support.

- *The renegade process:* Build a coalition of supporters, implement the innovation without formal permission, and argue for management approval based on demonstrated success (see Textbox 9.4).

Textbox 9.4   The Renegade

Malick worked at a community recreation center recently constructed by his city. The center offered a full range of exercise equipment at a reasonable membership cost. Although the population of his urban area is ethnically mixed, Malick noticed that few ethnic minorities registered for the exercise and nutrition classes he taught on Wednesday nights and Sunday afternoons. From his ethnic studies classes at the local college, the fitness instructor knew that African Americans and Hispanic Americans were at relatively high risk for diabetes, hypertension, and other obesity-related diseases. He wanted to recruit more minority students, but Malick's boss was reluctant to spend additional advertising dollars. So, Malick made his own advertising flyers and distributed them through the leaders of local churches with high minority populations. They told him that class times conflicted with church activities, so Malick scheduled an informal orientation session on a Tuesday night. More than two dozen people attended! Malick shared the impressive attendance figures with his fellow instructors. Together they shared the evidence with their supervisor, who agreed to change the class schedule and target advertising efforts to better reach minority residents.

All three processes eventually require innovators to make a persuasive case to key decision makers and engage in coalition building. Indeed, most employees simply lack the power to bring about change on their own, so they need to present convincing evidence and to develop the support of other employees. Obviously, the renegade approach, used by Malick, is most risky, as it calls for the employee to implement a change without approval. But as the textbox suggests, some changes can be made "below the radar," with limited risk exposure. They just require the employee to think creatively and invest additional effort in developing evidence and building coalitions of supportive coworkers.

Those who succeed as champions often have established a degree of technical expertise, experience, and cross-organizational connectivity. Less experienced employees might take a more cautious approach. We suggest the following tactics as ways to transform the risk associated with innovation, particularly if you are dealing with a reluctant boss.

- *Hypothetical scenario:* Ask your boss or more experienced coworkers to humor you as you offer a "what-if" scenario ("I wonder how our customers would respond it we used a Web site for ordering rather than the telephone system we use now.").

- *Trial balloon:* Suggest that your idea be tried on a small scale, so that disruption to current work processes is minimal and failure has limited consequences ("Could we try the new random sampling approach for just one week, then compare to the usual saturation sampling techniques?").

- *Advice seeking:* Give experienced coworkers the opportunity to advise you, so they have the opportunity to shape the innovation and possibly get behind it ("I know you have been doing this for years. Can you see any holes in this plan or maybe suggest some improvements?").

- *Enlist the help of a credible champion:* Take your idea to an experienced innovation champion in your organization. Ask for his or her advice and support. Do this informally, before you make any formal approach to management.

Thus, there is a range of communication options available pertaining to proposing new ideas. We provide a summary of these options in Textbox 9.5.

Textbox 9.5   Communication Options

Communication Processes in Creative Teams (Hargadon & Bechky, 2006)

   Help seeking
   Help giving
   Reflective reframing
   Reinforcing

Lessons From Theater Directors (Ibbotson & Darso, 2008)

Introduce challenging creative constraints
Trust and nurture the talent as they define their roles
Carefully observe and listen for creative interpretations
Accept that "false starts" are inevitable and helpful
Add new constraints when creativity ebbs
Develop synergy from the interactions of the actors
Incorporate emerging ideas into your evolving vision

Championing Behaviors (Howell & Higgins, 1990; Howell & Shea, 2006)

Articulate an exciting, compelling vision for the future
Link the innovation to organizational values and goals
Encourage risk taking in coworkers
Grant the freedom to experiment and develop potential ideas
Give recognition to risk takers and early adopters
Scout for outside information and resources
Protect the creative effort from unnecessary interference
Build communication links across functional units

Risk Management Tactics

Hypothetical situation
Trial balloon
Advice seeking
Enlisting the help of a credible champion

❖ PROPOSING NEW IDEAS AND THE RISK NEGOTIATION CYCLE

Communicating innovation can be a risky business, particularly in organizations that value top-down decision making and traditional thinking. It is possible that your new ideas will be resisted, appropriated, or simply neglected. In fact, because organizational systems are designed in part to promote stability, you should *expect* that the promotion of new ideas will be a challenging and lengthy process, more like an extended communication campaign than a brilliant and persuasive brainstorm. That reality is not a bad thing. After all, not all ideas are good ones, and poorly conceived changes can wreak havoc on an organization's employees and customers. New employees in particular should expect to use communication competence not just to spark creativity but also to present evidence in support of innovations and to manage the risks associated with organizational change. We look to the risk negotiation cycle to help employees think through the risk management process (see Figure 9.1).

Figure 9.1 Proposing New Ideas and the Risk Negotiation Cycle

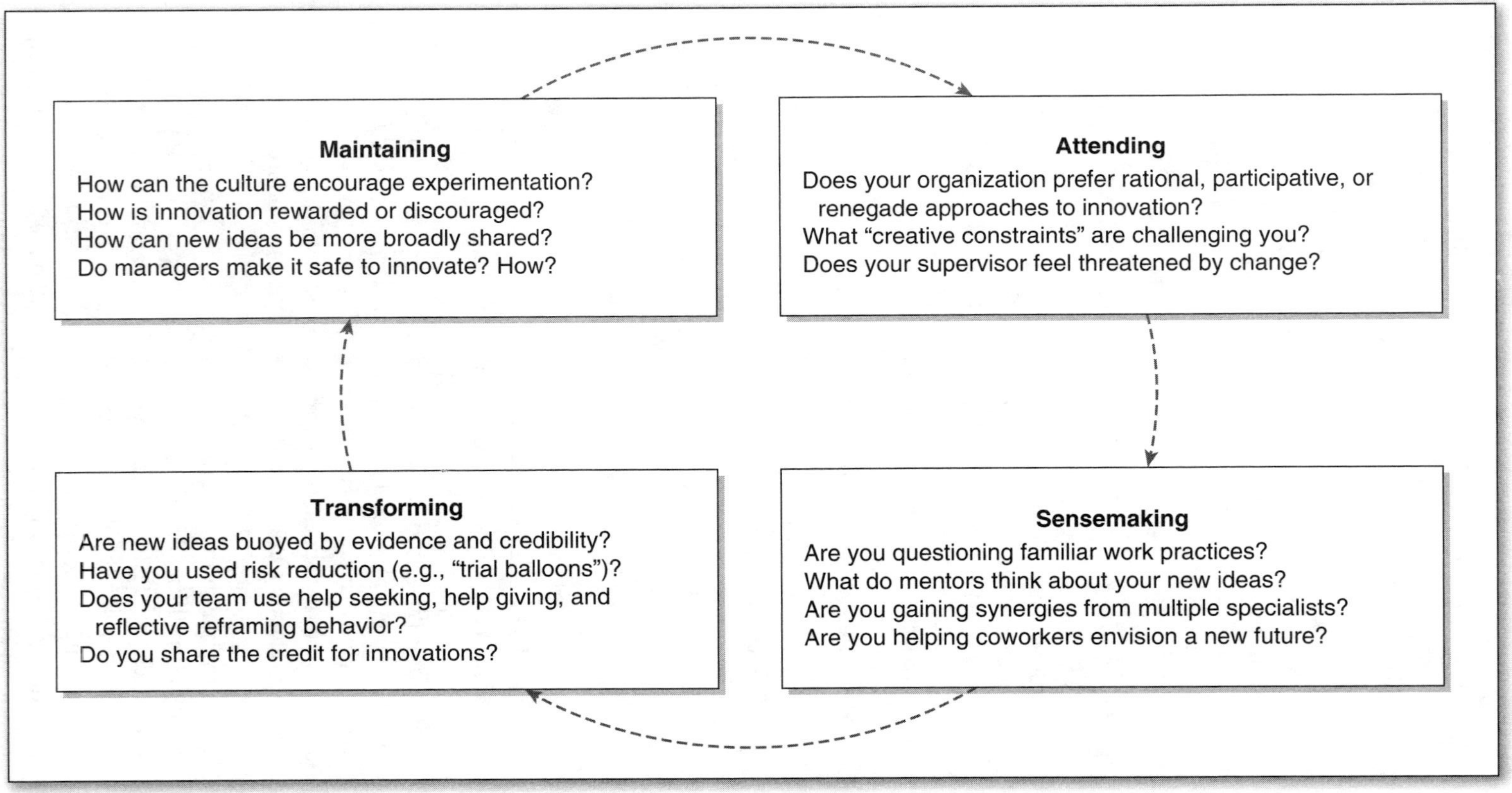

Attending

Does your organization prefer rational, participative, or renegade approaches to innovation?

What "creative constraints" are challenging you?

Does your supervisor feel threatened by change?

Sensemaking

Are you questioning familiar work practices?

What do mentors think about your new ideas?

Are you gaining synergies from multiple specialists?

Are you helping coworkers envision a new future?

Maintaining

How can the culture encourage experimentation?

How is innovation rewarded or discouraged?

How can new ideas be more broadly shared?

Do managers make it safe to innovate? How?

Transforming

Are new ideas buoyed by evidence and credibility?

Have you used risk reduction (e.g., "trial balloons")?

Does your team use help seeking, help giving, and reflective reframing behavior?

Do you share the credit for innovations?

Attending

A key message in the innovation literature is to attend to the culture of your organization. Some organizations encourage innovation and actually reward it. Others resist it. Some reward individual creativity, while others reward a collective approach through processes of help seeking, help granting, and reframing. Innovation champions adapt their approaches to organizational preferences. As we learned from the research, some organizations will respond positively to logical arguments, while others will want innovators to build consensus before making a pitch for new ideas.

Another theme is to entertain tough questions about the current status of an organization's work processes and products. Social observer Daniel Pink (2005), in his popular book *A Whole New Mind*, argues that we are entering a new age defined by abundance (consumers have nearly unlimited choices), outsourcing, and automation. To spur innovation in the face of these conditions, he suggests we ask these questions: Can someone overseas do it cheaper? Can a computer do it for you? Is what I'm offering in demand in an age of abundance? If the answers are yes, yes, and no, employees need to rethink the products and services they are providing and the work processes they are using. Pink's questions may be a version of the creative constraints used so effectively by artistic directors. In essence, American workers must increasingly challenge themselves to work in ways that are different, creative, and efficient. Like talented actors, employees who can embrace and transcend these constraints and the managers who can direct them will be highly valued in the emerging economy.

Finally, it is clear that innovators must attend to personal relationships. They recognize, for example, that some coworkers or supervisors become defensive or insecure at the prospect of change, and they adjust their tactics accordingly. Innovations are often collective efforts. Therefore, innovators must seek and offer help to fellow team members. They encourage brainstorming, share the credit, and recognize those who are willing to take risks. All of this is to say that innovators manage risk by making innovation less risky for others. They attend to relational and identity goals, as well as their own innovative impulses.

Sensemaking

Sensemaking is the process of making meaning. Interestingly, innovation requires us to put aside familiar ways of thinking, at least for the moment, to make space for creativity, ambiguity, and difference. As we learned earlier, creative collectives engage in a kind of reflective reframing, an intentional effort to question familiar or unproductive ways of problem solving. As a communicative practice, this process can take many forms. One is the answering of questions with questions. In our work as educators, we might ask, "Is it online or face-to-face communication that is more convenient for students?" But a host of other questions might spur more creative approaches to education. Do our students value efficiency over other qualities of the learning process? Can't learning be offered in *both* face-to-face and online formats? Are other formats not being considered? How can we learn from other industries that provide instructional services to large numbers of people (e.g., religious communities, newsmagazines)? As the Pump shoe design team demonstrated, creativity sometimes emerges from the brainstorming communication of very different specialists. In some cases, the key is to explore how a solution that has been designed for a much different problem (e.g., water circulation) can be applied to a new one (i.e., tennis shoe design).

Innovators use their communication to help coworkers make sense of new ideas. They do it by linking the innovation to organizational values, creating a motivating vision of what the future might be like if the new idea were accepted, and introducing the creative constraints that keep team members focused. In these ways, they help their peers manage unsettling feelings of uncertainty and offer assurance to those who fear the consequences of change. In other words, through their sensemaking communication, innovators make changes feel less risky.

Transforming

The process of innovation is inherently transformative. That is, it literally produces change in the ways an organization conducts its business. But our notion of transformation extends to the relationships and identities of organizational members. Proposing an innovation—taking the risk of questioning the status quo—can change an employee's status in an organization. The organizational member who makes a well-prepared pitch for a new idea has the opportunity to display both task-related knowledge and commitment to the organization's success. If the persuasive effort is successful, the innovator is likely to gain visibility, credibility, responsibility, and perhaps, financial recognition.

At the same time, employees who are overeager, underprepared, or highly individualistic in their approach may be less esteemed in the eyes of peers or supervisors. As we have seen, successful innovators share the credit, respect the talent, and build supportive coalitions. Interviews with innovation champions suggested that they found the process intrinsically rewarding. But they pressed for a new idea only after being convinced that it was sound. Most were aware of the risks involved but few regretted trying. Nonetheless, it is one thing to conceive of an idea and another to champion it through a lengthy process of adoption. Recall that communication of innovation is more like a communication campaign than a single persuasive episode, more like playing out an entire season than a single game.

Maintaining

We argued earlier that innovation can't be forced by management. It is not a top-down process. However, the risk of innovation has much to do with the organizational culture fostered by powerful people, the problem-solving procedures they endorse, and the rewards they provide. The key is to maintain an environment that is safe for innovation. Such an environment welcomes experimentation, encourages collective creativity, and rewards (rather than penalizes) those who question the status quo. Rather than keep employees confined within narrow roles and highly discrete organizational units, innovation-safe organizations encourage cross-fertilization. They draw more broadly on the human resources that form the heart of any innovation effort and find synergies among people with differing areas of expertise.

At the individual level, employees must examine their own communicative reactions to proposed innovation. For some, the knee-jerk reaction is to reject change, to assume that familiar ways of doing things are the best ways. Of course, traditions sometimes serve good purposes. It is quite possible to embrace change too uncritically or for all of the wrong reasons. Nevertheless, employees may be exhibiting unreasonable rigidity when they react to change proposals with superficial criticism, defensiveness, unrealistic doom, or "here we go again" cynicism. In some cases, well-intended innovation champions are derailed due to professional jealousy, insecurity, or a simple lack of open-mindedness to the possibility that someone else has a better idea. When these risk-aversive responses predominate in the workforce, the organization itself is put at risk. For if an organization fails to innovate, one of its competitors will.

❖ CONCLUSION

The concepts discussed in this chapter have very real implications for a host of American industries. We have mentioned the U.S. automotive industry, which is currently in a dire financial condition. Other examples come for various "green industries" in which companies are seeking new and improved products and more profitable business models; utility companies are scrambling to integrate solar and wind energy into their traditional models of delivering electricity. No company has succeeded in developing a truly long-lasting and affordable battery for running electric cars. Finally, the local newspaper is becoming a fading institution in America (see below), as industry executives struggle to make money in a world where most people find their news, free of charge, on the Internet.

In closing this chapter, we take a closer look at the contrast between Google, the massively successful Internet company, and the rapidly fading newspaper industry (see Textbox 9.6). Look for the concepts presented in this chapter as you consider why Google has been so successful and why even the most storied newspapers are struggling so mightily.

Textbox 9.6   Google and the Print Newspaper Industry

"Incumbents very seldom invent the future"

—Erich Schmidt, Google CEO

This quote was reported by *New York Times* columnist Maureen Dowd (2009), who interviewed the Google CEO about the fading prospects of the print newspaper industry. Google, Craigslist, and other companies make newspaper content available to Internet users for free, so readers have no incentive to buy the actual newspaper, and advertisers have little incentive to advertise in it. The nation's newspapers are closing at a rapid rate, and many are limiting publication to just a few days a week. Many argue that the loss of newspapers would be a crushing blow to our democracy because newspaper reporters do the investigative work required to filter good from bad information. Through their coverage of the local political process, newspapers support our democracy by keeping voters informed and politicians accountable. But Schmidt's message was blunt: If newspapers are to survive, they must invent new products, just as Google has done with its steady stream of innovative search tools, such as Google Street View. Thus far, traditional newspapers have been at a loss in imagining what those new products might be. Most papers have created their own Web sites, where much of their content is simply made available without charge. Those who have tried to charge for access to special content, such as the columns written by famous journalists, have not been successful.

In contrast, Google continues to add market share and new employees. It produces a steady stream of new and appealing products. How does Google do it? Well, for one thing, Google encourages employees to spend up to 20% of their time working on new ideas of personal interest. Many of these informal inventions are cultivated by Google to become new products. Marissa Mayer, Google's 32-year-old vice president for search products, recently explained Google's "nine rules for innovation." Her comments were widely reported on the Internet (e.g., Salter, 2008).

1. Innovation, not perfection. It is OK to make mistakes; to produce some "duds."

2. Ideas come from everywhere. All employees suggest and comment on innovations.

3. A license to pursue your dreams. Google engineers spend about 20% of their time working on whatever they want. They are trusted to build creative products.

4. Morph products, don't kill them. Failed but promising ideas are reworked to meet user needs.

5. Share as much information as you can. Ideas are constantly shared on the company's intranet, so like-minded innovators can find each other easily.

6. Users, users, users. If you create something that users really like, they will pay for it (or advertisers will pay to reach your community of users).

7. Data are apolitical. To decide which design or product is best, Google pilot tests them on a sample of users. The research results determine which design is deployed.

8. Creativity loves constraints. Employees are challenged to create new products within demanding design constraints.

9. You're brilliant, we're hiring. The company consistently seeks people who have new ideas and want to make them a reality in Google's innovation-friendly environment.

In terms of how organizations attend to risk, we can see differences between Google and the newspaper industry. For example, Google seems to be responsive to changing consumer preferences. How could newspapers do the same? How could they respond to current trends such as social media, citizen journalism, and new information delivery technologies? Who are the "users" of existing and potential newspaper services? And what new products might they want?

Consider the rational, participative, and renegade approaches to innovation. Are there elements of these in Google's nine rules of innovation? What creative constraints are faced by Google? The newspaper industry?

With regard to sensemaking, Google fosters a climate of information sharing and collaboration. We suggested that "creative collectives" draw synergies from the contributions of various specialists. How might the local newspaper put a creative collective into place? What types of employees could be enlisted? What functional units should be linked? Could newspapers learn from other industries? As we learned from the research on creative teams, reflective reframing is a kind of communication that promotes innovative thinking. How could newspapers rethink existing services and products? For example, could the local newspaper become a social networking site, or could the actual paper be reduced in size so that it is more portable?

Google seems to be particularly successful at transforming the risk associated with innovation. What evidence of help seeking and help giving is apparent at Google? We learned from theater directors that a key to innovation is trusting the talent. How does Google implement this idea?

What kinds of talent are available in a newspaper organization, and how could it facilitate innovation? Does Google display a tolerance for failure and false starts? How does this contribute to innovation? Imagine working at the local newspaper. What if you wanted to champion the social networking idea mentioned above. Which risk reduction tactics would you use? What championing behaviors would prove valuable?

And finally, Google maintains an environment that not only makes innovation seem relatively safe but views it as an optimal outcome. Is innovation rewarded at Google? How so? What steps does Google take to encourage experimentation? Google has put in place systems to share innovation and to connect innovators. What are these? Google chooses not to micromanage every minute of its employees' working lives. What message does this communicate to employees? Google consistently attracts innovative employees. What might the newspaper industry do to attract innovators?

❖ REFERENCES

Dowd, M. (2009, April 14). Dinosaur at the gate. *New York Times*. Retrieved from http://www.nytimes.com/2009/04/15/opinion/15dowd.html?_r=1

Fine, A. (2006). *Momentum: Igniting social change in the connected age*. San Francisco: Jossey-Bass.

Getz, I., & Robinson, A. G. (2003). Innovate or die: Is that a fact? *Creativity and Innovation Management, 12*, 130–136.

Hargadon, A. B., & Bechky, B. A. (2006). When collections of creatives become creative collectives: A field study of problem solving at work. *Organization Science, 17*, 484–504.

Howell, J. M., & Higgins, C. A. (1990). Champions of change: Identifying, understanding, and supporting champions of technological innovations. *Organizational Dynamics, 19*, 40–55.

Howell, J. M., & Shea, C. M. (2006). Effects of champion behavior, team potency, and external communication activities on predicting team performance. *Group & Organization Management, 31*, 180–211.

Ibbotson, P., & Darso, L. (2008). Directing creativity: The art and craft of leadership. *Journal of Management and Creativity, 14*, 548–560.

Nanda, T., & Singh, T. P. (2009). Determinants of creativity and innovation in the workplace: A comprehensive review. *International Journal of Technology Policy and Management, 9*, 84–106.

Peters, T. (1999). *The circle of innovation*. New York: Vintage.

Pink, D. (2005). *A whole new mind: Why right-brainers will rule the future*. New York: Penguin.

Salter, C. (2008, March 18). 9 rules of innovation from Google. Retrieved from http://specials.rediff.com/money/2008/mar/11google1.htm

Thompson, L. L., & Hoon-Seok, C. (2006). *Creativity and innovation in organizational teams*. New York: Routledge.

10

Responding to Difficult Team Members

It has been brought to my attention many times that one of my team teachers does not help out the students, especially the bilingual students who are struggling with language. Most of the students who have complained are hardworking students who end up getting Ds and Fs in her room. Many parents have also expressed their concern to me and my other team members. We have asked them to contact my supervisor/principal about the situation, but I feel they are intimidated. She [the teacher in question] has an excellent knowledge base, yet seems to have a hard time helping out the kids. My supervisor has known this, but I have seen no change.

Lesley, age 59

A nyone who has been part of a work team can relate to Lesley's concerns. How do you get a difficult or poor-performing team member to contribute to the team and the organization? Because many organizations have moved to team-based structures, employees find themselves highly interdependent on coworkers. Our success as employees is tied to collective efforts and achievements. We depend on the performance of our team to achieve personal, collective, and organizational goals. This trend presents an interesting challenge for employees, as not all organizational members are comfortable working in teams. In fact, some people are downright reluctant to do so.

This chapter explores the risks associated with difficult team members. Ideally, management would step in and make the necessary personnel adjustments when members experience serious conflicts. However, as our scenario above reveals, this is not always the case. Management either fails to get involved or decides not to get involved. Members are expected to work through these issues as they strengthen team unity and cohesion. This expectation may be quite justified, as dealing with problematic members is an essential team development task. Nevertheless, difficult team members can undermine performance and morale. In other words, they put the team at risk.

Lesley and her teammates can choose several strategies for managing the risk created by the problematic teacher. They can ostracize her with the hope that she may eventually quit or resign. They can confront her with the hope that she will begin to pull her weight. They can threaten to sanction her if she does not shape up. Or they can work collaboratively to help her develop the necessary skills and work practices required to perform her job more effectively. These approaches vary widely. Each has the potential to exacerbate or reduce risk. What if the ostracized team member is comfortable being on the periphery of the team, only minimally filling his or her responsibilities? What if the member reacts negatively to being confronted and counters with increasingly difficult behavior? In these instances, the communication strategy used by members could put the team at risk of losing productivity and cohesion. What if the team invests the time and energy necessary to help the poor-performing member improve, but the team member still fails to meet the expectations of the team? Here the team risks time, energy, and resources that could have been devoted elsewhere.

❖ WHY IS RESPONDING TO DIFFICULT TEAM MEMBERS IMPORTANT?

The Prevalence of Teams

Assessments over the past two decades show that organizations are generally moving toward more team-based approaches. For example, a national survey of *Fortune* 1000 companies conducted from 1987 to 1993 revealed that the percentage of organizations reporting the use of self-managed teams jumped from 27% to 68% (Lawler, Mohrman, & Ledford, 1995). In another study, 48% of randomly sampled organizations reported using teams in some capacity. Moreover, ongoing or standing teams were used more often than ad hoc teams brought together to address particular issues (Devine, Clayton, Philips, Dunford, & Melner, 1999). Thus, it has become more likely that employees will be asked or tasked with working in a team-based setting as teams have become recognized as a powerful tool for achieving organizational success. See the case of the Rx Team at Southwest Airlines in Textbox 10.1 for an example of how effective successful teams can be.

Textbox 10.1	The Power of Teams: The Rx Team at Southwest Airlines

To stay competitive in the airline industry amid rising fuel costs, new competitors, and more complex and costly operations, Southwest Airlines introduced the Rx Team. The team operates as part of a larger Rx Program that centers on tracking performance by the hour rather than by the month. The Rx Team, which started with seven handpicked employees, conducts "process mapping," or the measurement and analysis of everyday operations such as how long passengers wait in line to check in for a flight and how long it takes them to board the plane after the last passenger from the previous flight has deplaned.

Employees spend 1 week training in process mapping before joining the team. The team then spends a month in a designated airport, shadowing airport employees and collecting and recording data with stopwatches and clipboards to develop benchmarks for various operations. The team then engages employees in brainstorming sessions to develop ideas to address concerns the team noted in their data collection and analysis. Subsequent months are devoted to testing the viable ideas generated through the earlier process with the intention of implementing those that show the greatest promise.

The achievements at the Phoenix airport attest to the success of the team. After a visit from the Rx Team, on-time performance was up 11%, passenger wait times were cut from 31 minutes to 13.7 minutes, and the average wait time for passengers to receive their luggage declined by 20%.

The Permeability of Teams

We find it useful to consider organizational teams from the bona fide group perspective (Putnam & Stohl, 1990). This perspective suggests that to best understand how a team operates, one must consider its boundaries, natural context, and unique identity. Therefore, a management team will differ from a sales team, and both will differ from a production team. However, all may influence one another because teams have permeable boundaries. So a change in the management team may affect the sales and production teams or vice versa. Equally important, a change in the external environment may influence team performance. An economic downturn, for instance, may cause middle managers to worry about whether their positions will be eliminated. This type of preoccupation can alter performance and cooperation among members of a management team. Similarly, a highly publicized recall may make members of a production team extra diligent. Even events occurring in members' personal and family relationships can affect how a work team functions.

Mutual Accountability in Teams

When employees work in a team, they are accountable not only for themselves but also for the contributions and efforts of others. This is so because team performance exceeds the sum of individual contributions and because performance measures take into account collective rather than individual work products (Katzenbach & Smith, 1998). Thus, it is to the benefit of team members to work together effectively and collaboratively to be as productive as possible. Yet not all members will be comfortable or happy working on a team or will work collaboratively as team members. Moreover, "bad apples" or problematic team members can seriously hamper team effectiveness, leading management in some cases to disband teams (Felps, Mitchell, & Byington, 2006). Thus, the stakes for working effectively on a team are high for all team members. But not all members contribute equally or well. Those who fail to contribute are sometimes referred to as social loafers (see Textbox 10.2).

Textbox 10.2	Troublesome Team Members and Social Loafing

Teams often have to deal with underperforming members who practice *social loafing*. "Social loafing is the reduction in motivation and effort when individuals work collectively compared with when they work individually" (Karau & Williams, 1993, p. 681). Karau and Williams (1993) found that, across studies, group members consistently engaged in social loafing and that they were more likely to loaf when they expected their coworkers to perform well. This can present some serious challenges for a team. These challenges can be compounded further when the social loafer fails to recognize the lack of his or her contributions to the group. Generally, people are unable to recognize or unwilling to acknowledge that they loaf in groups. Fortunately, social loafing can be curbed when employees work in close-knit groups and possibly eliminated when teammates value their workplace teams.

Identification in Teams

The common wisdom suggests that employees are more productive in teams because they develop a sense of belonging and shared identity.

Barker and Tompkins (1994) found this to be the case in their study of workplace teams. They also observed that long-term employees reported identifying with their teams considerably more than mid-range and short-term employees. Furthermore, they found that employees reported greater loyalty to their team than to their organization regardless of job tenure. One's identification with an organization or team "creates a very important social identity for many individuals" (Craig, 2007, p. 125), an identity that emerges through the communication practices of the group or organization. Many of these communication practices are not formal but rather informal or "backstage" interactions—that is, interactions that take place among team members outside of the formal team communication and functions. An examination of health care teams revealed that backstage communication, which involved team members' make possessive sharing of and requests for both information and opinions, facilitated the achievement of team goals (Ellingson, 2003). Thus, working on a team can have a direct relationship to how we feel about our organization, our coworkers, and ourselves.

Obviously, working in teams is a challenge. Having a dysfunctional team member can make the experience even more challenging. Stohl and Schell (1991) suggested that teams plagued by dysfunctional members exhibit the following characteristics:

> (a) decision making procedures are often complicated and compromised as a result of preventive actions designed to avoid or accommodate one member; (b) issues are redefined against the backdrop of the member; (c) a great deal of energy is expended talking about the particular organizational member (whether or not he or she is present or directly involved in the decision-making process); (d) members become so worn out in dealing with issues related to this one member that they often fail to deal with task issues and priorities become confused; and (e) members often leave such meetings angry, depressed, or frustrated with both the individual and the group. (pp. 91–92)

The human component of teams makes them viable but also vulnerable. In the field of robotics (see Textbox 10.3), researchers are attempting to capture the viability of what makes human teams successful (e.g., compensating for one another when necessary) while avoiding those aspects that make teams vulnerable (e.g., personality conflicts).

A group of scholars recently reported about advances in robotics by testing a team of robots in a box-pushing task (Pham, Awadalla, & Eldukhrl, 2007). In this work, the scholars developed the infrastructure necessary for a robot team to perform missions over long periods of time and in changing environments. Moreover, robots in this system adapted their actions without human intervention and monitored and evaluated their performance and the performance of their teammates. This mutual monitoring allowed the robots to compensate when a team member's capability degraded.

Can we be replaced by robot teams? Perhaps for some tasks, but certainly not for all of them. Keep in mind that a team of computer scientists worked to develop the infrastructure necessary to instruct the robots in teamwork in the first place. We suspect that this human team, like all teams, suffered and benefited from the dynamics of teamwork.

❖ KEY RESEARCH STUDIES

The Characteristics of Difficult Team Members

What constitutes a difficult team member? One typology suggests difficult team members can be classified in terms of negative interpersonal behaviors as either *withholders of effort*, or those who intentionally shirk responsibilities and depend on or take credit for the efforts of others. *Affectively negative* group members consistently express negative mood states, attitudes, or both, and *interpersonal deviants* are those who violate interpersonal norms of respect (Felps et al., 2006). These negative interpersonal behaviors lead to particular negative outcomes that teams must address. Withholders of effort create equity issues within teams, affectively negative team members threaten the emotional stability of teams and team members, and interpersonal deviants undermine and damage trust among group members.

Each of these negative interpersonal behaviors appears in the stories posted to simplyfired.com. Consider this fictionalized narrative, which we have modeled after typical complaints posted about difficult teammates.

Mateo worked in the customer service division of a large credit card company alongside a coworker who claimed to suffer from back problems. Citing his back troubles, Dwight left his desk for extended periods throughout the day. As a result, the team had to pick up the slack by handling his customers. Despite his teammates' help, Dwight was impatient with customers and often left them on hold for too long. Dwight's low productivity was excused by management because they were aware of his supposed medical limitations. Mateo and his coworkers began to feel as if Dwight was taking advantage of the situation. In addition, Dwight complained constantly about company policy. When teammates defended the company, he accused them of being "brownnosers." It all came to a head one weekend when a supervisor questioned Dwight about his tendency to complain within earshot of customers. Dwight lost his temper and let loose a series of expletives. He was fired on the spot. While Mateo was pleased to see him go, he was disappointed that it hadn't happened sooner.

Dwight appears to exhibit all three negative interpersonal behaviors (Felps et al., 2006). He withholds effort and expects his teammates to cover for him. In addition, Dwight is persistently negative and critical of the company and coworkers. If this were not enough to put the difficult team member's employment in jeopardy, he displays interpersonally deviant behavior when he disrespects a supervisor.

Making Attributions About Poor Performance

Poor-performing individuals in interdependent teams affect both the behavior of other team members and overall team achievements (Taggar & Neubert, 2004). How employees account for the attributions they make about team members then plays a key role in how employees respond to poor-performing teammates. LePine and Van Dyne (2001) provided a rather comprehensive model for how workgroups respond to poor-performing members. They reasoned that the presence of a poor-performing team member sets the attribution process in motion. Attributions in turn lead to emotional and cognitive reactions and behavioral responses on the part of team members to the poor performer.

Attributions have three dimensions: locus of causality, controllability, and stability. *Locus of causality* concerns whether the cause of an event is the actor (internal attribution) or the situation (external attribution). Judging the locus of causality serves to focus people's attention with regard to assigning initial responsibility for poor performance. Is poor performance due to a characteristic or quality of the employee such as selfishness or to mitigating circumstances such as lack of sleep due to having a newborn at home? Interestingly, when observers attribute poor performance to external causes, they feel empathy and sympathy toward their coworkers, and they spend little time making further inferences about coworkers' behaviors. In contrast, internal attributions lead employees to seek further information about the character of the individual, which involves consideration of the controllability and stability dimensions.

Another attributional variable is *controllability*. Is a teammate's poor performance due to poor training (uncontrollable) or to low motivation (controllable)? The former leads to empathy and efforts to help or redress the situation, the latter to anger. *Stability*, in turn, refers to whether the cause of an event appears to be permanent (stable) or variable over time and context (unstable). Is low motivation relatively stable in all situations or variable, only appearing with regard to certain tasks? When peers attribute greater degrees of stability to poor performance, they are less likely to intervene in an effort to correct the behavior. Conversely, there are greater possibilities for behavioral alteration when team members perceive that behavior is unstable.

Jobschmob.com allows employees to voice their frustrations in an anonymous online forum. Difficult team members are a common topic of concern. The following post is fictionalized, but it resembles many of those we found.

> Ashanti worked on one of two sales teams at a large auto dealership. To ensure that the sales floor was fully covered at all times, the sales manager asked everyone to coordinate their lunch schedules. Everyone complied with exception of Carl, a disgruntled senior member of the sales team. Carl refused on the grounds that he had earned the right to take lunch whenever he wanted. Because as Carl sees it, he's the star of the sales force—management needs him, and sales would tank if it weren't for his efforts. One afternoon, Ashanti, knowing that they were short staffed, asked Carl if he would cover for her while she took her assigned lunch break. Carl was annoyed by her request and refused to help out. Shortly thereafter, he left for his own lunch break without making sure the sales floor was covered. Ashanti was incensed and proceeded to let her teammates know that she thought Carl was uncooperative and selfish—a real detriment to the sales team.

The attribution about being a difficult team member in this case clearly stems from an internal attribution about the uncooperative nature of Carl. Moreover, Carl's behavior appears to occur in situations that are within his control (i.e., when to take lunch versus cover the sales floor). Carl's continued overestimation of his value to the group displays behavioral stability; that is, his displays of bravado recur over time. Thus, it is not surprising that Ashanti is fed up with Carl and prefers not to have him as a teammate.

The Importance of Roles

According to Stohl and Schell (1991), dysfunction in teams stems from the role a member fulfills in a group and the interplay with other group members. Personality traits alone rarely account for dysfunction. The dysfunctional member behaves in a way that others perceive to be socially inappropriate and organizationally problematic. The authors offer three behavioral habits that potentially lead to dysfunction. *Interpretive omnipotence* occurs when one operates from the premise that he or she has a privileged claim to a singular explanation for what is appropriate or correct. It manifests in dismissing and trivializing others' points of view and in displaying disdain and self-righteousness. *Heroic stance* refers to an authoritarian and paternalistic posture one assumes and espouses in the best interest of the group while casting alternative perspectives as ill-advised and self-serving. *Undifferentiated passion* involves intense devotion to the group that exceeds the time and energy demanded by one's role in the group, thereby positioning other members as lacking in commitment and concern for the group.

Keyton (1999) highlighted the importance of distinguishing primary and supporting roles in dysfunctional workgroups. She used the terms *primary provoker* to label the difficult team member and *secondary provokers* to identify those who either provoke or avoid the primary provoker. Peers earn the secondary provoker distinction when they create and maintain ineffective relationships with the primary provoker. For example, a group member becomes the team's scapegoat after other workgroup members repeatedly point fingers at the targeted employee. In this way, the dysfunction is created and reinforced through social interaction patterns, through the acceptance and performance of particular roles.

Because of the interactive nature of roles, the effects of difficult team members can quickly escalate to entire groups. Felps et al. (2006) describe how this happens. *Additive defensiveness* occurs when a difficult team member deals poorly with multiple members of a team. When this occurs, defensiveness toward the difficult team member compounds and over time becomes additive. *Spillover effects* arise when team members model the behavior of others who find dealing with the team member in question difficult. Thus, when team members witness others ostracizing or confronting a difficult team member, they may do the same.

Responding to Poor-Performing Peers

LePine and Van Dyne (2001) identified four different responses to underperforming peers: train, motivate, reject, and compensate. Peers are most likely to *train* an underperforming teammate when they attribute poor performance to an inability to master a specific task due to poor training rather than the person's capacity or lack of effort. The appropriate response then is to train, teach, and instruct the team member better.

Peers *motivate* when they perceive that poor-performing team members display inconsistent behavior yet appear in control of their actions. Communicatively, this may take the form of providing pep talks or threats. For example, peers will become frustrated with the employee who comes to work tired and performs poorly on the workdays following his band's late-night gigs. They want the band member to recognize that he is also a team member and that his behavior affects the entire group. Performing intermittently takes away from group effectiveness and moves the team to motivate the coworker to perform more consistently.

But what if a team believes that the behavior underlying poor performance is in fact consistent and under the control of the offending team member? They can become angered in these cases and, as a consequence, tend to engage in behaviors that ostracize or *reject* the coworker. One approach is to criticize and complain about the team member in the presence of a supervisor, other team members, or directly to the poor performer with the intention of eliminating him or her from the team. Eliminating a team member can be risky and should be undertaken with considerable caution (see Textbox 10.4 for some important considerations).

Textbox 10.4   Replacing a Difficult Team Member?

According to Cook and Goff (2002), if team members are deciding about the removal of a difficult member, they must first give some thought to the following considerations.

1. Does the team need the expertise that the person offers?

2. Is the team in a position in its own formation and its work that a new person can be accepted?

3. Is there any person in the organization who has the qualities that are needed and who can adapt to the existing team structure?

Finally, teams may feel at times that it is necessary to *compensate* for a poor-performing member by helping with certain duties. This can happen in two possible conditions. First, it will occur with internal attributions deemed to be unstable and uncontrollable. For example, peers will be sympathetic to a team member whose performance is suffering because of a chronic medical condition that on occasion disrupts a fellow team member's work. Compensation also can occur when external attributions explain a coworker's performance, initially casting it as something beyond his or her control. For example, peers will compensate when a dip in a coworker's sales numbers results from one of her major accounts filing for bankruptcy.

Stohl and Schell (1991) provided several means by which employees deal with dysfunctional group members. For example, when employees are motivated to protect themselves and reluctant to engage the dysfunctional group member, they may practice *abdicating* (i.e., seeking someone else to help with the dysfunctional group member), *evading* or avoiding interaction with the dysfunctional group member while waiting for someone else to fix the problem, or simply *diminishing investment* in the group by "checking out" emotionally and minimizing contact with group members. In contrast, if they desire to preserve the group, they may practice reframing, discounting, and repairing. *Reframing* involves reinterpreting the dysfunctional group member's behavior in a way that makes it more palatable and tolerable, whereas *discounting* entails diminishing the effect the dysfunctional member's behavior has on the group. *Repairing*, on the other hand, concerns efforts to help other group members feel better about themselves and the group.

Effective Communication Skills in Teams and Workgroups

The opposite of dysfunction in workgroups is effectiveness. According to Hirokawa and Keyton (1995, p. 435), group effectiveness is a composite of individual, group, and organizational properties. The group properties are particularly relevant with regard to dealing with a difficult team member. These include the following:

1. Setting group goals that are compatible with individual goals

2. A collective commitment to performance excellence

3. Norms that emphasize group achievement and success

4. Cooperative and collaborative attitudes among group members

5. Competent group leadership

Textbox 10.5   Successful Workgroup Communication Skills

Hawkins and Fillion (1999) interviewed personnel managers to determine those communication skills that were deemed most important to successful workgroup contexts. The following is a list of the top five skills that emerged from their work.

1. Practicing effective listening

2. Understanding one's role in the workgroup

3. Actively contributing to the workgroup

4. Asking clear questions to attain necessary information and feedback

5. Establishing and maintaining good professional rapport with one's fellow workgroup members

---

The assets of effective groups reveal communication practices that can be used to address dysfunction in workgroups. For example, a frank discussion with a difficult team member about goal compatibility or group norms could help curb dysfunction in a team. In other work, Hawkins and Fillion (1999) interviewed personnel managers and determined that key communication skills deemed most important to successful workgroup contexts involved basic interaction skills such as listening and asking appropriate questions but also included more complex skills such as building rapport with fellow workgroup members (see Textbox 10.5). Coopman's (2001) investigation of democratic communication practices in health care teams showed that involvement in decision making, listening among team members, and sharing feelings between team members were strongly linked to perceptions of team cohesiveness. Thus, there are communication options available to us for dealing with a difficult team member (see Textbox 10.6 for a list of those covered in this chapter).

Textbox 10.6   Communication Options

Responding to Poor Performance (LePine & Van Dyne, 2001)

    Motivate (e.g., pep talk, threaten)
    Teach/train (e.g., instruct, explain)
    Reject (e.g., complain, criticize)
    Compensate

Reacting to Dysfunctional Group Members (Stohl & Schell, 1991)

   Abdicating
   Evading
   Diminishing investment
   Reframing
   Discounting
   Repairing

Effective Team Communication (Coopman, 2001; Hirokawa & Keyton, 1995)

   Setting compatible group and individual goals
   Committing to performance excellence
   Developing norms that emphasize group achievement and success
   Fostering cooperative and collaborative attitudes
   Ensuring involvement in decision making
   Listening
   Sharing feelings

❖ RESPONDING TO A DIFFICULT TEAM MEMBER AND THE RISK NEGOTIATION CYCLE

Dealing with a difficult team or workgroup member can be risky. Confronting or negatively responding to a difficult team member can result in continued strained relationships, heightened emotional states that detract from team performance, and withdrawal behaviors from some members of the group. In contrast, if the risk is managed effectively, the team may benefit in terms of cohesion, motivation, and perhaps even performance. We use the risk negotiation cycle (see Figure 10.1) to analyze the factors that heighten or reduce risk in interactions with difficult team members.

Attending

When attending to risk, the first task is to determine if the team's cohesion and performance are threatened. If they are, then employees will need to address the situation. They can begin by asking whether the issue with the difficult team member is performance based or personality based. If poor performance is the concern, members should examine the attributions they have made about the difficult coworker. Perhaps they believe the performance issue is uncontrollable and

Figure 10.1 Responding to a Difficult Team Member (DTM) and the Risk Negotiation Cycle

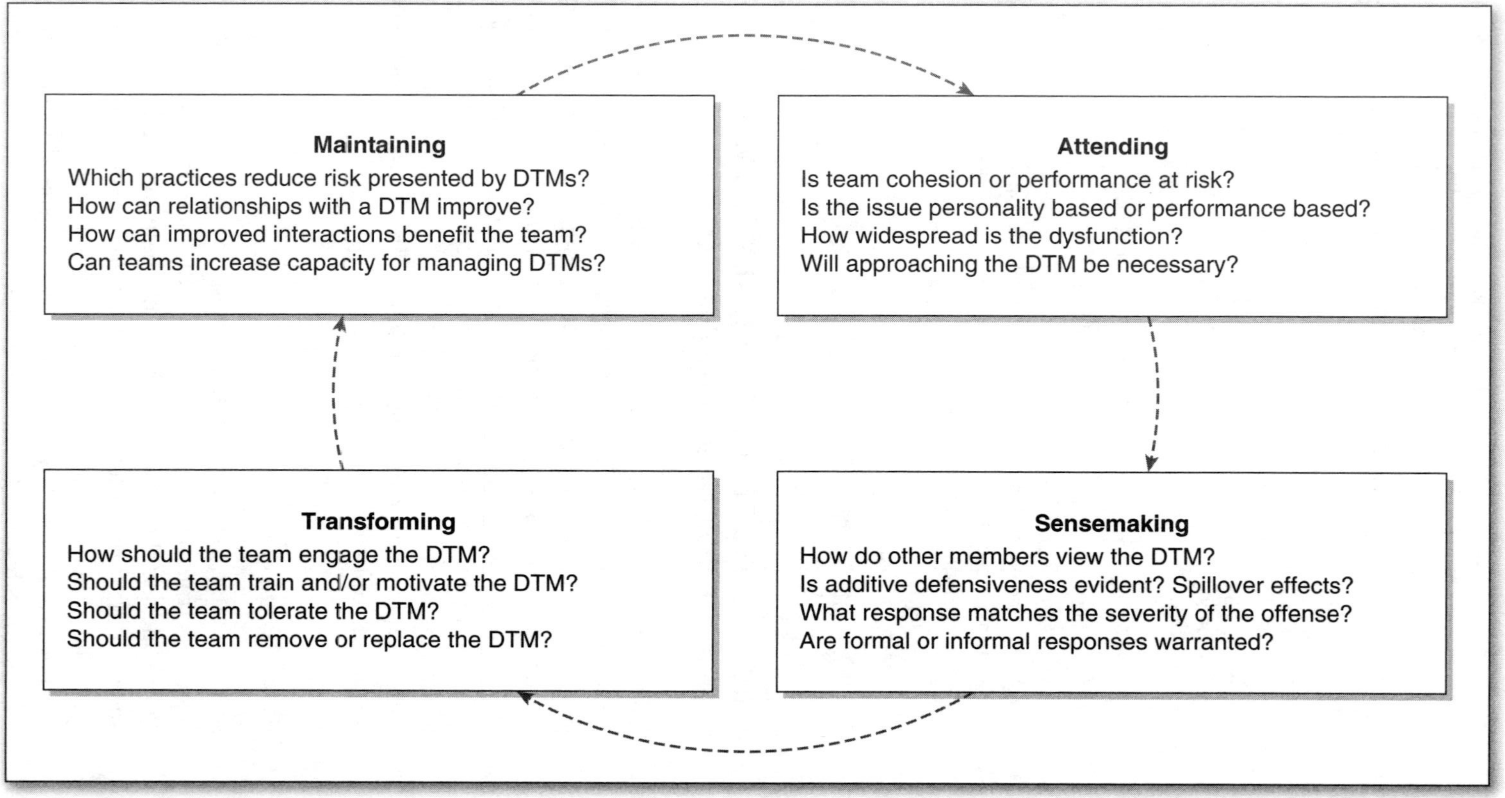

Attending

Is team cohesion or performance at risk?
Is the issue personality based or performance based?
How widespread is the dysfunction?
Will approaching the DTM be necessary?

Sensemaking

How do other members view the DTM?
Is additive defensiveness evident? Spillover effects?
What response matches the severity of the offense?
Are formal or informal responses warranted?

Maintaining

Which practices reduce risk presented by DTMs?
How can relationships with a DTM improve?
How can improved interactions benefit the team?
Can teams increase capacity for managing DTMs?

Transforming

How should the team engage the DTM?
Should the team train and/or motivate the DTM?
Should the team tolerate the DTM?
Should the team remove or replace the DTM?

unstable (e.g., an employee is late because she had to take an ailing parent to the emergency room). In this instance, the performance issue is unlikely to affect the group. In contrast, the behavior of the chronically late band member mentioned earlier is more problematic, and it will require a communicative response.

Once team members have determined that the group is truly at risk, they need to assess the extent of potential damage to team morale and cohesion. How extensive is the dysfunction in the team? And perhaps more important, how much of it can be linked to the disruption presented by the difficult team member? The team will want to determine if inequity, negative emotions, and/or damaged trust are present. For example, the group may be experiencing inequity because they work with a team member who routinely slacks on his responsibilities and often takes credit for others' work. Perhaps there is a member of the work group or team that employees no longer trust because she fails to respect the team, attacks team members in front of coworkers, and criticizes peers behind their backs. When the dysfunction is widespread and the difficult team member is clearly implicated, employees should consider engaging him or her. In contrast, if the dysfunction is minimal and not always linked to the member, confrontation may only make the situation worse.

Sensemaking

Before confronting a difficult team member, employees should initiate discussions with peers to affirm their perceptions of risk. Are their perceptions shared by peers who enjoy some degree of emotional distance from the trying situation? Do other team members feel anger as well? Or are they more sympathetic to the difficult team member? Perhaps our teammates know something about the team member's motives and external circumstances. They may know, for example, that a group member has been preoccupied and agitated because she is going through a divorce and custody battle. Sensemaking reveals the biases behind our perceptions and encourages us to review the evidence. It may keep us from reacting too quickly or harshly and encourage us to manage risk wisely. Our peers may help us be empathetic, patient, and willing to overlook smaller infractions in the interest of larger goals.

In contrast, our interactions with peers may reveal evidence of additive defensiveness and spillover effects. Coworkers may find the difficult team member's behavior to be problematic and threatening to team well-being. Are these effects mild, severe, or something in between? With workgroup peers, we can explore alternatives for managing the risks presented by the difficult team member. In less severe cases, employees on a team might suggest informal communication techniques. One approach would be for the team leader to convey the concerns quietly during a private lunchtime conversation. In more severe cases, there may be formal sanctions in place that would be applicable. For instance, team members could identify and report a poor-performing team member in a multisource feedback process (see Chapter 2).

Transforming

Teams transform risk when they take action to deal with a difficult team member. Can the issue be resolved through increased training? Can the team teach the difficult team member how to improve his or her performance? Can the member learn improved group interaction skills? For example, the team might instruct a disruptive peer to show restraint and to practice effective turn taking in team discussions. Should the team motivate the member through pep talks or possibly threats? Pep talks, if effective, can transform risk because they may lead to behavioral or performance corrections on the part of the member without appearing too threatening. Direct threats, although more risky, have a certain shock value. They transform risk by forcing a member to reflect on the serious consequences of his or her dysfunctional behavior.

In some cases, a team may need to tolerate difficult members because they make necessary and valuable contributions. In such instances, employees might launch repair efforts to bolster team morale (e.g., planning a night for the group to meet for happy hour). It might be helpful if peers collectively discount the effects of the difficult team member's behaviors. This occurs, for example, when groups agree to tolerate chronic tardiness, self-indulgent storytelling, or occasional tactlessness. The may also reframe the impact the difficult team member has had on the group. For example, a colleague's enduring stubbornness could be reinterpreted as a valuable check on hasty decision making. These strategies can be transformative in that they provide momentum for the group to move forward while sidestepping the risk associated with dysfunctional member behavior.

Another potential route to transforming risk may involve group efforts to remove the difficult team member. This may be the appropriate response when members suspect that further confrontation will lead to additional decline in team effectiveness and morale—and when no measure of training or motivation seems to change or improve dysfunctional behavior patterns. However, a team should give full consideration to the risk associated with losing the skill set of the problematic team member, the likelihood of finding a replacement, and the difficulty of socializing a new member. If removal is imminent, the team can draw management's attention to the difficult team member's disruptiveness in the hope that the offender will be removed. Team members also can communicate in ways that signal that the difficult member is no longer welcome in the group (e.g., through limiting access to group meetings, social events, etc.). This strategy transforms risk by increasing the likelihood that the difficult team member will depart of his or her own accord. Of course, not all difficult team members will go easily or quietly. Thus, a combination of alerts to management and exclusionary cues may be effective.

Maintaining

A team can maintain risk at acceptable levels when they successfully encourage a difficult team member to become more active, to be a better contributor, and to be less disruptive. This may involve bringing competing individual and group goals into alignment, socializing members to achievement norms of the team, or fostering collaborative and cooperative attitudes among group members. It also may take the form of ensuring that all members, regardless of previous history and role enactment, listen well to each other, share their feelings openly, and participate equally in decision making.

Careful and conscientious efforts to deal effectively and fairly with difficult team members can lead to optimization. Previously threatened relationships may improve and strengthen as a result. For example, the team member who previously displayed verbal aggressiveness toward colleagues might experience marked improvements in her relationships with peers once she interacts more constructively. As a result, team productivity, morale, and effectiveness stand to benefit. An additional optimal outcome will be the team's capacity for dealing with difficult team members in the future, which could be valuable as team membership ebbs and flows over time. Individual members and the collective team may develop norms regarding how to deal effectively with difficult team members. For example, members will learn and understand the value of talking with one another to confirm their attributions about poor-performing peers. At the same time, working through risk associated with difficult, poor-performing, or problematic peers will remind us that not all people prove troublesome for the same reasons. Recall that some difficulties are personality related, whereas others are performance based. Also consider that mitigating circumstances may be affecting the performance and interaction of peers. Thus, employees need to be fully versed in the communication options available for dealing with difficult team members.

❖ CONCLUSION

In closing, we provide Gloria's account of how a difficult member made life miserable for her team, caused members to quit, and falsely reported about her to management. Although Gloria's story is disturbing and dramatic, it is not all that unusual. It demonstrates how a single difficult team member can erode a team's collective health and demoralize individual team members.

> The lead technician [on my team] was "micromanaging." She told the manager that new employees had complained I was difficult to work with. She caused people to quit and basically made life miserable. She targeted one person at a time to a point they quit. I tried talking to the person [difficult team member], then the manager, then the CEO. We went as a group too. We were told to "suck it up." Things calmed down for about 6 months. I got a new manager. She [the difficult team member] went to the new manager and basically told the same stories. She said the team was intimidated by me. My new manager went to the team. They told her they didn't have problems with me and that they hadn't said anything negative about me. The manager filed a harassment claim with HR. HR investigated this time and found her [the difficult team member] guilty. She was demoted.
>
> Gloria, age 54

Attend to the risk presented by this difficult team member. Has this individual put team performance at risk? Team cohesion? How widespread is the dysfunction she created? What seems to be the root issue with the difficult team member? Is it personality, performance, or some combination of the two? Should the group members have approached the difficult team member or overlooked the problem?

In making sense of the risk presented by this difficult team member, employees agreed that she was disruptive and difficult. But is this assessment fair? Is there additive defensiveness at work? Are there possible spillover effects? Is there reasonable and legitimate consensus about the concerns with the difficult team member? Once these questions have been answered, the team must consider a course of action. Given the perceived severity of the offense, was formal or informal action warranted? What formal courses of action were apparent in this case? What workgroup norms were evident?

The characters in this story take action to transform risk. What did they do? Were their actions successful? To what degree? How might the team have handled this situation differently? What other options were available to them to transform risk? Could they engage with the difficult team member? Offer to coach her? Motivate her? What could they have done to make the effects of the difficult team member more tolerable? Should the difficult team member have been replaced? How would this have transformed risk?

Finally, what can be done to maintain relative safety for the members of this team? What can the team learn from dealing with this difficult team member? What communication practices proved particularly effective? Ineffective? Which communication practices might they use in the future to improve relationships with the difficult team member? What norms could emerge from the group's experience that might inform how they would deal with difficult team members in the future?

❖ REFERENCES

Barker, J. R., & Tompkins, P. K. (1994). Identification in the self-managing organization: Characteristics of target and tenure. *Human Communication Research, 2,* 223–240.

Cook, R. A., & Goff, J. L. (2002). Coming of age with self-managed teams: Dealing with a problem employee. *Journal of Business Psychology, 16,* 485–496.

Coopman, S. J. (2001). Democracy, performance, and outcomes in interdisciplinary health care teams. *Journal of Business Communication, 3,* 261–284.

Craig, R. S. (2007). Communication and social identity theory: Existing and potential connections in organizational identification research. *Communication Studies, 58,* 123–138.

Devine, D. J., Clayton, L. D., Philips, J. L., Dunford, B. B., & Melner, S. B. (1999). Teams in organizations: Prevalence, characteristics, and effectiveness. *Small Group Research, 30,* 678–711.

Ellingson, L. L. (2003). Interdisciplinary health care teamwork in the clinic backstage. *Journal of Applied Communication Research, 31,* 93–117.

Felps, W., Mitchell, T. R., & Byington, E. (2006). How, when, and why bad apples spoil the barrel: Negative group members and dysfunctional groups. In B. M. Staw (Ed.), *Research in organizational behavior: An annual series of analytical essays and critical reviews* (Vol. 27, pp. 175–222). Burlington, MA: JAI/Elsevier.

Hawkins, K. W., & Fillion, B. P. (1999). Perceived communication skills needs for work groups. *Communication Research Reports, 16,* 167–174.

Hirokawa, R. Y., & Keyton, J. (1995). Perceived facilitators and inhibitors of effectiveness in organizational work teams. *Management Communication Quarterly, 8,* 424–446.

Karau, S. J., & Williams, K. D. (1993). Social loafing: A meta-analytic review and theoretical integration. *Journal of Personality and Social Psychology, 65,* 681–706.

Katzenbach, J. R., & Smith, D. K. (1998). *The wisdom of teams: Creating the high performance organization.* New York: Harper Business.

Keyton, J. (1999). Interaction patterns in dysfunctional teams. *Small Group Research, 30,* 491–518.

Lawler, E. E., III, Mohrman, S. A., & Ledford, G. E., Jr. (1995). *Creating high performance organizations: Practices and results of employee involvement and total quality management in Fortune 1000 companies.* San Francisco: Jossey-Bass.

LePine, J. A., & Van Dyne, L. (2001). Peer responses to low performers: An attributional model of helping in the context of groups. *Academy of Management Review, 26,* 67–84.

Pham, D. T., Awadalla, M. H., & Eldukhrl, E. E. (2007). Adaptive and cooperative mobile robots. *Journal of Systems and Control Engineering, 221,* 279–292.

Putnam, L. L., & Stohl, C. (1990). Bona fide groups: A reconceptualization of groups in context. *Communication Studies, 41,* 248–265.

Stohl, C., & Schell, S. E. (1991). A communication-based model of small-group dysfunction. *Management Communication Quarterly, 5,* 90–110.

Taggar, S., & Neubert, M. (2004). The impact of poor performers on team outcomes: An empirical examination of attribution theory. *Personnel Psychology, 57,* 935–968.

11

Conclusion

Risk and Next-Generation Challenges

I was thrilled when a local advertising agency, known for its quirky and creative ad campaigns, responded almost immediately to my request for an internship. Only later did I learn that it was my assertive and unconventional prose that got their attention. Within days, I was working a frantic 20 hours a week in the company's colorful but austere offices, located in a glass tower high above the city. Soon I understood why the company had developed its maverick reputation. Creative teams gathered continuously for brief, raucous brainstorming sessions in a room furnished in bean bag chairs and cabinets stocked with candy, trays of tropical fruit, and a huge collective peanut butter jar (Rule 1: Bring your own knife!). I was frequently baffled by my new work environment. No one seemed to be in charge, and no job description was provided to interns. My supervisors, the creative directors, worked at home frequently and sometimes conducted their business from a local coffee shop, pub, or fitness center. I could rarely anticipate what my tasks might be, but I knew the instruction would likely come in a blast of cryptic text messages or a brief Facebook chat.

I grew frustrated with one director who often sent me on unnecessary errands, including one sojourn to the health food store in search of creative new snacks for the office larder. That night, I shared my bewilderment on Facebook, wondering how my "crazy bosses" ever became so successful. Unfortunately, I had "friended" a fellow intern, who quickly shared the message around the office. Within 24 hours, I was invited to my first real conversation with a senior executive, who curtly informed me that my services "were no longer needed."

Santana, age 32

This final chapter examines new sources of risk, the kinds that employees are only beginning to encounter in a workplace that is rapidly changing. Santana was caught off guard by some of these. First, as an intern, she experienced the complications of temporary employment. Temporary employment arrangements are increasingly common, but these employees sometimes have trouble fitting themselves into an organizational culture created by permanent employees. Second, the blurring of personal and work life was routine for Santana's coworkers, but their blended lives created difficulties for Santana, who felt isolated from the creative staff and out of synch with their unpredictable schedules. Third, the routine use of communication technologies, such as text messaging and Facebook chat, creates both opportunities and risks. Due to the limitations of texting, Santana's task instructions were often terse and ambiguous. And by choosing Facebook as the medium for venting her understandable feelings of bewilderment and frustration, Santana made herself vulnerable. The tone of her message was probably misinterpreted as it passed from her network of friends to coworkers and, finally, to management.

In Chapter 1, we argued that competent communication practices are essential in managing the inevitable risks that we encounter at work. In subsequent chapters, we made that case more concretely, describing specific types of risk and the communication behaviors that exacerbate or ameliorate it. In preparing this final chapter, we pursued two objectives. First, we wanted to help our readers anticipate the future. To do so, we scanned the changing landscape of the workplace, looking for trends that might intensify or change the risks American workers will be facing in the next decade. Some of these are already widespread, while others are, for now, affecting only a limited number of workers in certain leading-edge industries. Our search revealed that new kinds of risk are emerging for individual employees, work relationships, and the larger society in which our organizations operate.

Our second purpose was to leave the reader with a cautionary tale—one that emphasizes the positive functions of risk and the dangers of ignoring it. Throughout this book, we have been careful to acknowledge the upside of risky situations. Imbued with what we earlier called transformative potential, risky situations really *matter*. When approached with care and skill, they offer the promise of positive change for employees and their organizations. But in recent months, we have come to respect the value of risk even more. Why? In the time it took to write this book, about a year, the American economy, indeed the world economy, has been in free fall. The United States entered its worst economic downturn since the Great Depression. American companies shed workers at an alarming rate, corporate profits plummeted, the housing market crashed, and some of our most respected financial institutions failed. The private sector faltered so badly that the U.S. government was forced to rescue it with untold billions of taxpayer dollars. Although the causes of this debacle are many, we argue that the most fundamental of these involves a failure by individuals, and organizations, to respond prudently to risk. Fortunately, the current economic debacle yielded a variety of important lessons. We explore them toward the end of this chapter.

As with all the risky communication situations examined in this book, the ones presented here have both positive and negative implications for workers. Our hope is that by anticipating challenges, we can help you prepare for them.

❖ INDIVIDUAL RISKS

Several of the trends we observed are particularly relevant to individual workers, as they hone their skills for the emerging economy and attend to their own well-being. Although grounded in individual risk, these emerging trends also have implications for relational and organizational risk.

Frequent Job Changes

It has long been conventional wisdom that the typical college graduate will switch careers multiple times, in response to changing personal interests and new economic realities. The Bureau of Labor Statistics (2008) recently reported a study of the youngest baby boomers (born 1957–1964). Between the ages of 18 and 42 years, these workers held an average of 10.8 jobs. So job switching has been a common phenomenon, and the trend is accelerating as younger workers neither expect nor want the "job for life" that was for so long the American ideal and the workplace standard.

What may be changing are the reasons for job switching. Certainly, workers change due to boredom or altered career goals. But many more American workers are being forced to change careers. Their jobs are at risk due to the intensifying use of outsourcing—the contracting out of nonessential tasks rather than performing them in-house. Other trends are important here. For example, America's manufacturing jobs have been migrating to cheaper overseas labor markets for many years, but now many technical and customer service tasks are moving to countries such as India, where an educated workforce can be accessed at comparatively low wages.

What are the implications? To manage the risk of forced job change, workers can take several steps. First, stay attuned to the trends in your industry. Don't get caught by surprise when jobs start moving overseas. Second, maintain your network of contacts, using traditional forms of communication as well as social networking sites, such as LinkedIn. Communication networks help you locate job opportunities and share your qualifications with a wide audience. Third, prepare yourself financially and emotionally for a world where job changes, and even periods of unemployment, are common. Finally, as Textbox 11.1 suggests, consider how your job skills could be applied within a career that can neither be outsourced nor exported.

Textbox 11.1   Outsource This!

Sylvia, a 43-year-old supply-chain manager with a county hospital, was growing bored of her job of 14 years. With limited opportunity for advancement beyond her current job level, Sylvia wondered if she should hang on for an early retirement or try something new. Her decision was made more urgent when a poor economy made it necessary for the county to cut positions. Although her job was in no immediate danger, Sylvia was asked to explore possibilities for outsourcing of her department's inventory, ordering, and delivery functions. These ominous signs prompted the experienced manager to revisit her dream of owning a small business. After carefully researching franchising opportunities, Sylvia eventually found an unfilled niche. Schools in her urban area were struggling to educate a growing population of students for whom English was a second language. New state regulations threatened these schools with closure if they failed to make adequate progress with these children. The state also was investing significantly in tutoring services for struggling students. Sylvia spoke excellent Spanish and her supply-chain training would help her develop a system to match student needs with tutors' teaching strengths. Sylvia purchased a tutoring franchise from a nationally known chain and soon left her job at the hospital.

Obsolete Skills

American employees have known for a long time that continuous learning is a key to job security. Due to changing technologies and morphing markets, this trend is accelerating. The technical knowledge that makes someone successful today won't suffice in just a few years. Those who choose not to keep learning put their careers at risk. A common reaction to the uncertainty of today's job market is to seek technical education. Interestingly, it may be the more liberal arts–based learning, courses in humanities, composition, or communication that will prove most useful. A longtime chronicler of NASA's technical culture, a pilot, and a prolific adventure writer, Lane Wallace (2009) makes this point in her role as a guest blogger for the *Atlantic* magazine. Wallace notes that "as the economy has worsened, and fears of joblessness have risen, the voices advocating pursuit of more 'practical' degrees have grown in both number and volume. . . . I passionately disagree." In defending her own liberal education, she argues that technical skills quickly become obsolete, but the capacity to make good arguments, understand other cultures, and manage ambiguity are more important in the long run.

A reader responded to Wallace's (2009) comments, affirming that his own technical training quickly became obsolete:

> Here's the thing—I'm only 33, and many of the technical skills I learned both in biology and in computer science courses in college are obsolete just 11 years later . . .
>
> I understand the need for technical skills, but frankly one can learn most of those raw technical skills in about a year at a decent community college. If you're going to commit four years of your life in your prime to education, it ought to be on skills that are going to last more than a decade. With the rate of technological change, there's not one technical course of study I would be willing to point to now and be confident that the skills learned there will be relevant 20 years from now. On the other hand, history, philosophy, sociology, economics, the outlines of scientific inquiry, mathematical theory, and yes, most of all, the ability to write, I have utmost confidence will serve the student well in any job discipline.

It won't surprise the reader that, as professors of communication studies, we agree with Lane Wallace and her reader. Whatever the future holds, you can reduce the risk of obsolescence by supplementing your technical training with a strong dose of liberal education. The other obvious hedge is to commit to a lifetime of learning.

Successful employees will be those who are continually updating their education.

Working 24–7

In his recent book, *Elsewhere, U.S.A.*, sociologist and trend spotter Dalton Conley (2009) observes one of the most sweeping developments in the American workplace—the blurring of private and working life. According to Dalton, workers increasingly conduct business at home, and they often pursue leisure at work (see Textbox 11.2). Santana, the intern we introduced earlier, observed this trend firsthand. The blurring effect is attributable in part to the ubiquitous and addictive nature of communication technologies—it is just so tempting to check that BlackBerry during a slow moment at your kid's soccer game; it is so easy to play a quick video game at your desk. E-mails and Facebook provide varied opportunities for constant social connections. Who wants to talk to me now? Has anyone left a message on my Facebook page?

Textbox 11.2   Welcome to the "Weisure" Class

A story posted recently to CNN's Web site (Patterson, 2009) explored Dalton Conley's notion of "weisure," the blurry space between work and play. Workers choose the weisure lifestyle when they monitor the BlackBerry while on vacation or post pictures to Facebook between business meetings. The blending of leisure and work is a creative and ubiquitous lifestyle choice, one that is likely to evolve and intensify. But Conley's interesting work encourages us to be mindful of what might be lost as the private sphere shrinks and our capacity to engage in uninterrupted work (and play) erodes.

Another factor blurring the work-family boundary is this: In our increasingly knowledge-based economy, work can be more consuming, creative, and engaging. It is not uncommon for employees to work in highly committed problem-solving teams in a race to create the next round of innovative and profitable products and services. Some organizations facilitate high levels of worker commitment by creating an environment that is informal, empowering, highly social, and, for many workers, fun. As Santana found at the advertising agency, in this kind of workplace, the boundaries between work and play are permeable. And for some employees, work is simply more interesting and rewarding than their home life. For that reason, the private lives of employees become integrated with their working life; "off-stage" moments are few and opportunities for traditional leisure limited. Although most workers experience this 24–7 as a lifestyle choice, they may not be fully aware of the potential risks. Among the possibilities: increased inability to focus, heightened levels of physiological arousal/agitation, fatigue, and failure to attend fully to the relational needs of family members.

One way to manage these risks is to establish (or reestablish) communication rules that help manage the boundaries between private and working life. Some of these rules seem hopelessly out of date, but they were developed to preserve the mental and social well-being of a previous generation of hard-driving executives (e.g., "Never mix business with pleasure" or "Don't do business with friends"). These traditional prescriptions may be worth revisiting and updating as a new generation of workers strikes the right blend of work and leisure, family life and professional life. For example, you might resolve to make time each week for uninterrupted face-to-face talk with valued friends or family members. Turning off the BlackBerry might be a good idea, especially when the kids need your attention or you are out for a night on the town. Checking your e-mail only once or twice a day may help you be more productive at work and get you home earlier. Choosing not to check it at night might help you sleep better and ward off the stress and the constant tension about what needs to be done next. Putting some boundaries back in place between our work life and home life will reduce the risk of falling prey to the 24–7 communication cycle.

❖ RELATIONAL RISKS

Intergenerational Conflict

The aging of the population is a major economic concern in certain parts of the world, including China and the United States. Prior to a recent economic downturn, the business pages of American newspapers worried over the retirement of the largest American generation—the baby boomers. Who would replace the droves of retiring teachers, engineers, and social workers? In China, with its "one-child" policy, the worry is even more acute, as fewer younger workers will be asked to support the economic needs of families and elders. Interestingly, the stresses of the current economic downturn have changed the nature of this discussion. In the United States, fewer older workers can afford to retire, and unemployment rates are increasing for recent college graduates. The result, at least for the moment, is increasing intergenerational tension, with older workers feeling pressure to step aside and younger workers growing impatient with their limited prospects for employment and promotion.

Even after current economic strains relax, intergenerational misunderstanding will represent a significant risk for work relationships. The problems are anticipated in a new wave of popular business books, including Bruce Tulgan's (2009) *Not Everyone Gets a Trophy: How to Manage Generation Y*. We would argue that the workplace is an important site for intergenerational communication and learning, more important than the home for the many workers who have limited contact with grandparents or other elders. Even so, the potential for conflict stems from two sources. First, social change has been so rapid in recent years that generational differences are more stark than in the past. To illustrate, workers in their 20s or 30s have ridden comfortably atop relentless waves of new communication technologies: iTunes, Bluetooth, Facebook, iPhones, Second Life, and iTouch. As middle-aged professors, we observe our younger colleagues with a mix of admiration and skepticism, even as we search in vain for a device that will play the tape recordings we collected as young researchers.

A second source of conflict is the rejection by younger workers of some traditional assumptions about work. We won't belabor the point here, but we note that in contrast to their baby boomer parents, employees born in the 1980s may (as examples) view gender equality as the normal state of affairs at work, have experienced democratic and emotionally nurturing parenting (and expect the same treatment from managers), conceive of work as a temporary commitment rather than lifetime career, and expect work to provide social as well as economic benefits. These differences needn't be problematic, but research on intergenerational communication suggests that intergenerational interactions can be dissatisfying and dysfunctional. The communicative predicaments of aging (CPA) model (Ryan, Giles, Bartolucci, & Henwood, 1986) offers a time-tested explanation of how intergenerational tensions develop and how they might be averted (see Textbox 11.3).

<table>
</table>

> **Textbox 11.3**   **Managing the Predicaments of Intergenerational Communication**
>
> The CPA model argues that it is age-related stereotypes that trigger difficulties in intergenerational relationships. Upon spotting certain age-related cues such as gray hair on an older colleague or headphones on a younger employee, observers engage certain stereotypes. For example, an older worker is assumed to be "grumpy" or the younger "self-absorbed." These cues lead to modified speech behavior (e.g., the older worker is treated with condescending kindness; the younger worker is ignored), which inadvertently constrains the behavior of the coworker. Thus, the older worker may feel compelled to protest or correct this condescension. This response confirms the grumpy stereotype. As a consequence, future interactions are marked by avoidance, discomfort, and even stronger stereotyping. The keys to breaking this cycle are both psychological and behavioral. The first involves recognition of aging stereotypes and a willingness to acknowledge the diversity of older and younger people. The second requires coworkers to approach intergenerational conversations with flexibility, avoiding behaviors that either overaccommodate or underaccommodate generational differences. When training older peers, for instance, younger employees should avoid simplistic "babytalk" explanations (overaccommodation). However, the use of generation-specific jargon (underaccommodation) is also problematic. For example, workers who are unfamiliar with the culture of Facebook may not know what "friending" means.

Intercultural Difference

Due to increasing globalization, workers who fail to develop intercultural competence will put their relationships with coworkers at risk. We discussed this issue in Chapter 7 in some detail, so here we will simply reinforce the point that your coworkers will increasingly differ from you in appearance, cultural background, and communication styles. The risk is in mindlessly applying your own cultural assumptions to those around you. Ignoring the tendencies of others to make assumptions based on your own cultural background can also be risky. What will help? First, learn as much as you can about specific cultures and the dimensions on which they are similar or different to your own. Understand that some cultures orient to the group, whereas others prioritize the individual. Some cultures embrace a short-term perspective when accomplishing tasks and conducting negotiations, whereas others adhere to a much longer term perspective. And cultures can differ markedly in their assignment of gender roles and expectations for men and women (Hofstede, 2001). Second, be mindful of diversity as a broad concept that stretches far beyond commonly held notions of racial and ethnic differences. Understand that (inter)cultural differences can be present when able-bodied and disabled people interact, when heterosexual and homosexual people interact, and even when men and women interact.

Another suggestion is to travel. Travel broadens your cultural experiences and provides a sense of perspective that will prove helpful in an increasingly intercultural workplace. Finally, learn a second language. For now, English remains the dominant language of business, but in the future, employees who speak multiple languages will be more successful in building peer relationships and working across cultures.

❖ ORGANIZATIONAL RISKS

The Temporary Workplace

The current trend of replacing permanent workers with temporary hires is likely to accelerate. To limit expenses and increase flexibility, employers hire "temps," contractors, and consultants. In at least one sense, these arrangements reduce risk for employers. In this era of rapidly changing business conditions, they avoid the risk of making a permanent commitment. Employers hedge their bets against change because it is easier to shed temporary workers in response to downturns. In many cases, employers reduce their financial risk by avoiding the obligation to pay a short-term employee's health care or retirement expenses.

For some employees, temporary work is ideal, particularly if the compensation is high enough. A series of transitory positions can broaden work experience and hone one's skill set. Some are leery of making a long-term commitment to an employer because they have witnessed the sometimes devastating effects on permanent employees of downsizing, mergers, and other drastic changes. They prefer to be nimble and independent.

The risks come to employers in the form of workers who lack commitment to the organization's future. Temporary workers sometimes fail to see the big picture, and they have little incentive to contribute beyond the narrowly defined scope of their temporary jobs. For temporary workers, an obvious risk is the lack of employer-paid benefits, such as health care. Some manage the risk by working for consulting companies or employment agencies that build the cost of benefits into their temporary contracts. Others must be careful to set aside earnings to cover the sometimes substantial costs of health care coverage. Temps face other risks. Unfamiliar with the culture of the workplace, they must be proactive in learning the cultural ropes from coworkers. Temporary employees may find it difficult to make meaningful social connections with coworkers who are reluctant to invest in temporary relationships. Resentment may be encountered as well, particularly if the temporary hire is replacing permanent workers who were laid off.

Temporary workers can manage these risks by tending to and relying on relationships outside of the workplace. For them, memberships in professional associations and interactions with occupational colleagues may be more important sources of support and advice than relationships with coworkers. In addition, temporary workers manage the risk of not fitting in through assertive uncertainty management. They seek well-defined roles, ask questions, and quickly develop mutually beneficial task relationships with their new peers.

The Virtual Workplace

In a recent special issue titled "The Future of Work," *Time* magazine (May 25, 2009) called on a variety of experts to describe the emerging workplace. Some of the trends have been described above; the bulk of the remaining changes are captured by the term *virtual workplace*. For many of us, work will become virtual in the sense that *where* we work will be much less important than the ways we are connected to our work and our coworkers. Physical workspaces are expensive to maintain, and so are the forms of transportation we use to reach them. In the future, more of us will be coordinating our activities through online connections. More work will be performed from home, as we monitor systems and coordinate activities via our laptops. Virtual teams—employees from around the world connected through increasingly powerful forms of "groupware"—will gather in hyperspace for intense but temporary collaborations. Increasingly, we won't really know the people we work with, even as our networks of online contacts increase exponentially.

Fewer of us will have a boss (literally) looking over our shoulder at the office. At the same time, nearly all of our work will be subject to surveillance, as our every keystroke is monitored from afar. Old-style hierarchical chains of authority will be increasingly supplanted by horizontal networks, lattices of interconnections based on expertise and common objectives. Opportunities for face-to-face communication with coworkers will become rare and presumably more valuable. Fundamental to the performance of many jobs will be competence in the use of a wide range of communication technologies. Some of these might include next-generation group decision-making systems, simulation and social gaming software, online customer support services, digital community management software, and language translation systems.

It seems unlikely that any one technical skill will prove dominant in this virtual landscape. But the personal satisfaction of workers and their success may depend on communication skills such as these. *Privacy management* will be important as workers come to understand surveillance and take steps to protect certain kinds of personal and business information. *Network sensitivity* is the capacity of an employee to be aware of and responsive to the extended set of social connections that develops online. Santana, the intern featured in the opening scenario, failed to appreciate how her personal thoughts could travel beyond her immediate Facebook network. A key consideration is anticipating how your messages will be interpreted by unintended readers who are several steps removed from the original communication context. A third skill would be *virtual relationship management*, which includes forming, maintaining, and regulating online ties. Advantaged employees will be those who can form online working relationships quickly, master the rules of professional communication within a particular medium, and create the right mix of interactions. This latter criterion includes striking the right balance between personal and professional content in online conversations. It might also include knowing when to supplement online communication with face-to-face meetings.

❖ SOCIETAL RISK

As we mentioned early in this final chapter, the economic crisis of 2008–2010 illustrates the important role that risk management plays in our larger society. Indeed, the risk management behaviors of organizations and individuals created a domino effect that placed whole industries at risk of failure and the American government in perilous debt. Some of the trends that exacerbated the crises will likely be present in the future. For example, short-term profits will continue to be emphasized over more prudent long-term plans. Government leaders will continue to be lobbied by those seeking to eliminate regulations, which govern risky behavior in the financial markets. Industries will continue to be consolidated into fewer and larger companies, making them more vulnerable to the failure of a single organization and more narrowly governed by select and perhaps not always ethical groups of executives.

As they sift through the financial wreckage looking for clues to an improved financial future, economic analysts make it clear that one important step will be more prudent management of risk. Consider the home mortgage industry. Traditionally, to reduce the risk that borrowers might default on their loans, lenders carefully scrutinized the financial health of potential home buyers. Even those who were judged to be at low risk of default were required to make a substantial down payment as a condition of receiving a mortgage, and some were required to purchase mortgage insurance to further reduce the risk assumed by the lender. All of these moves acknowledged the reality that large sums of money were at stake—that the long-term profitability of the loan would be compromised if imprudent lenders failed to do their homework. However, in recent years, some mortgage lenders turned a blind eye to the risk of default, offering huge loans to buyers who were patently unqualified. As the hot housing market inevitably cooled and unemployment numbers soared, many of these loans went bad. Buyers realized that they owed more money than their homes were actually worth on the open market. Straddled with unmanageable payments and unable to sell their homes, many of these new owners simply handed over the keys and walked away. Banks were left holding a huge inventory of distressed real estate. The burden of these bad loans became so great that previously well-respected banks failed, triggering a chain reaction of economic anxieties that is still reverberating in the economy (see Textbox 11.4).

Textbox 11.4	**What Went Wrong? A Lesson in Imprudent Risk-Taking**

The real estate market crashed for many reasons, most having to do with the mismanagement of risk. Some of the blame belongs with individual home buyers. You can protect yourself from similar mistakes by understanding what went wrong. We recommend the easy-to-follow analyses published by *BusinessWeek* (Steverman & Bogoslaw, 2008) and *Time* (Kiviat, 2008). See the reference list to locate these online resources.

❖ RISK REVISITED

As a risk management problem, the real estate crash is broadly instructive. It illustrates how mismanaged risk can ripple across multiple levels of analysis (as we discussed in Chapter 1), expanding to the point where it finally threatens the larger society. At the *individual* level, risky home loans created undue financial stress for borrowers. Their willingness to ignore the perils of overborrowing ended up ruining their credit records and creating untold levels of anxiety and distress. This extended to the *relational* level, where families and marriages were stressed to the breaking point by unmanageable mortgage payments. Business relationships were shattered as well. Mortgage brokers, realtors, appraisers—all of those businesspeople who were trusted by their customers to make the mortgage process safe—will find that trust harder to come by in the future.

At the *organizational* level, some of America's most respected financial institutions placed their employees and stockholders in the way of harm, largely because they failed to take risk seriously. Some did so by knowingly, issuing or purchasing risky loans, repackaging them in murky financial products called derivatives, and selling them to unwitting buyers further up the financial food chain. This pass-it-on process disguised the risk inherent in those loans and created a false sense of safety. Those making imprudent loans were shielded from the consequences. Another problem: short-term thinking. Highly paid financial wizards maximized short-term returns (in the form of yearly performance bonuses) while ignoring the longer term consequences of their risky financial behavior.

Finally, this chain of events created *communal* risk. In our area of the American Southwest, whole neighborhoods of new homes were built rapidly during the go-go years, largely funded by risky loans. Now plagued by silent blocks of repossessed homes, these communities stand in quiet, testament to the folly of risk ignored. At the level of *societal* risk, the U.S. government is partly to blame for relaxing the regulations that once subjected lenders and loans to scrutiny. The government plays an important role in ensuring the transparency and safety of our market-driven economy. As the public looked on complacently, oversight processes were undermined by the efforts of financial industry lobbyists and imprudent elected officials.

The financial crisis of the past few years is our cautionary tale. It reminds us that risk serves a valuable function. Through communication, we become aware of risk and help others assess it, manage it, and ultimately create conditions that are reasonably safe for ourselves, our peers, our organizations, and the larger communities in which we live. The larger objective isn't to reject risk in favor of security and safety. Successful people are often prudent risk takers. Rather, it is to be mindful of risk, to communicate in ways that exploit its important role in organizational life while also diminishing risk that is unnecessary or destructive. To help with this rather challenging task, we leave the reader to ponder how the lessons learned from the current financial crisis might be put to good use in the future. Some lessons are obvious, and they map clearly into the four elements of the risk negotiation cycle introduced in this book (see Figure 11.1).

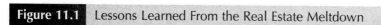

Figure 11.1   Lessons Learned From the Real Estate Meltdown

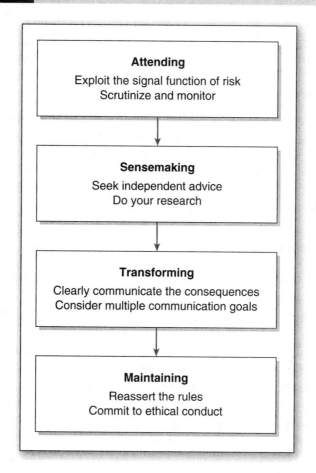

Attending

1. *Exploit the signal function of risk.* Many lenders and borrowers knew deep down that they were engaging in risky transactions. Failing to appreciate the signal function of risk, they ignored the emotions and suspicions that could have warned them away from dangerous investments and unethical behavior.

2. Scrutinize and monitor. Government oversight, the checks and balances that ensured safety in the mortgage markets, were gradually relaxed over the years. The lesson is that risky decisions should be subjected to outside scrutiny, continuous reevaluation, and transparency. Risky decisions should not be secret decisions.

Sensemaking

3. Seek independent advice. Borrower suspicions about questionable loans were often assuaged by realtors, property assessors, and mortgage brokers—all of whom accepted the same faulty assumptions and often worked in close association. Risk assessments are more realistic when objective outside parties are consulted.

4. Do your research. Some borrowers did manage to avoid unwise risk taking, even during this tumultuous period. How? They researched loan options, knew the historical trends for housing prices in their area, and understood the economic conditions that could make a mortgage an unmanageable burden. In other words, they made informed assessments of the potential for risk.

Transforming

5. Clearly communicate the consequences. In the real estate market, buyers and lenders obscured the consequences of risky behavior. Lenders hid the bad loans by bundling them in ambiguous financial instruments that could be sold to unwitting buyers. The very real risk of increased monthly payments was underemphasized when some lenders sold variable-rate loans to naive buyers. Unscrupulous lenders knew they would never be held accountable for the risks they took. Yet how many borrowers would have committed to such loans knowing the full scale of risk involved? In short, disaster might have been averted by explicit communication about the consequences of risk.

6. Consider multiple communication goals. The parties to the real estate meltdown focused too exclusively on their task goal—to make money quickly. But our business interactions also have implications for our identities (Are we perceived as honest?) and our relationships (Will family life be unduly stressed if we borrow more then we can afford?). Long-term success is unlikely if we put our identities and relationships at risk.

Maintaining

7. Reassert the rules. By establishing rules of communication, we add predictability and safety to our transactions and preserve the practices that we consider to be acceptable and good. Lenders and government regulators weakened rules that made mortgage lending safe (e.g., buyers should provide evidence of their income; property appraisers should make independent estimates of property values). It is certainly true that rule systems can morph into senseless bureaucracies if we are not careful. But some rules keep risk in check. We need them.

8. Commit to ethical conduct. At the height of the real estate fiasco, lenders and borrowers fudged on what most would consider core business values. Apparently, these time-honored commitments seemed outdated or irrelevant during the anything-goes boom times. Honesty is the best policy. Respect others. Be prudent. Don't pass the buck. These ethical principles may seem simplistic, but they make work relationships safe. We ignore them at our peril.

Although the mortgage meltdown was an involved unraveling of a complex system, at a very fundamental level, it simply boils down to how we managed risk. Unpacking the mortgage industry meltdown leaves us face-to-face with a simple conclusion: We all benefit when we carefully manage risk.

❖ REFERENCES

Bureau of Labor Statistics. (2008). *Number of jobs held, labor market activity, and earnings growth among the youngest Baby Boomers: Results from a longitudinal survey.* Retrieved May 21, 2009, from http://www.bls.gov/news.release/pdf/nlsoy.pdf

Conley, D. (2009). *Elsewhere, U.S.A.: How we got from the company man, family dinners, and the affluent society to the home office, BlackBerry moms, and economic anxiety.* New York: Pantheon.

Hofstede, G. (2001). *Culture's consequences: Comparing values, behaviors, institutions, and organizations across nations.* Thousand Oaks, CA: Sage.

Kiviat, B. (2008, November 5). Reassessing risk. *Time.* Retrieved on May 27, 2009, from http://www.time.com/time/magazine/article/0,9171,1856998,00.html

Patterson, T. (2009). *Welcome to the "weisure" lifestyle.* Retrieved September 10, 2009, from http://www.cnn.com/2009/LIVING/worklife/05/11/weisure/index.html?iref=newssearch

Ryan, E., Giles, H., Bartolucci, G., & Henwood, K. (1986). Psycholinguistic and social psychological components by and with the elderly. *Language and Communication, 6,* 1–24.

Steverman, B., & Bogoslaw, D. (2008, October, 18). The financial crisis blame game. *BusinessWeek.* Retrieved May 27, 2009, from http://www.businessweek .com/investor/content/oct2008/pi20081017_950382.htm?chan=top+news_ top+news+index+-+temp_top+story

Tulgan, B. (2009). *Not everyone gets a trophy: How to manage Generation Y.* San Francisco: Jossey-Bass.

Wallace, L. (2009, May 19). In defense of the liberal arts. *The Atlantic.* Retrieved May 23, 2009, from http://andrewsullivan.theatlantic.com/the_daily_dish/ 2009/05/in-defense-of-the-liberal-arts.html

Index

About the Authors

Vincent R. Waldron is Professor of Communication Studies at Arizona State University, where he teaches courses on communication in work and personal relationships. Professor Waldron received his Ph.D. from Ohio State University in 1989. Dr. Waldron's research explores how employees manage difficult workplace encounters, such as expressing intense emotion, exercising upward influence, and repairing damaged relationships. The author of two previous books on these subjects, Professor Waldron has published his work in such outlets as the *Journal of Social and Personal Relationships, Management Communication Quarterly,* and *Communication Yearbook.* Vince Waldron has been recognized as a Professor of the Year by the Carnegie Foundation for the Advancement of Teaching. He is chair-elect of the Interpersonal Communication Division of the National Communication Association. With his wife Kathleen and daughters Emily and Laura, Vince Waldron resides in Phoenix, Arizona.

Jeffrey W. Kassing is an Associate Professor of Communication Studies at Arizona State University, where he teaches graduate and undergraduate organizational, applied, and environmental communication courses, as well as research methods. He earned his Ph.D. from Kent State University with an emphasis in organizational communication in 1997. Dr. Kassing's primary line of research concerns how employees express dissent about organizational policies and practices. This work, which began with his dissertation and development of the Organizational Dissent Scale, now spans over a decade and appears in numerous scholarly outlets, including *Management Communication Quarterly, Communication Quarterly, Communication Studies, Journal of Business Communication,* and *The International Encyclopedia of Communication.* Before seeking a career as an academic, Dr. Kassing worked as an office manager in the real estate industry, as an area coordinator in residence life at a state college, as a sales agent in the bicycle business, and as a professional house painter.

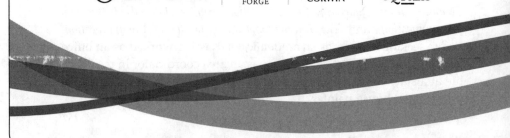